JUMP Math 3.1

Book 3 Part 1 of 2

D0474048

Contents

jump math™

MULTIPLYING POTENTIAL.

Copyright © 2016 JUMP Math

Excerpts from this publication may be reproduced under licence from Access Copyright, or with the express written permission of JUMP Math, or as permitted by law.

All rights are otherwise reserved, and no part of this publication may be reproduced, stored in a retrieval system, or transmitted in any form or by any means, electronic, mechanical, photocopying, scanning, recording or otherwise, except as specifically authorized.

JUMP Math
One Yonge Street, Suite 1014
Toronto, Ontario M5E 1E5
Canada
www.jumpmath.org

Writers: Dr. Anna Klebanov, Saverio Mercurio
Editors: Megan Burns, Liane Tsui, Julie Takasaki, Natalie Francis, Julia Cochrane, Jackie Dulson, Janice Dyer, Jodi Rauch
Layout and Illustrations: Linh Lam, Fely Guinasao-Fernandes, Sawyer Paul
Cover Design: Blakeley Words+Pictures
Cover Photograph: © Shutterstock/irin-k

ISBN 978-1-927457-95-5

Third printing July 2018

Printed and bound in Canada

Welcome to JUMP Math

Entering the world of JUMP Math means believing that every child has the capacity to be fully numerate and to love math. Founder and mathematician John Mighton has used this premise to develop his innovative teaching method. The resulting resources isolate and describe concepts so clearly and incrementally that everyone can understand them.

JUMP Math is comprised of teacher's guides (which are the heart of our program), interactive whiteboard lessons, student assessment & practice books, evaluation materials, outreach programs, and teacher training. All of this is presented on the JUMP Math website: **www.jumpmath.org**.

Teacher's guides are available on the website for free use. Read the introduction to the teacher's guides before you begin using these resources. This will ensure that you understand both the philosophy and the methodology of JUMP Math. The assessment & practice books are designed for use by students, with adult guidance. Each student will have unique needs and it is important to provide the student with the appropriate support and encouragement as he or she works through the material.

Allow students to discover the concepts by themselves as much as possible. Mathematical discoveries can be made in small, incremental steps. The discovery of a new step is like untangling the parts of a puzzle. It is exciting and rewarding.

Students will need to answer the questions marked with a 📓 in a notebook. Grid paper notebooks should always be on hand for answering extra questions or when additional room for calculation is needed.

Contents

Unit 4: Measurement: Length and Perimeter

Unit 5: Geometry: Shapes

Unit 6: Number Sense: Skip Counting and Multiplication

Unit 7: Number Sense: Multiplication

Unit 8: Measurement: Area

Unit 9: Probability and Data Management: Charts

PART 2
Unit 10: Number Sense: Division

Unit 11: Patterns and Algebra: Patterns and Equations

Unit 12: Number Sense: Fractions

Unit 13: Measurement: Time

Unit 14: Measurement: Capacity, Mass, and Temperature

Unit 15: Number Sense: Estimating

Unit 16: Number Sense: Money

Unit 17: Geometry: Transformation and 3-D Shapes

Unit 18: Probability and Data Management: Graphs and Probability

PA3-1 Counting On

COPYRIGHT © 2016 JUMP MATH: NOT TO BE COPIED.

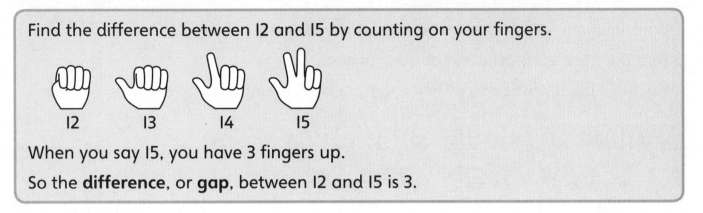

Find the difference between 12 and 15 by counting on your fingers.

| 12 | 13 | 14 | 15 |

When you say 15, you have 3 fingers up.

So the **difference**, or **gap**, between 12 and 15 is 3.

1. Find the difference between the numbers.

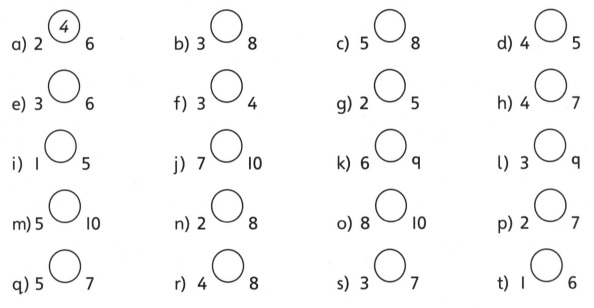

a) 2 (4) 6   b) 3 ◯ 8   c) 5 ◯ 8   d) 4 ◯ 5

e) 3 ◯ 6   f) 3 ◯ 4   g) 2 ◯ 5   h) 4 ◯ 7

i) 1 ◯ 5   j) 7 ◯ 10   k) 6 ◯ 9   l) 3 ◯ 9

m) 5 ◯ 10   n) 2 ◯ 8   o) 8 ◯ 10   p) 2 ◯ 7

q) 5 ◯ 7   r) 4 ◯ 8   s) 3 ◯ 7   t) 1 ◯ 6

2. Find the difference between the numbers.

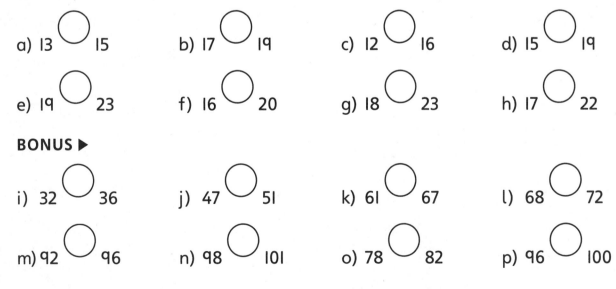

a) 13 ◯ 15   b) 17 ◯ 19   c) 12 ◯ 16   d) 15 ◯ 19

e) 19 ◯ 23   f) 16 ◯ 20   g) 18 ◯ 23   h) 17 ◯ 22

BONUS ▶

i) 32 ◯ 36   j) 47 ◯ 51   k) 61 ◯ 67   l) 68 ◯ 72

m) 92 ◯ 96   n) 98 ◯ 101   o) 78 ◯ 82   p) 96 ◯ 100

PA3-2 Number Patterns Made by Adding

What number is 4 more than 16? Or, what is 16 + 4?

Find the answer by counting on your fingers.

Say 16 with your fist closed. Then count on from 16 until you have raised 4 fingers.

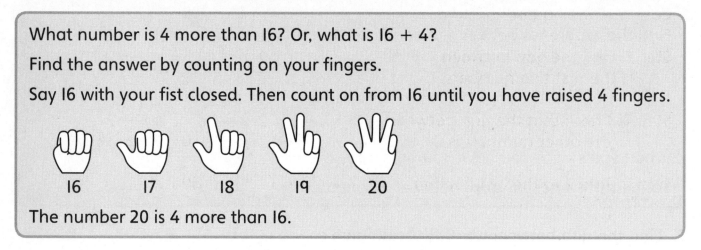

The number 20 is 4 more than 16.

1. Add the number in the circle to the number beside it.

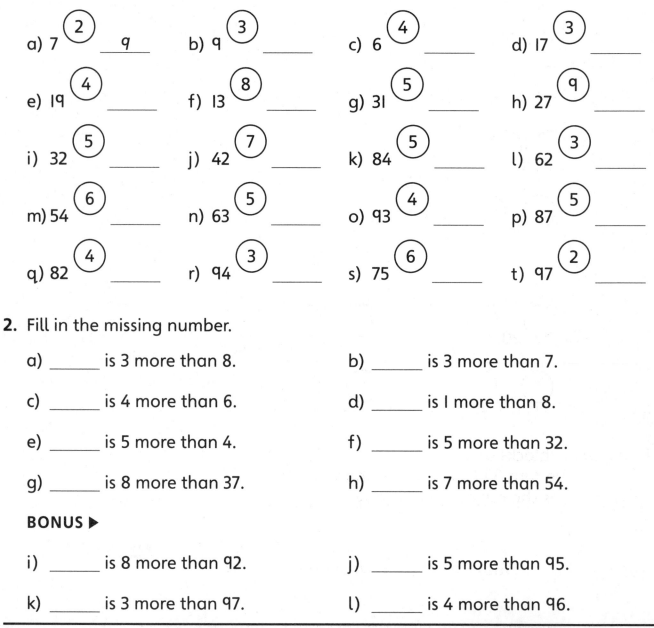

a) 7 ② 9   b) 9 ③ _____   c) 6 ④ _____   d) 17 ③ _____

e) 19 ④ _____ f) 13 ⑧ _____   g) 31 ⑤ _____   h) 27 ⑨ _____

i) 32 ⑤ _____ j) 42 ⑦ _____   k) 84 ⑤ _____   l) 62 ③ _____

m) 54 ⑥ _____ n) 63 ⑤ _____   o) 93 ④ _____   p) 87 ⑤ _____

q) 82 ④ _____ r) 94 ③ _____   s) 75 ⑥ _____   t) 97 ② _____

2. Fill in the missing number.

a) _____ is 3 more than 8.

b) _____ is 3 more than 7.

c) _____ is 4 more than 6.

d) _____ is 1 more than 8.

e) _____ is 5 more than 4.

f) _____ is 5 more than 32.

g) _____ is 8 more than 37.

h) _____ is 7 more than 54.

BONUS ▶

i) _____ is 8 more than 92.

j) _____ is 5 more than 95.

k) _____ is 3 more than 97.

l) _____ is 4 more than 96.

COPYRIGHT © 2016 JUMP MATH: NOT TO BE COPIED.

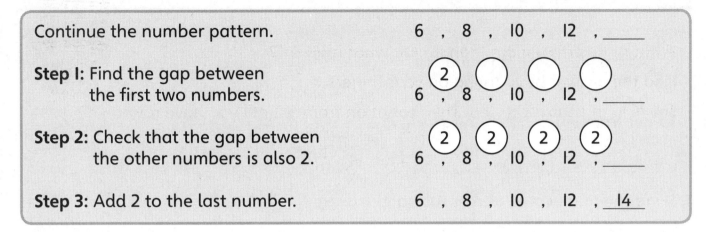

Continue the number pattern.   6 , 8 , 10 , 12 , _____

Step 1: Find the gap between
the first two numbers.
6 , 8 , 10 , 12 , _____

Step 2: Check that the gap between
the other numbers is also 2.
6 , 8 , 10 , 12 , _____

Step 3: Add 2 to the last number.   6 , 8 , 10 , 12 , __14__

3. Find the gap between the numbers. Then continue the
   number pattern.

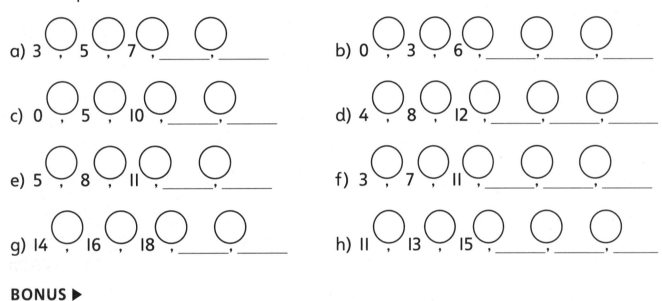

a) 3 , 5 , 7 , _____ , _____

b) 0 , 3 , 6 , _____ , _____ , _____

c) 0 , 5 , 10 , _____ , _____

d) 4 , 8 , 12 , _____ , _____ , _____

e) 5 , 8 , 11 , _____ , _____

f) 3 , 7 , 11 , _____ , _____ , _____

g) 14 , 16 , 18 , _____ , _____

h) 11 , 13 , 15 , _____ , _____ , _____

BONUS ▶

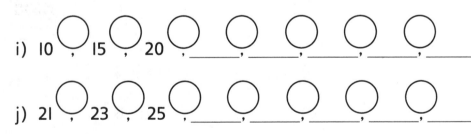

i) 10 , 15 , 20 , _____ , _____ , _____ , _____ , _____

j) 21 , 23 , 25 , _____ , _____ , _____ , _____ , _____

4. Jane runs 14 blocks on Monday.
   Each day she runs 2 blocks farther than the day before.
   How far does she run on Wednesday?

__14__   _____   _____
Monday   Tuesday   Wednesday

COPYRIGHT © 2016 JUMP MATH: NOT TO BE COPIED.

PA3-3 Counting Backwards

To get from 12 to 16, Ethan adds 4.

$\widehat{+4}$

12   16

To get from 16 to 12, he subtracts 4.

$\widehat{-4}$

16   12

1. Find the numbers to add or subtract.

a) 12 $\overset{+2}{\frown}$ 14 and 14 $\overset{-2}{\frown}$ 12

b) 11 ◯ 15 and 15 ◯ 11

c) 2 ◯ 5 and 5 ◯ 2

d) 10 ◯ 18 and 18 ◯ 10

e) 7 ◯ 14 and 14 ◯ 7

f) 9 ◯ 14 and 14 ◯ 9

What number do you subtract from 18 to get 15?

Count backwards on your fingers to find out. A number line can help you count.

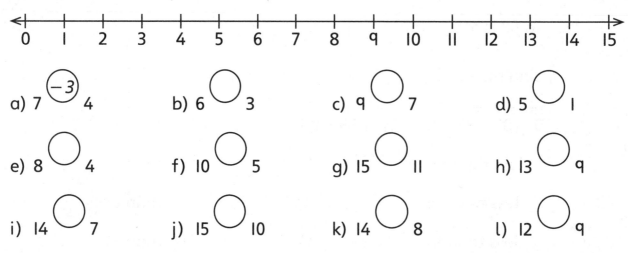

18   17   16   15

13 14 15 16 17 18

You have 3 fingers up, so 3 subtracted from 18 is 15.

2. What number must you subtract?

0   1   2   3   4   5   6   7   8   9   10   11   12   13   14   15

a) 7 $\overset{-3}{\frown}$ 4

b) 6 ◯ 3

c) 9 ◯ 7

d) 5 ◯ 1

e) 8 ◯ 4

f) 10 ◯ 5

g) 15 ◯ 11

h) 13 ◯ 9

i) 14 ◯ 7

j) 15 ◯ 10

k) 14 ◯ 8

l) 12 ◯ 9

COPYRIGHT © 2016 JUMP MATH: NOT TO BE COPIED.

3. Find the gap between the numbers.

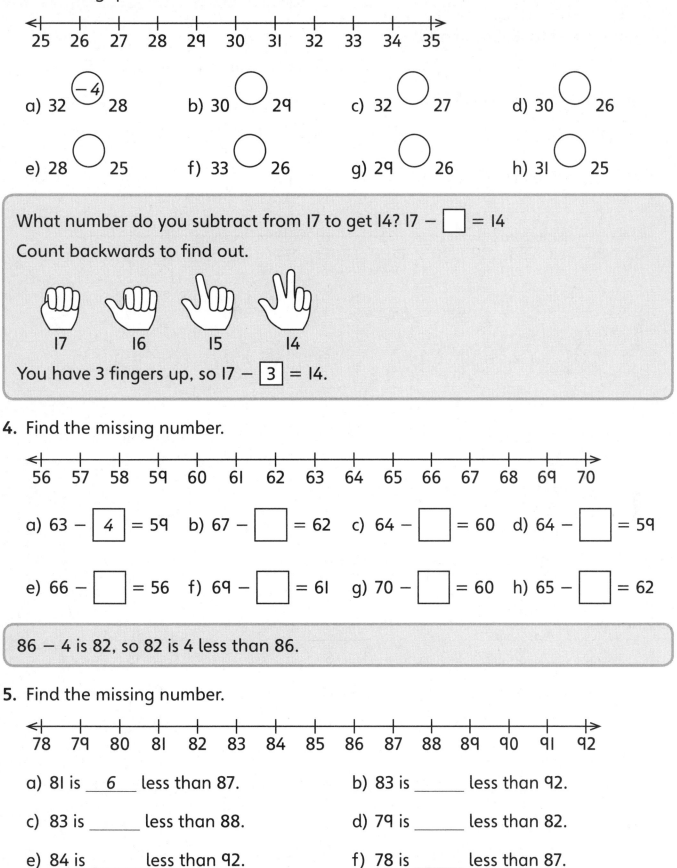

a) 32 (−4) 28   b) 30 ◯ 29   c) 32 ◯ 27   d) 30 ◯ 26

e) 28 ◯ 25   f) 33 ◯ 26   g) 29 ◯ 26   h) 31 ◯ 25

What number do you subtract from 17 to get 14? $17 - \square = 14$

Count backwards to find out.

17   16   15   14

You have 3 fingers up, so $17 - \boxed{3} = 14$.

4. Find the missing number.

a) $63 - \boxed{4} = 59$ b) $67 - \square = 62$ c) $64 - \square = 60$ d) $64 - \square = 59$

e) $66 - \square = 56$ f) $69 - \square = 61$ g) $70 - \square = 60$ h) $65 - \square = 62$

$86 - 4$ is 82, so 82 is 4 less than 86.

5. Find the missing number.

a) 81 is ___6___ less than 87.   b) 83 is _____ less than 92.

c) 83 is _____ less than 88.   d) 79 is _____ less than 82.

e) 84 is _____ less than 92.   f) 78 is _____ less than 87.

COPYRIGHT © 2016 JUMP MATH: NOT TO BE COPIED.

PA3-4 Number Patterns Made by Subtracting

I. Find the gap between the numbers.

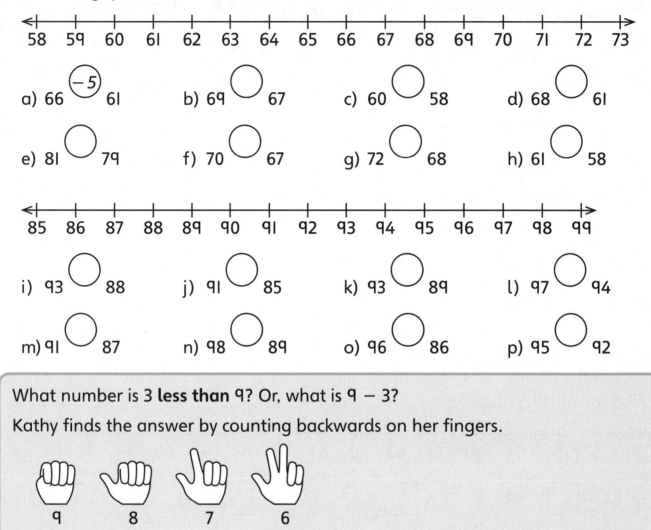

a) 66 $\bigcirc$−5 61   b) 69 $\bigcirc$ 67   c) 60 $\bigcirc$ 58   d) 68 $\bigcirc$ 61

e) 81 $\bigcirc$ 79   f) 70 $\bigcirc$ 67   g) 72 $\bigcirc$ 68   h) 61 $\bigcirc$ 58

i) 93 $\bigcirc$ 88   j) 91 $\bigcirc$ 85   k) 93 $\bigcirc$ 89   l) 97 $\bigcirc$ 94

m) 91 $\bigcirc$ 87   n) 98 $\bigcirc$ 89   o) 96 $\bigcirc$ 86   p) 95 $\bigcirc$ 92

What number is 3 **less than** 9? Or, what is 9 − 3?

Kathy finds the answer by counting backwards on her fingers.

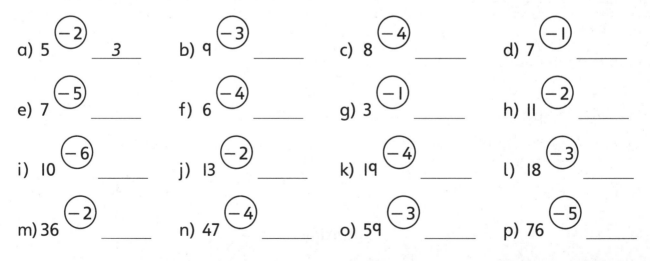

Kathy has 3 fingers up. The number 6 is 3 less than 9. So 9 − 3 = 6.

2. Subtract.

a) 5 $\bigcirc$−2 __3__   b) 9 $\bigcirc$−3 ____   c) 8 $\bigcirc$−4 ____   d) 7 $\bigcirc$−1 ____

e) 7 $\bigcirc$−5 ____   f) 6 $\bigcirc$−4 ____   g) 3 $\bigcirc$−1 ____   h) 11 $\bigcirc$−2 ____

i) 10 $\bigcirc$−6 ____   j) 13 $\bigcirc$−2 ____   k) 19 $\bigcirc$−4 ____   l) 18 $\bigcirc$−3 ____

m) 36 $\bigcirc$−2 ____   n) 47 $\bigcirc$−4 ____   o) 59 $\bigcirc$−3 ____   p) 76 $\bigcirc$−5 ____

COPYRIGHT © 2016 JUMP MATH: NOT TO BE COPIED.

3. Find the missing number.

a) _____ is 2 less than 6.

b) _____ is 2 less than 8.

c) _____ is 3 less than 8.

d) _____ is 5 less than 17.

e) _____ is 4 less than 20.

f) _____ is 6 less than 20.

g) _____ is 7 less than 28.

h) _____ is 4 less than 32.

i) _____ is 5 less than 40.

j) _____ is 4 less than 57.

In a number pattern made by subtracting, each number is less than the number before it.

Extend the number pattern.

11 , 9 , 7 , _____ , _____

Step 1: Find the gap.

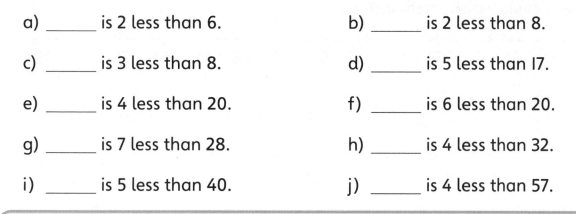

Step 2: Extend the number pattern.

11 , 9 , 7 , _5_ , _3_

4. Extend the number pattern by subtracting.

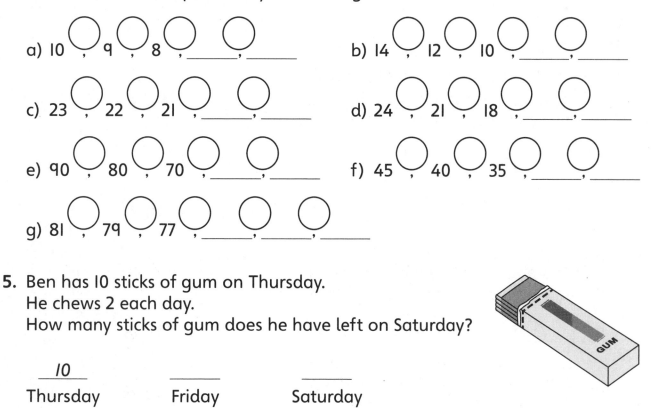

a) 10 , 9 , 8 , _____ , _____

b) 14 , 12 , 10 , _____ , _____

c) 23 , 22 , 21 , _____ , _____

d) 24 , 21 , 18 , _____ , _____

e) 90 , 80 , 70 , _____ , _____

f) 45 , 40 , 35 , _____ , _____

g) 81 , 79 , 77 , _____ , _____ , _____

5. Ben has 10 sticks of gum on Thursday.
He chews 2 each day.
How many sticks of gum does he have left on Saturday?

_10_   _____   _____
Thursday   Friday   Saturday

COPYRIGHT © 2016 JUMP MATH: NOT TO BE COPIED.

PA3-5 Number Patterns Made by Adding or Subtracting

1. Extend the number pattern using the gap.

a) 6 (+1), 7 (+1), _8_, _9_ (+1), _10_

b) 8 (−2), 6 (−2), _4_, _2_ (−2), _0_

c) 5 (+5), 10, _____, _____, _____

d) 3 (+3), 6, _____, _____, _____

e) 8 (+2), 10, _____, _____, _____

f) 14 (+2), 16, _____, _____, _____

g) 18 (−2), 16, _____, _____, _____

h) 25 (−5), 20, _____, _____, _____

i) 9 (−2), 7, _____, _____, _____

j) 22 (−3), 19, _____, _____, _____

k) 15 (+5), 20, _____, _____, _____

l) 13 (−1), 12, _____, _____, _____

m) 29 (−5), 24, _____, _____, _____

n) 32 (+5), 37, _____, _____, _____

o) 41 (+4), 45, _____, _____, _____

p) 46 (−3), 43, _____, _____, _____

2. a) Rani has a box of 24 crayons. She gives her brother 3 crayons each day for 4 days. How many crayons does she have left?

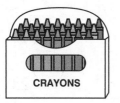
CRAYONS

24 (−), _____, _____, _____, _____

Day 1   Day 2   Day 3   Day 4

b) Amir has read 22 pages in his book. He reads 5 pages each day for 5 days. How many pages does he read in total?

22 (+), _____, _____, _____, _____, _____

Day 1   Day 2   Day 3   Day 4   Day 5

COPYRIGHT © 2016 JUMP MATH: NOT TO BE COPIED.

Extend the number pattern.   3 , 5 , 7 , _____

Step 1: Does the pattern go up or down? This
pattern goes up, so you need to add.

3 , 5 , 7 , _____

Step 2: Find the gap. Check that the gap
is always the same.

3 , 5 , 7 , _____

Step 3: Add or subtract to continue the
pattern.

3 , 5 , 7 , _9_

3. Find the gap. Then extend the number pattern.

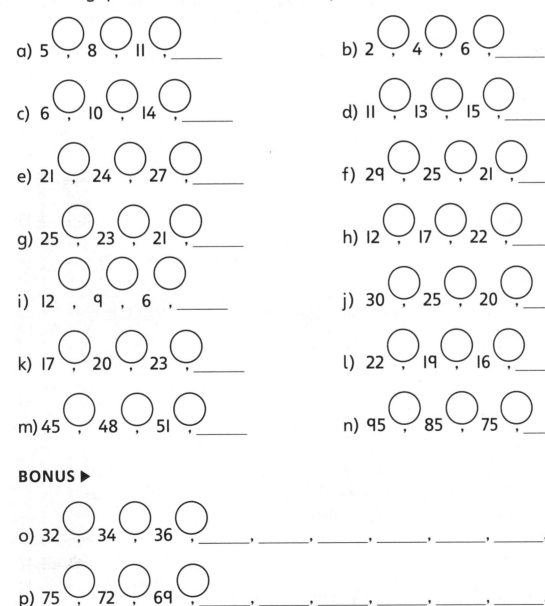

a) 5 , 8 , 11 , _____

b) 2 , 4 , 6 , _____

c) 6 , 10 , 14 , _____

d) 11 , 13 , 15 , _____

e) 21 , 24 , 27 , _____

f) 29 , 25 , 21 , _____

g) 25 , 23 , 21 , _____

h) 12 , 17 , 22 , _____

i) 12 , 9 , 6 , _____

j) 30 , 25 , 20 , _____

k) 17 , 20 , 23 , _____

l) 22 , 19 , 16 , _____

m) 45 , 48 , 51 , _____

n) 95 , 85 , 75 , _____

BONUS ▶

o) 32 , 34 , 36 , _____, _____, _____, _____, _____, _____, _____

p) 75 , 72 , 69 , _____, _____, _____, _____, _____, _____, _____

COPYRIGHT © 2016 JUMP MATH: NOT TO BE COPIED.

PA3-6 Number Patterns and Rules

1. Extend the number pattern by adding.

a) Add 3.   30, 33, _36_ , _39_ , _42_   b) Add 4.   60, 64, _____, _____, _____

c) Add 2.   26, 28, _____, _____, _____   d) Add 3.   20, 23, _____, _____, _____

e) Add 3.   12, 15, _____, _____, _____   f) Add 5.   46, 51, _____, _____, _____

g) Add 4.   83, 87, _____, _____, _____   h) Add 5.   74, 79, _____, _____, _____

i) Add 3.   76, 79, _____, _____, _____   j) Add 5.   80, 85, _____, _____, _____

k) Add 4.   62, 66, _____, _____, _____   l) Add 2.   89, 91, _____, _____, _____

2. Extend the number pattern by subtracting.

a) Subtract 2.   12, 10, _____, _____   b) Subtract 3.   40, 37, _____, _____

c) Subtract 4.   55, 51, _____, _____   d) Subtract 3.   63, 60, _____, _____

e) Subtract 2.   88, 86, _____, _____   f) Subtract 5.   79, 74, _____, _____

g) Subtract 4.   30, 26, _____, _____   h) Subtract 4.   66, 62, _____, _____

i) Subtract 3.   87, 84, _____, _____   j) Subtract 5.   100, 95, _____, _____

k) Subtract 5.   74, 69, _____, _____   l) Subtract 3.   98, 95, _____, _____

BONUS ▶ Circle the number patterns made by adding 3.
Hint: Check the gap between each pair of numbers.

A.   3, 7, 9, 11   B.   3, 6, 9, 11   C.   3, 6, 9, 12

D.   19, 22, 25, 28   E.   15, 18, 21, 24   F.   18, 21, 24, 29

3. Look at the number pattern 2, 6, 10, 14, 18.
Marcel says the pattern was made by adding 4 each time.
Is he correct? Explain how you know.

_____

COPYRIGHT © 2016 JUMP MATH: NOT TO BE COPIED.

4. What number do you add to make the number pattern?

a) 2, 4, 6, 8   Add _____.   b) 3, 6, 9, 12   Add _____.

c) 15, 18, 21, 24   Add _____.   d) 42, 44, 46, 48   Add _____.

e) 41, 46, 51, 56   Add _____.   f) 19, 23, 27, 31   Add _____.

g) 43, 45, 47, 49   Add _____.   h) 21, 27, 33, 39   Add _____.

5. What number do you subtract to make the number pattern?

a) 16, 14, 12, 10   Subtract _____.   b) 30, 25, 20, 15   Subtract _____.

c) 100, 99, 98, 97   Subtract _____.   d) 42, 39, 36, 33   Subtract _____.

e) 17, 14, 11, 8   Subtract _____.   f) 99, 97, 95, 93   Subtract _____.

6. Write the number to add or subtract.

a) 97, 90, 83, 76, 69   _Subtract 7_.   b) 1, 9, 17, 25, 33, 41   _____.

c) 81, 85, 89, 93   _____.   d) 99, 88, 77, 66   _____.

7. Fill in the **rule** for the number pattern. Extend the pattern.

Number Pattern	Pattern Rule
a) 13, 18, 23, _____, _____, _____	Start at _____ and add _____.
b) 38, 36, 34, _____, _____, _____	Start at _____ and subtract _____.
c) 63, 60, 57, _____, _____, _____	Start at _____ and subtract _____.
d) 56, 61, 66, _____, _____, _____	Start at _____ and add _____.
e) 10, 17, 24, _____, _____, _____	Start at _____ and add _____.
f) 76, 72, 68, _____, _____, _____	Start at _____ and subtract _____.
g) 85, 82, 79, _____, _____, _____	Start at _____ and _____.
h) 23, 29, 35, _____, _____, _____	Start at _____ and _____.
i) 76, 86, 96, _____, _____, _____	Start at _____ and _____.

COPYRIGHT © 2016 JUMP MATH: NOT TO BE COPIED.

8. Use the rule to make the pattern. Write 5 numbers in the pattern.

a) Start at 3 and add 4 each time. _3, 7, 11, 15, 19_____

b) Start at 4 and add 5 each time. _____

c) Start at 68 and subtract 2 each time. _____

d) Start at 45 and add 3 each time. _____

e) Start at 97 and subtract 10 each time. _____

f) Start at 10 and add 7 each time. _____

g) Start at 99 and subtract 8 each time. _____

BONUS ▶ Start at 17 and add 100 each time. _____

9. Nora makes a pattern for the rule. She makes some mistakes.
Correct the pattern and explain her mistakes.

a) Start at 4 and add 3 each time. Nora's pattern is 4, 7, 11, 13, 16.

b) Start at 89 and subtract 2 each time. Nora's pattern is 89, 85, 83, 81, 79.

c) Start at 94 and subtract 10 each time. Nora's pattern is 94, 84, 64, 54.

d) Start at 20 and add 10 each time. Nora's pattern is 10, 20, 30, 40.

e) Start at 5 and add 6 each time. Nora's pattern is 6, 11, 16, 21, 26.

10. Look at the number pattern 5, 8, 11, 14, 17.

Tom's Rule

Start at 5. Subtract 3 each time.

Amy's Rule

Start at 4. Add 3 each time.

Jayden's Rule

Start at 5. Add 3 each time.

a) Whose pattern rule is correct?

b) What mistakes did the others make? Explain.

COPYRIGHT © 2016 JUMP MATH: NOT TO BE COPIED.

PA3-7 Ordinal Numbers

> **Ordinal numbers** tell the positions of objects.
>
> first, second, third, fourth, fifth, sixth, seventh, eighth, ninth, tenth
>
> 1st   2nd   3rd   4th   5th   6th   7th   8th   9th   10th

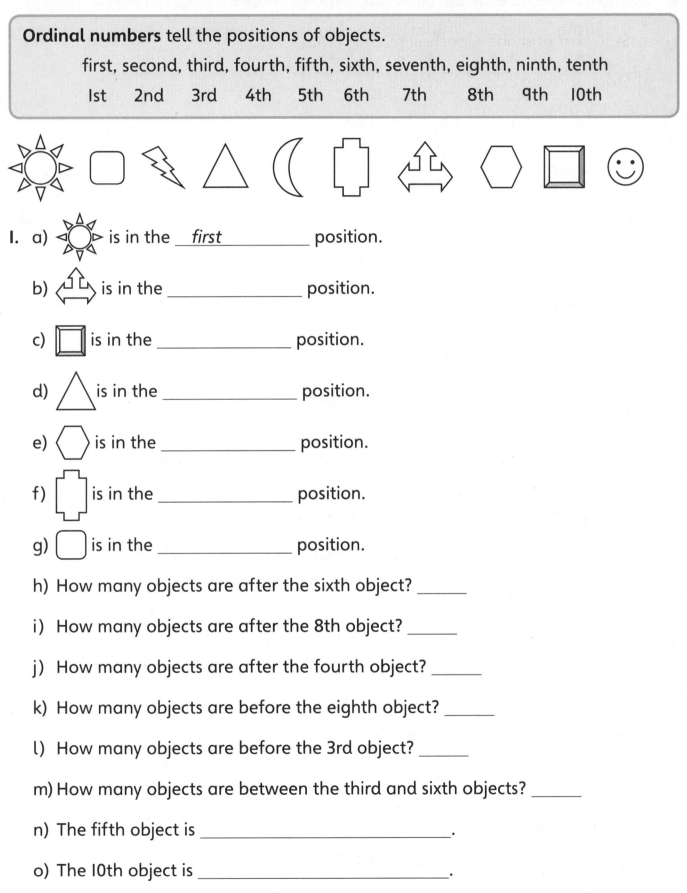

1. a) ☀ is in the ___first___ position.

   b) ⇱ is in the _____ position.

   c) ▢ is in the _____ position.

   d) △ is in the _____ position.

   e) ⬡ is in the _____ position.

   f) ⬚ is in the _____ position.

   g) ▢ is in the _____ position.

   h) How many objects are after the sixth object? _____

   i) How many objects are after the 8th object? _____

   j) How many objects are after the fourth object? _____

   k) How many objects are before the eighth object? _____

   l) How many objects are before the 3rd object? _____

   m) How many objects are between the third and sixth objects? _____

   n) The fifth object is _____.

   o) The 10th object is _____.

COPYRIGHT © 2016 JUMP MATH: NOT TO BE COPIED.

2. Liz and her friends took part in a race with 40 people.

a) Who came in 32nd in the race? _____

b) Who finished in the 17th position? _____

c) Who finished in the 24th position? _____

d) In which position did Tasha finish the race? _____

e) In which position did Arsham finish the race? _____

f) Liz came in 11th in the race. How many places before Sam

was Liz? _____

g) How many people are between Liz and Sam? _____

h) How many people are between Tasha and Sam? _____

i) How many people are between Sam and Arsham? _____

j) Jake was 4 places behind Jen. Mark the number line above

to show Jake's position. _____

3. a) What is the first letter of your name? _____

b) What is the third letter in "apple"? _____

c) What is the 5th letter in "Nunavut"? _____

d) Circle the 2nd **a** in "Manitoba."

e) Circle the 2nd **o** in "books."

f) What is the 7th letter of the alphabet? _____

COPYRIGHT © 2016 JUMP MATH: NOT TO BE COPIED.

PA3-8 Number Patterns in Tables

Columns run up and down. They are numbered from left to right.
The 2nd column is shaded.

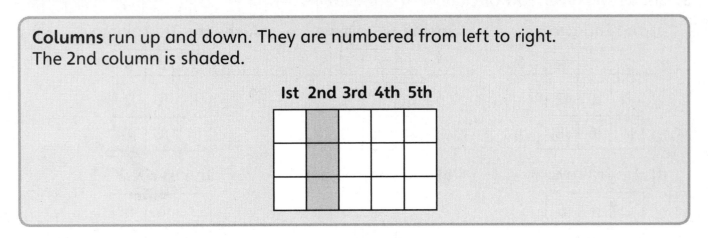

1. Shade the given column.

a) the 1st column

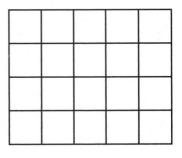

b) the 5th column

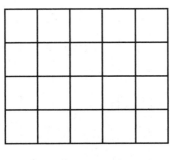

c) the 3rd column

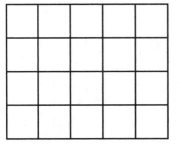

Rows run sideways. They are numbered from top to bottom.
The 3rd row is shaded.

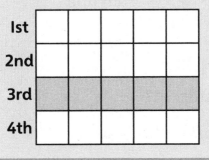

2. Shade the given row.

a) the 1st row

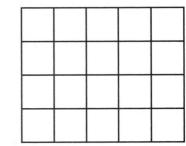

b) the 4th row

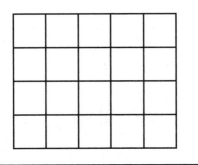

c) the 2nd row

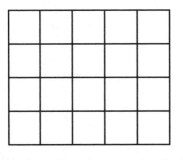

COPYRIGHT © 2016 JUMP MATH: NOT TO BE COPIED.

3. Shade the given row or column.

a) the 2nd row

2	4	6
8	10	12
14	16	18

b) the 1st column

2	4	6
8	10	12
14	16	18

c) the 3rd column

2	4	6
8	10	12
14	16	18

d) the 3rd row

2	4	6
8	10	12
14	16	18

e) the 2nd column

2	4	6
8	10	12
14	16	18

f) the 1st row

2	4	6
8	10	12
14	16	18

g) the 4th row

2	4	6	8
10	12	14	16
18	20	22	24
26	28	30	32

h) the 4th column

2	4	6	8
10	12	14	16
18	20	22	24
26	28	30	32

i) the 2nd row and the 3rd column

2	4	6	8
10	12	14	16
18	20	22	24
26	28	30	32

4. a) Write the pattern in the 1st row.

__1__ __3__ _____ _____

What number did you start at? _____

What number did you add each time? _____

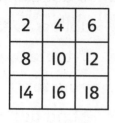

1	3	5	7
3	5	7	9
5	7	9	11
7	9	11	13

b) Write a rule for the pattern in the 3rd column.

_____

_____

c) Describe two other patterns you see.

_____

_____

COPYRIGHT © 2016 JUMP MATH: NOT TO BE COPIED.

PA3-9 T-tables

Nina saved 10 dollars in January.

She saves 5 dollars every month after that.

Nina uses a **T-table** to keep track of her money.

She writes a rule for the table:

Start at 10 and add 5 each time.

Month	Dollars Saved
January	10
February	15
March	20

⑤
⑤

Nina writes the number of dollars saved each month.

1. Write the gaps in the circles. Then write the rule for the pattern.

a)

Month	Dollars Saved
January	4
February	7
March	10
April	13

③

Rule: Start at _____ and add _____.

b)

Month	Dollars Saved
January	2
February	5
March	8
April	11

Rule: Start at _____ and add _____.

c)

Month	Dollars Saved
January	3
February	5
March	7
April	9

Rule: Start at _____ and add _____.

d)

Month	Dollars Saved
January	2
February	6
March	10
April	14

Rule: Start at _____ and add _____.

e)

Month	Dollars Saved
March	4
April	6
May	8
June	10

Rule: Start at _____ and add _____.

f)

Month	Dollars Saved
May	1
June	5
July	9
August	13

Rule: Start at _____ and add _____.

COPYRIGHT © 2016 JUMP MATH: NOT TO BE COPIED.

2. Complete the T-table.

a)

Month	Dollars Saved
January	2
February	5
March	8
April	
May	
June	

3

b)

Month	Dollars Saved
February	6
March	9
April	12
May	
June	
July	

c)

Month	Dollars Saved
July	1
August	6
September	11
October	
November	
December	

d)

Month	Dollars Saved
August	4
September	9
October	14
November	
December	
January	

3. How many young would 4 animals have? Complete the table to find out.

a)

Number of Cats	Number of Kittens
1	6
2	12
3	
4	

b)

Number of Foxes	Number of Kits
1	4
2	8
3	
4	

c)

Number of Bears	Number of Cubs
1	2
2	4
3	
4	

COPYRIGHT © 2016 JUMP MATH: NOT TO BE COPIED.

4. How much money would Shelly earn for 4 hours of work? Complete the T-table to find out.

a)
Hours Worked	Dollars Earned
1	7

b)
Hours Worked	Dollars Earned
1	8

c)
Hours Worked	Dollars Earned
1	6

5. It costs 5 dollars to rent a canoe for the first hour. It costs 4 dollars for each hour after that.

a) How much does it cost to rent a canoe for 4 hours? _____

b) Carl has 20 dollars. Can he rent the canoe for 5 hours? _____

Hours	Dollars Paid
1	
2	
3	

6. Marla makes figures with squares.

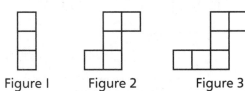

Figure 1   Figure 2   Figure 3

a) Complete the T-table to show how many squares Marla uses for each figure.

b) Marla has 12 squares. Can she make Figure 5 in this pattern? Explain.

Figure	Number of Squares
1	3
2	
3	

_____

_____

7. Marko saves 6 dollars each month.

a) How much will he save in 3 months?

b) How many months will it take for Marko to save 30 dollars?

COPYRIGHT © 2016 JUMP MATH: NOT TO BE COPIED.

PA3-10 Attributes

Anna makes a pattern with shapes. She uses different colours. The shapes have different sizes. Shape, colour, and size are examples of **attributes**.

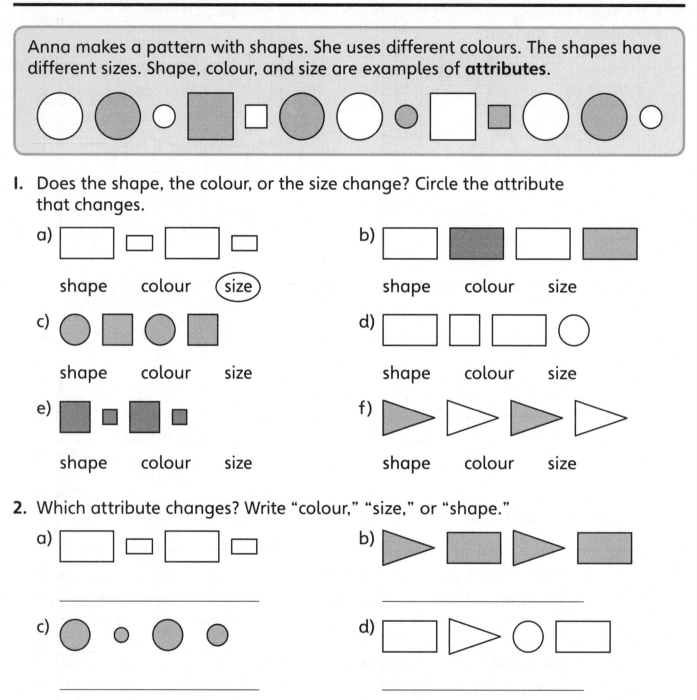

1. Does the shape, the colour, or the size change? Circle the attribute that changes.

a) shape   colour   (size)

b) shape   colour   size

c) shape   colour   size

d) shape   colour   size

e) shape   colour   size

f) shape   colour   size

2. Which attribute changes? Write "colour," "size," or "shape."

a) _____

b) _____

c) _____

d) _____

3. Circle two attributes that change.

a) size   shape   colour

b) size   shape   colour

c) size   shape   colour

d) size   shape   design

COPYRIGHT © 2016 JUMP MATH: NOT TO BE COPIED.

4. Which two attributes change? Write "colour," "size," "design," or "shape."

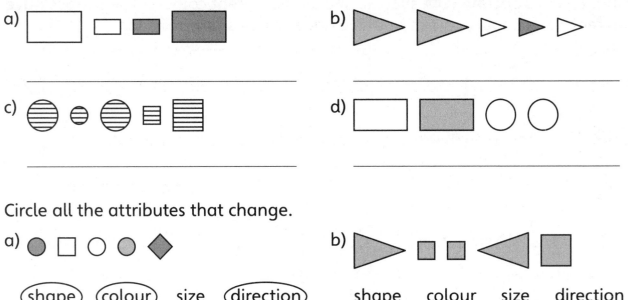

a) _____

b) _____

c) _____

d) _____

5. Circle all the attributes that change.

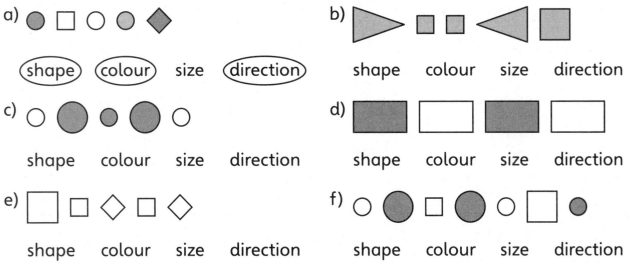

a) (shape) (colour) size (direction)

b) shape colour size direction

c) shape colour size direction

d) shape colour size direction

e) shape colour size direction

f) shape colour size direction

6. Draw five shapes with the given attributes.

a) same shape, same size, different colours

b) same shape, same colour, different sizes

c) same colour, different shapes, different sizes

d) same size, different shapes, different colours

e) one attribute is the same, two attributes change

COPYRIGHT © 2016 JUMP MATH: NOT TO BE COPIED.

PA3-II Repeating Patterns

This is a **repeating pattern.**

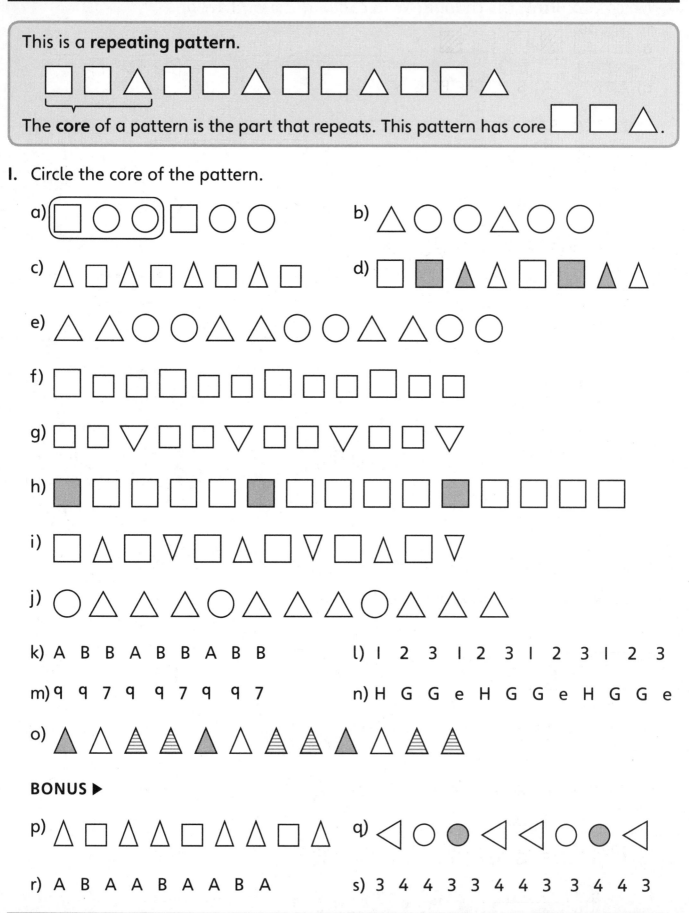

The **core** of a pattern is the part that repeats. This pattern has core ☐ ☐ △.

I. Circle the core of the pattern.

a) ☐ ○ ○ ☐ ○ ○

b) △ ○ ○ △ ○ ○

c) △ ☐ △ ☐ △ ☐ △ ☐

d) ☐ ▣ ▲ △ ☐ ▣ ▲ △

e) △ △ ○ ○ △ △ ○ ○ △ △ ○ ○

f) ☐ ☐ ☐ ☐ ☐ ☐ ☐ ☐ ☐ ☐ ☐ ☐

g) ☐ ☐ ▽ ☐ ☐ ▽ ☐ ☐ ▽ ☐ ☐ ▽

h) ▣ ☐ ☐ ☐ ☐ ▣ ☐ ☐ ☐ ☐ ▣ ☐ ☐ ☐ ☐

i) ☐ △ ☐ ▽ ☐ △ ☐ ▽ ☐ △ ☐ ▽

j) ○ △ △ △ ○ △ △ △ ○ △ △ △

k) A B B A B B A B B

l) 1 2 3 1 2 3 1 2 3 1 2 3

m) 9 9 7 9 9 7 9 9 7

n) H G G e H G G e H G G e

o) ▲ △ △ △ ▲ △ △ △ ▲ △ △ △

BONUS ▶

p) △ ☐ △ △ ☐ △ △ ☐ △

q) ◁ ○ ● ◁ ◁ ○ ● ◁

r) A B A A B A A B A

s) 3 4 4 3 3 4 4 3 3 4 4 3

COPYRIGHT © 2016 JUMP MATH: NOT TO BE COPIED.

2. Circle the core of the pattern. Then continue the pattern.

a) □ ■ ▨ □ ■ ▨ ____ ____ ____ ____ ____ ____

b) A B C A B C A B C A ____ ____ ____ ____

c) 2 7 9 5 2 7 9 5 ____ ____ ____ ____

d) 3 0 0 1 3 0 0 1 3 0 ____ ____ ____ ____ ____

e) A B b A B b A B b ____ ____ ____ ____ ____

f) 5 3 3 3 3 5 3 3 3 3 5 3 3 ____ ____ ____ ____

g) □ ○ △ ■ □ ○ △ ■ ____ ____ ____ ____

h) ▨ ▽ △ □ ▨ ▽ △ □ ____ ____ ____ ____

i) △ ◬ ◬ △ ◬ ◬ △ ____ ____ ____ ____ ____

j) ↑ → ↓ ← ↑ → ↓ ← ____ ____ ____ ____ ____

Ray wants to describe this pattern. □ ● ☰ □ ● ☰ The core is □ ● ☰.
He describes the pattern as white square, black circle, striped square, then repeat.

---

3. Circle the core. Then describe the pattern.

a) □ ○ ○ □ ○ ○ □

_____

_____

b) □ ▨ □ ▨ □ ▨

_____

_____

c) △ ○ ▲ □ △ ○ ▲ □

_____

_____

d) ↑ → ↓ ↑ → ↓ ↑ →

_____

_____

e) A B B A A B B A A B

A, B, B, A, then repeat

f) 1 2 3 4 1 2 3 4 1 2 3

_____

g) E G G E G G E G G E

_____

h) 6 7 6 6 7 6 6 7 6 6 7 6 6

_____

COPYRIGHT © 2016 JUMP MATH: NOT TO BE COPIED.

4. Draw a pattern for the rule. Repeat the core three times.

  a) large white square, small dark square, striped circle, then repeat

  b) A, c, h, then repeat   c) 3, 4, 4, 3, then repeat

  _____   _____

> **REMINDER ▶** Colour, shape, size, design, and direction are examples of attributes.

5. Circle the attributes that change in the pattern.

  a) ↑ → ↓ ← ↑ → ↓ ←   b) □ ○ △ ■ □ ○ △ ■

      colour shape size direction   colour shape direction size

  c) ▨ ▽ △ □ ▨ ▽ △ □   d) ◁ ○ ● ▷ ◁ ○ ● ▷

      shape size design direction   shape colour size direction

6. Make a repeating pattern. Draw the core 3 times. Have a partner draw 5 more shapes in your pattern.

  a) The core has 4 circles. Size and colour change.

  b) The core has 5 shapes of the same size. Colour and shape change.

  c) The core has 3 triangles. Design and direction change.

  d) Two attributes change, and two attributes stay the same.

7. Make your own repeating pattern. Use three different shapes and two different colours. Describe your pattern.

8. The pattern rule is circle, square, triangle, then repeat.

  Iva's pattern is ○ ■ △ ○ ■ △. Jay's pattern is ○ □ ▽ ○ □ ▽.

  Why are the patterns not the same? Write a better rule for each pattern.

BONUS ▶ The pattern is 2, 4, 6, 8.

        Megan thinks the pattern is 2, 4, 6, 8, 2, 4, 6, 8, 2, 4, 6, 8.

        Rick thinks the pattern is 2, 4, 6, 8, 10, 12, 14, 16.

        Who is correct? Explain. Write the rule for each person's pattern.

COPYRIGHT © 2016 JUMP MATH: NOT TO BE COPIED.

PA3-12 Exploring Patterns

1. The core of a pattern is circled. Continue the pattern.

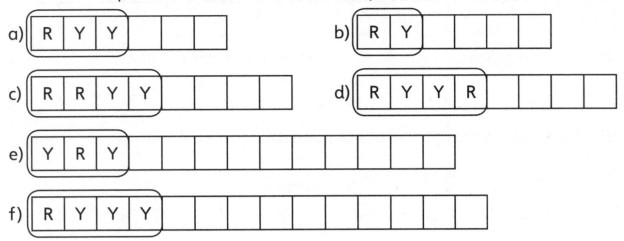

a) | R | Y | Y | | | |

b) | R | Y | | | | |

c) | R | R | Y | Y | | | | |

d) | R | Y | Y | R | | | | |

e) | Y | R | Y | | | | | | | |

f) | R | Y | Y | Y | | | | | | |

2. The core of a pattern is circled. Glen tries to extend the pattern.
Write ✓ if he extends the pattern correctly. Write ✗ on his mistakes.

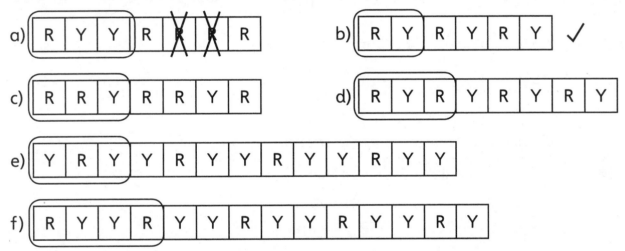

a) | R | Y | Y | R | ✗ | ✗ | R |

b) | R | Y | R | Y | R | Y | ✓

c) | R | R | Y | R | R | Y | R |

d) | R | Y | R | Y | R | Y | R | Y |

e) | Y | R | Y | Y | R | Y | Y | R | Y | Y | R | Y | Y |

f) | R | Y | Y | R | Y | Y | R | Y | Y | R | Y | Y | R | Y |

3. Kim circled the core of a pattern. Did she do it correctly?
Write ✓ for "yes" and ✗ for "no."

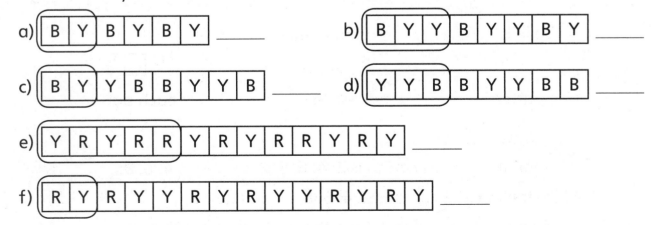

a) | B | Y | B | Y | B | Y | _____

b) | B | Y | Y | B | Y | Y | B | Y | _____

c) | B | Y | Y | B | B | Y | Y | B | _____

d) | Y | Y | B | B | Y | Y | B | B | _____

e) | Y | R | Y | R | R | Y | R | Y | R | R | Y | R | Y | _____

f) | R | Y | R | Y | Y | R | Y | R | Y | Y | R | Y | R | Y | _____

COPYRIGHT © 2016 JUMP MATH: NOT TO BE COPIED.

4. a) Continue the pattern to 18 squares.

1	2	3	4	5	6	7	8	9	10	11	12	13	14	15	16	17	18
R	Y	R	Y	R	Y	R	Y	R	Y								

b) What letter is in each square?

12th square _____   14th square _____   15th square _____   18th square _____

c) What letter is in the squares of the **even** numbers (2, 4, 6, …)? _____

d) If you extend the pattern, what letter would be in each square?

20th square _____   23rd square _____   35th square _____   78th square _____

In some patterns, the number of terms in the core changes.

○ △ ○ △ △ ○ △ △ △ ○ △ △ △ ○ △ △ △ △

5. Draw the next five terms in the pattern.

a) △ ○ △ △ ○ ○ △ △ △ ○ ○ ○

b) ○ ● ○ ○ ● ○ ○ ○ ● ○ ○ ○

c) ▥ □ □ □ ▥ ▥ ▥ ▥ ▥ □ □ □

d) □ ▨ ▨ ▨ ▨ □ ▨ ▨ ▨ ▨ □ ▨ ▨ ▨

6. Write the next five terms in the pattern.

a) A, B, A, B, B, A, B, B, B, _____

b) A, B, B, C, C, C, D, D, D, D, _____

c) Z, z, Y, y, X, x, _____

d) 1, 1, 2, 2, 3, 3, 4, 4, _____

e) 1, 1, 1, 1, 2, 2, 2, 2, 3, 3, 3, 3, _____

f) 9, 8, 8, 7, 7, 7, _____

g) 1, 3, 3, 5, 5, 5, 7, _____

COPYRIGHT © 2016 JUMP MATH: NOT TO BE COPIED.

Aputik makes bead patterns. She has the following 8 types of beads.

To make a pattern, Aputik changes the attributes of the beads she chooses.

7. Use Aputik's beads to make a bead pattern. Change the attributes.
   Then write a rule for the pattern.

   a) Start with ◯. Change size. Change colour. Repeat.

   Rule _Large white circle, small white circle, small grey circle, large grey circle,_
   then repeat.

   b) Start with ▭. Change size. Change colour. Repeat.

   Rule _____

   _____

   c) Start with ▭. Change shape. Change colour. Repeat.

   Rule _____

   _____

   d) Start with ▮. Change shape. Repeat.

   Rule _____

   _____

   e) **BONUS** ▶ Start with ◯. Change shape. Change size. Change size. Repeat.

   f) Make your own pattern by changing attributes. Describe your pattern.

COPYRIGHT © 2016 JUMP MATH: NOT TO BE COPIED.

NS3-I Place Value—Ones, Tens, and Hundreds

You can write a number in a place value chart. Example: 431

Hundreds	Tens	Ones
4	3	I

I. Write the number in the place value chart.

	Hundreds	Tens	Ones
a) 65	0	6	5
c) 408			
e) 17			
g) 372			
i) 0			

	Hundreds	Tens	Ones
b) 283			
d) 130			
f) 4			
h) 900			
j) 825			

3   7   5

hundreds   tens   ones

2. Write the place value of the underlined digit.

a) 1<u>7</u>   ones   b) 9<u>8</u>   c) <u>2</u>4

d) <u>6</u>3   e) <u>3</u>81   f) 97<u>2</u>

g) 4<u>2</u>5   h) 25<u>6</u>   i) <u>1</u>08

3. Write the place value of the digit 5.

a) 50   tens   b) 15   c) 251

d) 586   e) 375   f) 584

g) 935   h) 563   i) 153

COPYRIGHT © 2016 JUMP MATH: NOT TO BE COPIED.

The number 586 is a **3-digit number**.

- The **digit** 5 stands for 500.
- The **digit** 8 stands for 80.
- The **digit** 6 stands for 6.

4. Fill in the blank.

a) In the number 657, the **digit** 5 stands for ___50___.

b) In the number 248, the **digit** 2 stands for _____.

c) In the number 129, the **digit** 9 stands for _____.

d) In the number 108, the **digit** 0 stands for _____.

e) In the number 803, the digit _____ is in the **hundreds** place.

f) In the number 596, the digit _____ is in the **tens** place.

g) In the number 410, the digit _____ is in the **ones** place.

5. What number does each digit stand for?

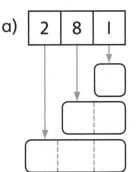

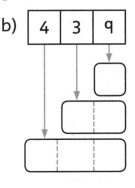

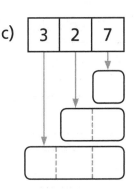

6. What number does the digit 3 stand for?

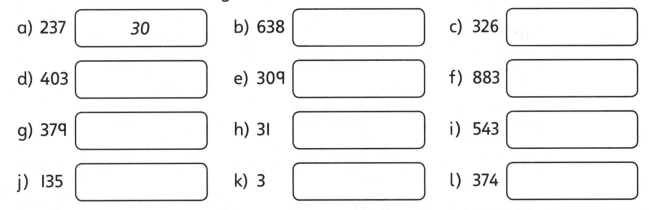

a) 237 ⟨ 30 ⟩   b) 638 ⟨ ⟩   c) 326 ⟨ ⟩

d) 403 ⟨ ⟩   e) 309 ⟨ ⟩   f) 883 ⟨ ⟩

g) 379 ⟨ ⟩   h) 31 ⟨ ⟩   i) 543 ⟨ ⟩

j) 135 ⟨ ⟩   k) 3 ⟨ ⟩   l) 374 ⟨ ⟩

COPYRIGHT © 2016 JUMP MATH: NOT TO BE COPIED.

NS3-2 Base Ten Blocks

Hundreds block	Tens block	Ones block
= 100	= 10	□ = 1

1. Write the number of hundreds, tens, and ones. Then write the number.

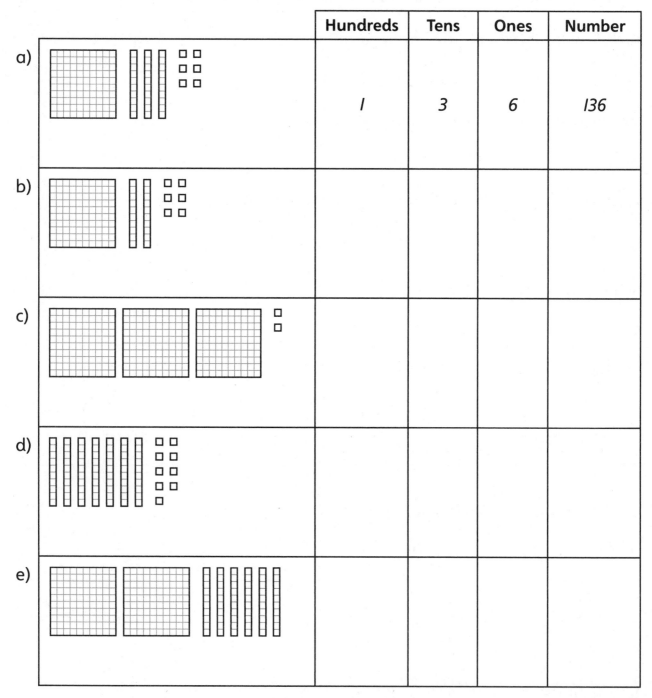

	Hundreds	Tens	Ones	Number
a)	1	3	6	136
b)				
c)				
d)				
e)				

COPYRIGHT © 2016 JUMP MATH: NOT TO BE COPIED.

2. Sketch the number using base ten blocks.

a) 342

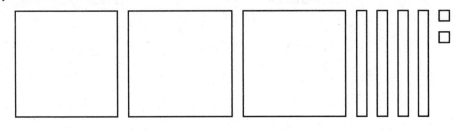

b) 237

c) 113

d) 206

e) 130

COPYRIGHT © 2016 JUMP MATH: NOT TO BE COPIED.

3. Sketch the missing base ten blocks to show the number.

a) 583

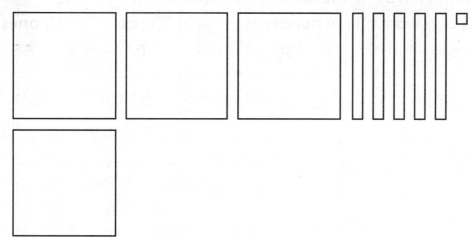

b) 467

4. Fill in the blanks.

a) 472 has ___4___ hundreds, ___7___ tens, and ___2___ ones.

b) 573 has _____ hundreds, _____ tens, and _____ ones.

c) 821 has _____ hundreds, _____ tens, and _____ one.

d) 409 has _____ hundreds, _____ tens, and _____ ones.

BONUS ▶ 3 has _____ hundreds, _____ tens, and _____ ones.

5. How many more tens blocks do you need to draw 452 than to draw 422? Explain.

COPYRIGHT © 2016 JUMP MATH: NOT TO BE COPIED.

NS3-3 Expanded Form

You can write the number **475** in **expanded form** in two ways.
- Using **numerals** and words: **4 hundreds**   +   **7 tens**   +   **5 ones**
- Using numerals only: **400**   +   **70**   +   **5**

1. Write "hundreds," "tens," or "ones" for each digit. Then write in expanded form.

a) 658   6 _hundreds_

      5 _tens_

      8 _ones_

  _600_ + _50_ + _8_

b) 493   4 _____

      9 _____

      3 _____

  _____ + _____ + _____

2. Fill in the blanks.

a) 267 = __2__ hundreds + __6__ tens + __7__ ones

b) 381 = _____ hundreds + _____ tens + _____ one

c) 709 = _____ hundreds + _____ ones

d) 727 = _____ hundreds + _____ tens + _____ ones

e) 53 = _____ tens + _____ ones

f) 640 = _____ hundreds + _____ tens

3. Write the number in expanded form using numerals and words.

a) 547 = _5 hundreds + 4 tens + 7 ones_

b) 239 = _____

c) 73 = _____

d) 190 = _____

e) 605 = _____

f) 420 = _____

COPYRIGHT © 2016 JUMP MATH: NOT TO BE COPIED.

4. Write the number for the expanded form.

a) 3 hundreds + 4 tens + 7 ones

[347]

b) 9 hundreds + 8 tens + 2 ones

[ ]

c) 5 tens + 6 ones

[ ]

d) 2 hundreds + 7 tens

[ ]

e) 6 hundreds + 1 ten + 4 ones

[ ]

f) 1 hundred + 8 ones

[ ]

5. Write the number in expanded form using numerals only.

a) 762 = __700 + 60 + 2__

b) 845 = _____

c) 72 = _____

d) 503 = _____

e) 431 = _____

f) 978 = _____

6. Write the number for the expanded form.

a) 400 + 50 + 3 = __453__

b) 800 + 70 + 1 = _____

c) 40 + 8 = _____

d) 600 + 20 = _____

e) 900 + 1 = _____

f) 400 + 40 + 4 = _____

g) 500 + 40 + 9 = _____

h) 300 + 10 + 5 = _____

7. Write the missing numbers for the expanded form.

a) 247 = 200 + __40__ + 7

b) 598 = 500 + 90 + _____

c) 651 = _____ + 50 + 1

d) 843 = 800 + _____ + _____

e) 352 = _____ + 50 + _____

f) 400 + 50 + _____ = 458

g) 300 + _____ + 7 = 367

h) _____ + 2 = 702

i) 57 = _____ + 7

j) 700 + 80 + _____ = 788

k) _____ + 20 + _____ = 924

l) _____ + _____ + _____ = 835

COPYRIGHT © 2016 JUMP MATH: NOT TO BE COPIED.

NS3-4 Writing and Reading Number Words

> Number words from 0 to 9:
>
> zero   one   two   three   four   five   six   seven   eight   nine

1. Write the number word.

   a) 2 _two_

   b) 4 _____

   c) 5 _____

   d) 3 _____

   e) 9 _____

   f) 8 _____

   g) 0 _____

   h) 6 _____

   i) 1 _____

   j) 7 _____

> Number words from 10 to 19:
>
> ten   eleven   twelve   thirteen   fourteen
> fifteen   sixteen   seventeen   eighteen   nineteen

2. Write the number word.

   a) 12 _twelve_

   b) 14 _____

   c) 15 _____

   d) 13 _____

   e) 19 _____

   f) 18 _____

   g) 11 _____

   h) 16 _____

3. Write the numeral for the number word.

   a) nineteen = _1_ _9_

   b) eighteen = ___ ___

   c) sixteen = ___ ___

   d) fifteen = ___ ___

   e) thirteen = ___ ___

   f) twelve = ___ ___

   g) seventeen = ___ ___

   h) fourteen = ___ ___

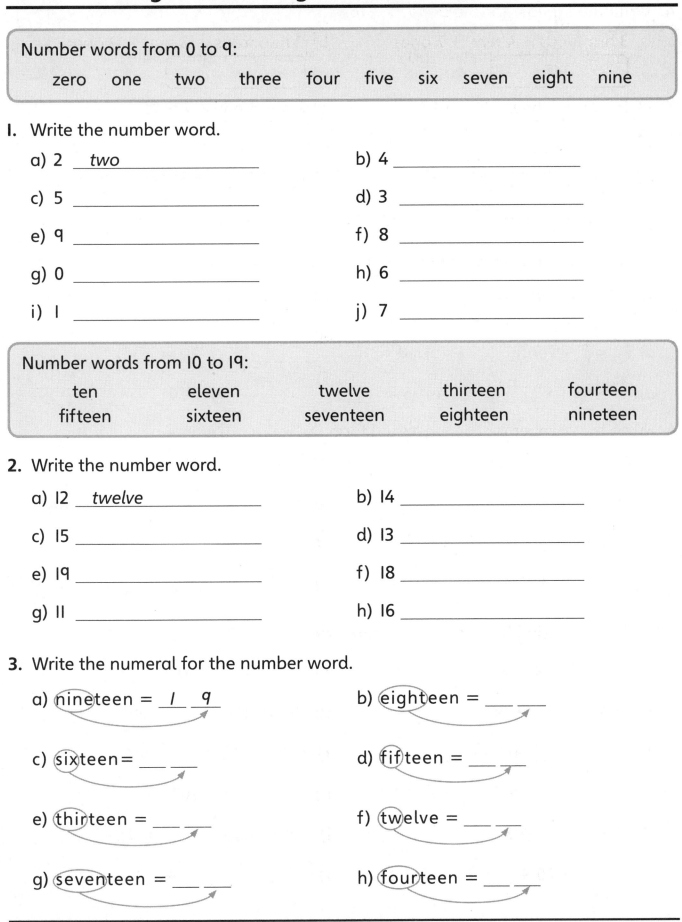

COPYRIGHT © 2016 JUMP MATH: NOT TO BE COPIED.

Number words for the tens place:

twenty   thirty   forty   fifty   sixty   seventy   eighty   ninety

4. Write the ending for the number word.

a) 60 = six _ty_____

b) 16 = six _teen_____

c) 40 = for_____

d) 14 = four_____

e) 50 = fif_____

f) 20 = twen_____

g) 13 = thir_____

h) 18 = eight_____

i) 70 = seven_____

j) 30 = thir_____

k) 19 = nine_____

l) 90 = nine_____

5. Write the number word for the numeral.

a) 70 = ___seventy____

b) 60 = _____

c) 90 = _____

d) 17 = _____

e) 16 = _____

f) 19 = _____

g) 40 = _____

h) 50 = _____

i) 30 = _____

j) 20 = _____

k) 15 = _____

l) 80 = _____

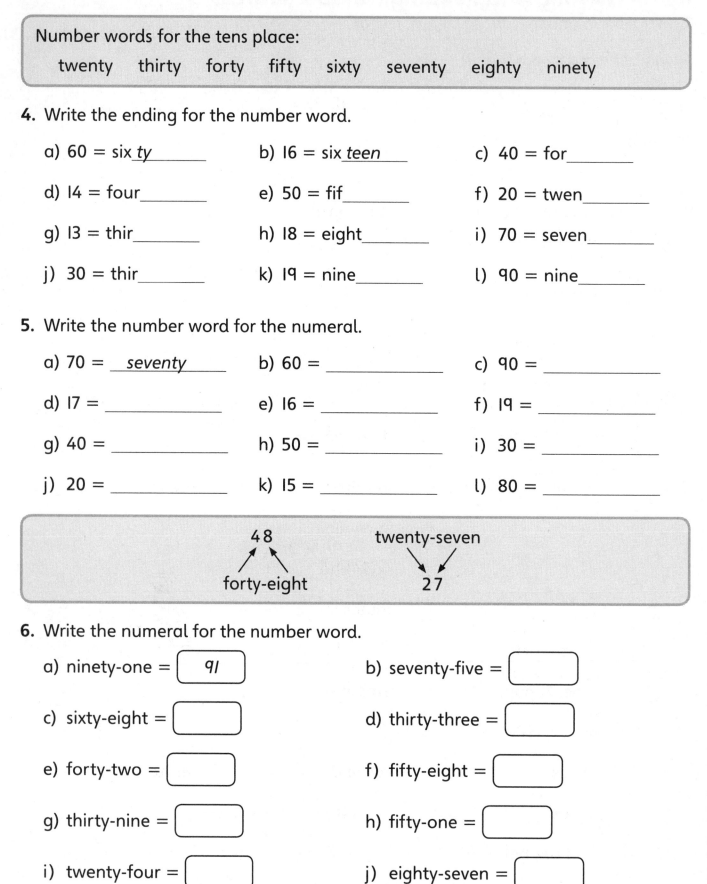

6. Write the numeral for the number word.

a) ninety-one = [91]

b) seventy-five = [ ]

c) sixty-eight = [ ]

d) thirty-three = [ ]

e) forty-two = [ ]

f) fifty-eight = [ ]

g) thirty-nine = [ ]

h) fifty-one = [ ]

i) twenty-four = [ ]

j) eighty-seven = [ ]

COPYRIGHT © 2016 JUMP MATH: NOT TO BE COPIED.

7. Write the number word for the numeral.

a) 43 = ___*forty-three*___   b) 22 = _____

c) 73 = _____   d) 37 = _____

e) 64 = _____   f) 96 = _____

8. Underline the number words in the sentence.

a) Avril has three pet fish.

b) Lewis buys thirty grapes.

c) A bus can seat sixty-four children.

d) Pat runs three kilometres in forty-five minutes.

e) Arsham will be nine years old in two weeks.

9. Write the number words for the numeral to complete the sentence.

a) There are _____ (7) days in a week.

b) There are _____ (24) hours in a day.

c) There are _____ (60) minutes in an hour.

d) In checkers, each side has _____ (12) pieces.

e) April, June, September, and November each have

_____ (30) days.

f) Canada has _____ (10) provinces and _____ (3) territories.

g) Canada has _____ (46) national parks.

h) Teenagers are between _____ (12) and

_____ (20) years old.

COPYRIGHT © 2016 JUMP MATH: NOT TO BE COPIED.

NS3-5 Writing and Reading 3-Digit Numbers

> 3 0 0 → three hundred
>
> seven hundred → 7 0 0

1. Write the number word for the numeral.

a) 100 _one hundred_

b) 600 _____

c) 500 _____

d) 800 _____

e) 700 _____

f) 200 _____

g) 400 _____

h) 900 _____

> 3 4 8 → three hundred forty-eight
>
> seven hundred twenty-nine → 7 2 9

2. Underline the hundreds digit. Draw a box around the last 2 digits. Write the number words for the numeral.

a) 4 2 3 _four hundred_ _twenty-three_

b) 3 7 5 _____ _____

c) 9 6 8 _____ _____

d) 1 3 4 _____ _____

BONUS ▶ 6 0 8 _____ _____

3. Write the numeral for the number words.

a) three hundred fifty-four _3 5 4_

b) six hundred seventy-eight _____

c) two hundred thirty-nine _____

d) five hundred sixty-two _____

BONUS ▶

e) one hundred eighteen _____

f) seven hundred six _____

COPYRIGHT © 2016 JUMP MATH: NOT TO BE COPIED.

NS3-6 Showing Numbers in Different Ways

1. Write the numeral for the expanded form.

   a) 200 + 50 + 3 = [ ]

   b) 400 + 60 + 8 = [ ]

   c) 20 + 7 = [ ]

   d) 900 + 90 + 9 = [ ]

   e) 600 + 7 = [ ]

   f) 500 + 60 = [ ]

2. Write the missing numbers for the expanded form.

   a) 800 + __20__ + 7 = 827

   b) 400 + _____ + 5 = 475

   c) _____ + 30 + 5 = 735

   d) 500 + 20 + _____ = 526

   e) 600 + _____ + 1 = 681

   f) 200 + _____ = 202

   g) 300 + _____ = 320

   h) 100 + _____ + _____ = 173

3. Write the number word.

   a) 623 _____

   b) 412 _____

   c) 803 _____

4. Write the numeral for the number word.

   a) four hundred seventy-three = _____

   b) seven hundred eleven = _____

   c) eight hundred fifty = _____

5. Kim's class brings 118 cans to school for a food drive. Write the number of cans in words.

   _____

COPYRIGHT © 2016 JUMP MATH: NOT TO BE COPIED.

6. Draw a base ten model. Then write the number in expanded form. Use squares for hundreds, lines for tens, and dots for ones.

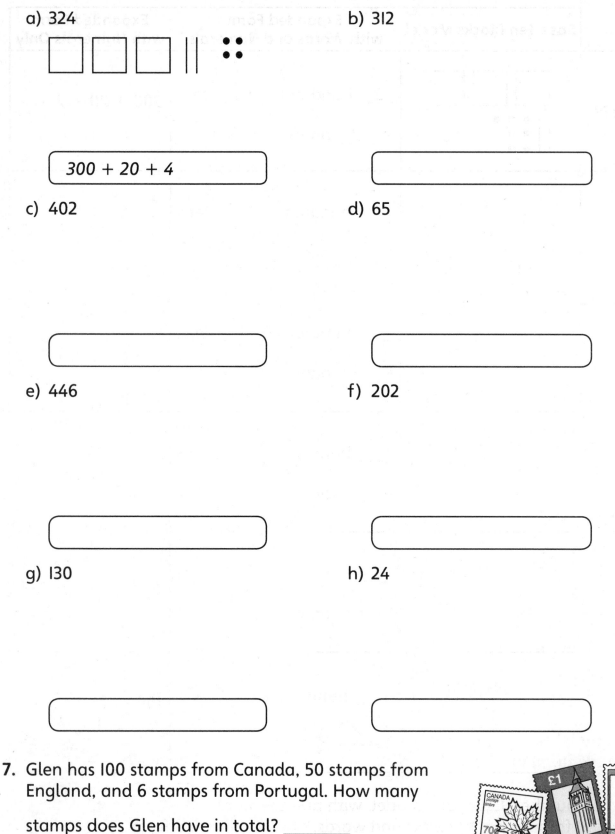

a) 324

300 + 20 + 4

b) 312

c) 402

d) 65

e) 446

f) 202

g) 130

h) 24

7. Glen has 100 stamps from Canada, 50 stamps from England, and 6 stamps from Portugal. How many stamps does Glen have in total? _____

COPYRIGHT © 2016 JUMP MATH: NOT TO BE COPIED.

8. Fill in the table. Use squares for hundreds, lines for tens, and dots for ones.

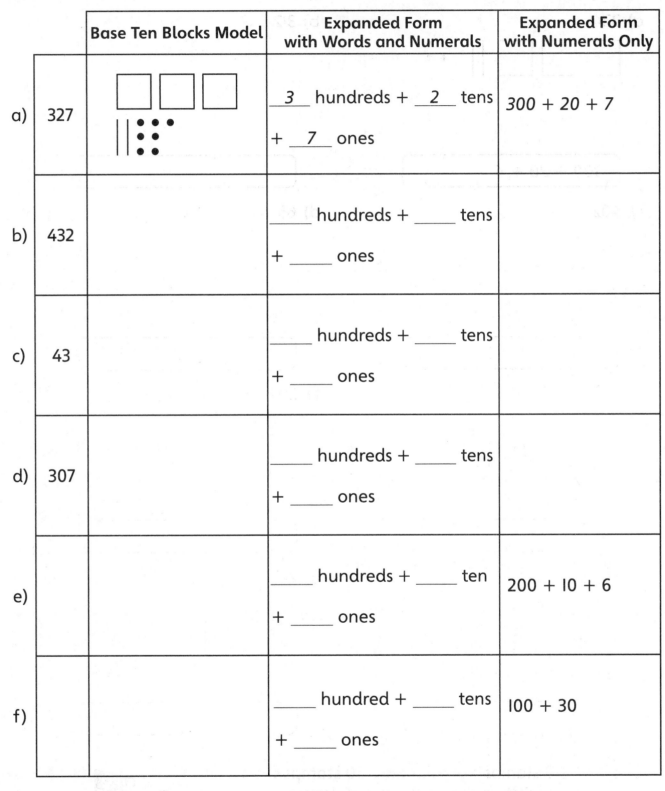

		Base Ten Blocks Model	Expanded Form with Words and Numerals	Expanded Form with Numerals Only
a)	327		__3__ hundreds + __2__ tens + __7__ ones	300 + 20 + 7
b)	432		____ hundreds + ____ tens + ____ ones	
c)	43		____ hundreds + ____ tens + ____ ones	
d)	307		____ hundreds + ____ tens + ____ ones	
e)			____ hundreds + ____ ten + ____ ones	200 + 10 + 6
f)			____ hundred + ____ tens + ____ ones	100 + 30

9. Show the number 358 with a model, with number words, in expanded form using numerals and words, and in expanded form using numerals only.

COPYRIGHT © 2016 JUMP MATH: NOT TO BE COPIED.

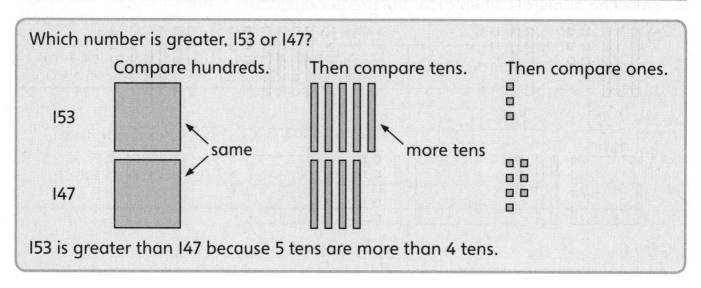

Which number is greater, 153 or 147?

Compare hundreds. Then compare tens. Then compare ones.

153

147

same   more tens

153 is greater than 147 because 5 tens are more than 4 tens.

1. Write the numerals. Then circle the greater number.

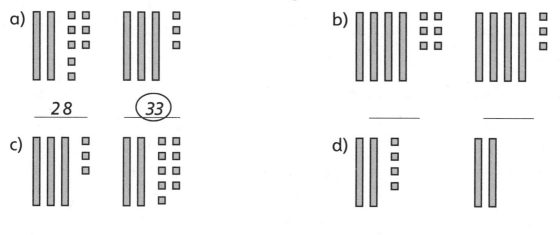

a)   28   (33)

b)   _____   _____

c)   _____   _____

d)   _____   _____

2. Write the numerals. Compare the hundreds, then the tens, then the ones. Circle the greater number.

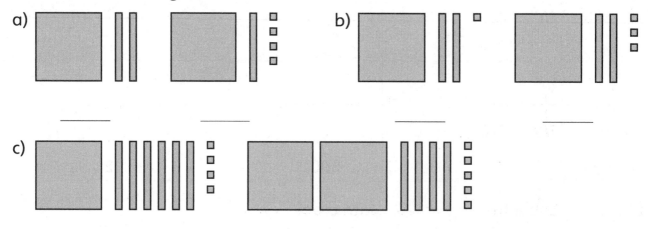

a)   _____   _____

b)   _____   _____

c)   _____   _____

COPYRIGHT © 2016 JUMP MATH: NOT TO BE COPIED

3. Write the numerals. Then circle the greater number.

a)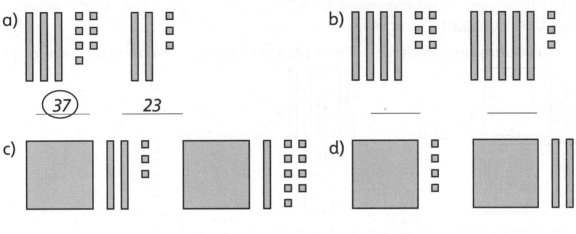

(37)   23 _____

b) _____   _____

c)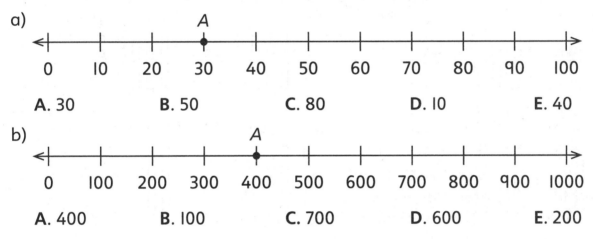

_____   _____

d) _____   _____

4. Label each number with a dot on the **number line**.

a)

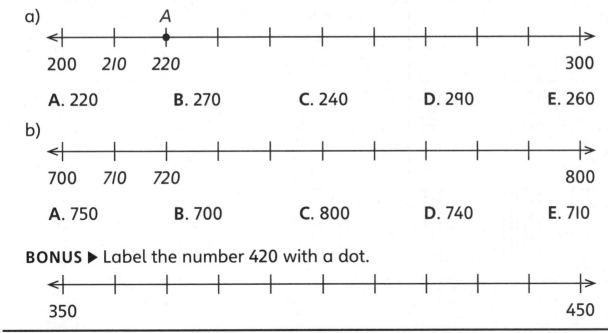

0 10 20 30 40 50 60 70 80 90 100

A. 30   **B.** 50   **C.** 80   **D.** 10   **E.** 40

b)

0 100 200 300 400 500 600 700 800 900 1000

A. 400   **B.** 100   **C.** 700   **D.** 600   **E.** 200

5. Complete the number line. Then label each number with a dot.

a)

200 210 220   300

A. 220   **B.** 270   **C.** 240   **D.** 290   **E.** 260

b)

700 710 720   800

A. 750   **B.** 700   **C.** 800   **D.** 740   **E.** 710

BONUS ▶ Label the number 420 with a dot.

350   450

COPYRIGHT © 2016 JUMP MATH: NOT TO BE COPIED.

NS3-8 Comparing Numbers by Place Value

I. Write the number that each digit stands for. Then fill in the blanks.

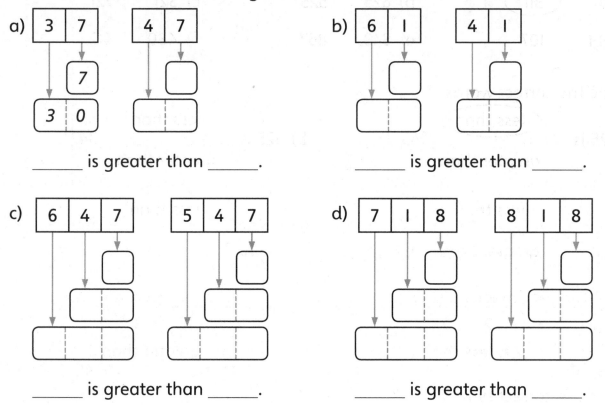

a)

| 3 | 7 |

| | 7 |

| 3 | 0 |

| 4 | 7 |

_____ is greater than _____.

b)

| 6 | 1 |

| 4 | 1 |

_____ is greater than _____.

c)

| 6 | 4 | 7 |

| 5 | 4 | 7 |

_____ is greater than _____.

d)

| 7 | 1 | 8 |

| 8 | 1 | 8 |

_____ is greater than _____.

2. Circle the first two digits that are different.
Then write the **greater** number in the box.
Hint: Remember to read the numbers from left to right.

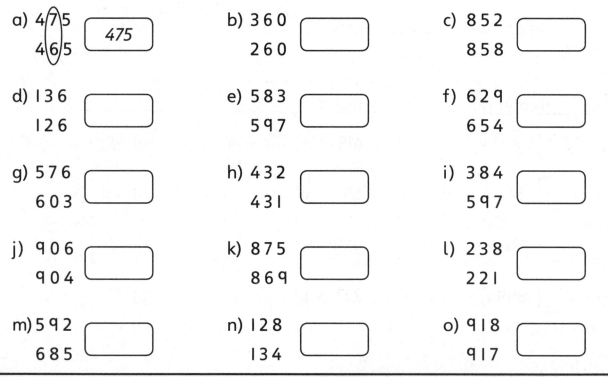

a) 4⑦5   475
   4⑥5

b) 3 6 0
   2 6 0

c) 8 5 2
   8 5 8

d) 1 3 6
   1 2 6

e) 5 8 3
   5 9 7

f) 6 2 9
   6 5 4

g) 5 7 6
   6 0 3

h) 4 3 2
   4 3 1

i) 3 8 4
   5 9 7

j) 9 0 6
   9 0 4

k) 8 7 5
   8 6 9

l) 2 3 8
   2 2 1

m) 5 9 2
   6 8 5

n) 1 2 8
   1 3 4

o) 9 1 8
   9 1 7

COPYRIGHT © 2016 JUMP MATH: NOT TO BE COPIED.

3. Circle the greater number.

a) 111   (311)   b) 625   525   c) 321   721

d) 99   107   e) 843   867   f) 480   412

4. Circle the correct words.

a) 25 is   (less than)   43   b) 425 is   less than / greater than   347
     greater than

c) 625 is   less than / greater than   647   d) 958 is   less than / greater than   951

< means **less than**	> means **greater than**
2 < 7	5 > 3
2 is less than 7	5 is greater than 3

---

5. Circle the correct symbol.

a) 35   (<) / >   47   b) 430   < / >   417   c) 35   < / >   47   d) 430   < / >   417

e) 635   < / >   647   f) 351   < / >   347   g) 789   < / >   879   h) 42   < / >   402

6. Circle the greater number. Then write < or > in the box.

a) 41   <   (301)   b) 427 ☐ 419   c) 821 ☐ 88   d) 999 ☐ 107

e) 643 ☐ 647   f) 580 ☐ 69   g) 219 ☐ 220   h) 456 ☐ 32

i) 125 ☐ 122   j) 854 ☐ 859   k) 336 ☐ 330   l) 530 ☐ 503

m) 401 ☐ 399   n) 272 ☐ 227   o) 454 ☐ 445   p) 778 ☐ 787

COPYRIGHT © 2016 JUMP MATH: NOT TO BE COPIED.

7. Write "**less than**" or "**greater than**."

a) 423 is ___*greater than*___ 268.   b) 48 is _____ 103.

c) 307 is _____ 312.   d) 983 is _____ 981.

8. Use both digits to write 2-digit numbers.

a) 4 and 5   b) 6 and 1   c) 3 and 9   d) 6 and 7

__4__ __5__   _____ _____   _____ _____   _____ _____

__5__ __4__   _____ _____   _____ _____   _____ _____

9. Use both digits to write the largest possible 2-digit number.

a) 2, 3   b) 8, 9   c) 4, 1   d) 4, 7

__3__ __2__   _____ _____   _____ _____   _____ _____

10. Fill in the table using the digits to make numbers.

a)

Digits	Greatest Number	Smallest Number
5, 7, 2		

b)

Digits	Greatest Number	Smallest Number
3, 6, 4		

11. Write the numbers in order from smallest to greatest.

a) 75, 62, 87   b) 251, 385, 256

_____ , _____ , _____   _____ , _____ , _____

12. Write the lengths of these ocean animals from smallest to greatest.

   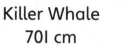

Octopus   Dolphin   Killer Whale   Grey Reef Shark
488 cm   396 cm   701 cm   183 cm

COPYRIGHT © 2016 JUMP MATH: NOT TO BE COPIED.

You can use a number line to place numbers in order.
Example: 38, 49, 41, 47, 32

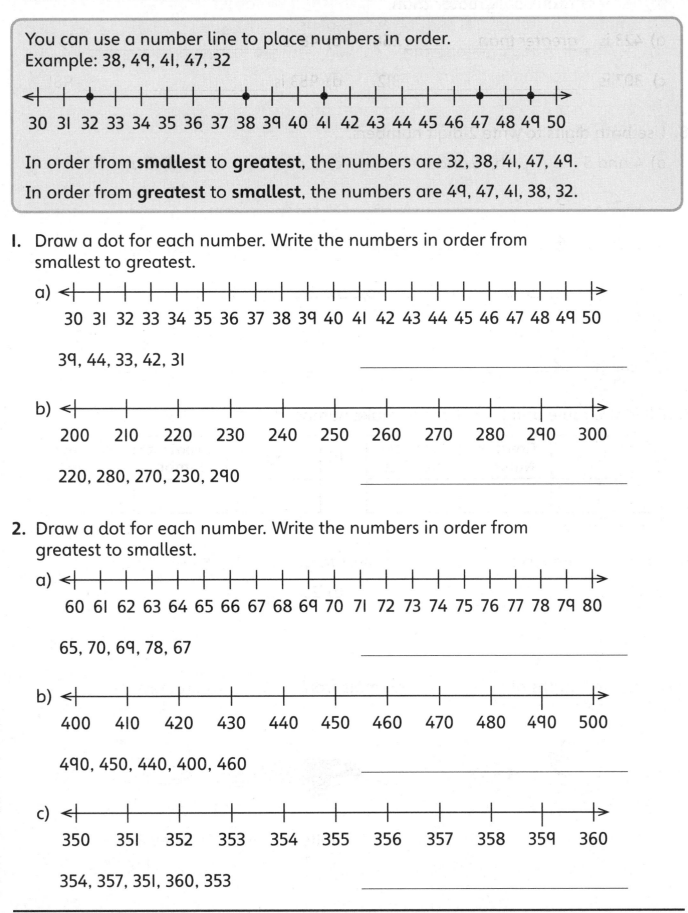

30 31 32 33 34 35 36 37 38 39 40 41 42 43 44 45 46 47 48 49 50

In order from **smallest** to **greatest**, the numbers are 32, 38, 41, 47, 49.

In order from **greatest** to **smallest**, the numbers are 49, 47, 41, 38, 32.

1. Draw a dot for each number. Write the numbers in order from smallest to greatest.

a)

30 31 32 33 34 35 36 37 38 39 40 41 42 43 44 45 46 47 48 49 50

39, 44, 33, 42, 31 _____

b)

200 210 220 230 240 250 260 270 280 290 300

220, 280, 270, 230, 290 _____

2. Draw a dot for each number. Write the numbers in order from greatest to smallest.

a)

60 61 62 63 64 65 66 67 68 69 70 71 72 73 74 75 76 77 78 79 80

65, 70, 69, 78, 67 _____

b)

400 410 420 430 440 450 460 470 480 490 500

490, 450, 440, 400, 460 _____

c)

350 351 352 353 354 355 356 357 358 359 360

354, 357, 351, 360, 353 _____

COPYRIGHT © 2016 JUMP MATH: NOT TO BE COPIED.

3. a) Mary thinks the numbers 78, 72, 71, 75, 79 are in order from smallest to greatest. Is she correct? Explain.

b) Frank thinks the numbers 590, 540, 560, 520, 510 are in order from greatest to smallest. Is he correct? Explain.

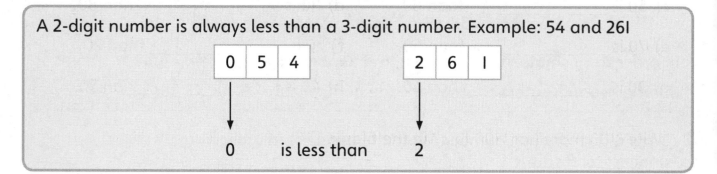

A 2-digit number is always less than a 3-digit number. Example: 54 and 261

| 0 | 5 | 4 |

| 2 | 6 | 1 |

0   is less than   2

4. Write the numbers in order from smallest to greatest.

a) 240, 250, 70, 40, 270   *40, 70, 240, 250, 270*

b) 340, 10, 90, 310, 320   _____

c) 200, 80, 300, 90, 500   _____

d) 310, 20, 70, 60, 890   _____

e) 50, 210, 90, 320, 280   _____

5. Write the numbers in order from greatest to smallest.

a) 80, 390, 340, 20, 310   *390, 340, 310, 80, 20*

b) 25, 430, 85, 490, 410   _____

c) 231, 431, 91, 131, 61   _____

d) 143, 287, 43, 98, 526   _____

e) 75, 123, 185, 68, 234   _____

6. John thinks the numbers 250, 310, 430, 90, 520 are in order from smallest to greatest. Is he correct? Explain.

_____

_____

COPYRIGHT © 2016 JUMP MATH: NOT TO BE COPIED.

1. Write "10 more" or "10 less" in the blank.

   a) 80 is ___10 more___ than 70.   b) 20 is _____ than 30.

   c) 50 is _____ than 60.   d) 90 is _____ than 80.

   e) 70 is _____ than 60.   f) 10 is _____ than 20.

   g) 30 is _____ than 40.   h) 40 is _____ than 30.

2. Write "100 more" or "100 less" in the blank.

   a) 500 is _____ than 400.   b) 300 is _____ than 400.

   c) 700 is _____ than 600.   d) 800 is _____ than 900.

   e) 400 is _____ than 500.   f) 100 is _____ than 200.

3. Write what each digit stands for. Compare the numbers.

   a) | 6 | 4 | 7 | | 6 | 5 | 7 |

   647 is ___10 less___ than 657.

   b) | 4 | 8 | 2 | | 3 | 8 | 2 |

   482 is _____ than 382.

   c) | 3 | 2 | 7 | | 3 | 1 | 7 |

   327 is _____ than 317.

   d) | 6 | 5 | 2 | | 7 | 5 | 2 |

   652 is _____ than 752.

COPYRIGHT © 2016 JUMP MATH: NOT TO BE COPIED.

4. Circle the digits that are different. Then fill in the blank.

a) 2⑥5
   2⑦5

265 is ___10 less___ than 275.

b) 3 9 2
   4 9 2

392 is _____ than 492.

c) 6 8 7
   6 7 7

687 is _____ than 677.

d) 3 6 2
   2 6 2

362 is _____ than 262.

e) 4 0 5
   4 1 5

405 is _____ than 415.

f) 5 8 7
   6 8 7

587 is _____ than 687.

g) 3 2 5
   3 3 5

325 is _____ than 335.

h) 4 2 9
   4 1 9

429 is _____ than 419.

5. Fill in the blank.

a) _____ is 10 more than 475.

b) _____ is 10 less than 263.

c) _____ is 10 less than 387.

d) _____ is 10 more than 482.

e) _____ is 100 more than 583.

f) _____ is 100 less than 402.

g) _____ is 100 more than 687.

h) _____ is 100 less than 291.

i) _____ is 100 less than 305.

j) _____ is 100 more than 851.

6. Fill in the blank.

a) 385 + _____ = 395

b) 201 + _____ = 301

c) 483 + _____ = 493

d) 617 + _____ = 717

e) 286 − _____ = 276

f) 837 − _____ = 737

COPYRIGHT © 2016 JUMP MATH: NOT TO BE COPIED.

7. Fill in the blank.

a) 375 + 10 = _____   b) 252 + 10 = _____   c) 972 + 10 = _____

d) 127 + 100 = _____   e) 863 + 100 = _____   f) 821 + 100 = _____

g) 357 − 10 = _____   h) 683 − 10 = _____   i) 932 − 10 = _____

j) 487 − 100 = _____   k) 901 − 100 = _____   l) 316 − 100 = _____

m) 301 − 10 = _____   n) 507 − 10 = _____   o) 397 + 10 = _____

8. Circle the digits that are different. Then fill in the blanks.

a) 2 4 1
   2 3 1

   _231_ is _10_ less than _241_ .

b) 4 8 5
   5 8 5

   _____ is _____ greater than _____ .

c) 6 8 2
   6 9 2

   _____ is _____ less than _____ .

d) 7 2 7
   8 2 7

   _____ is _____ less than _____ .

e) 3 5 4
   3 6 4

   _____ is _____ less than _____ .

f) 5 2 7
   5 3 7

   _____ is _____ greater than _____ .

9. Fill in the blanks for the number pattern.

a) 508, 518, 528, _____, _____   b) 772, 672, 572, _____, _____

c) 512, 502, _____, 482, _____   d) 363, _____, _____, 393, 403

e) 214, _____, _____, 514, 614   f) 627, 617, _____, 597, _____

g) 865, 875, _____, _____, 905   h) 410, 510, _____, _____, 810

i) 219, _____, 199, _____, 179   j) 311, 301, _____, _____, 271

k) 544, _____, _____, 844, 944   l) 227, 217, _____, 197, _____

COPYRIGHT © 2016 JUMP MATH: NOT TO BE COPIED.

NS3-11 Regrouping of Ones, Tens, and Hundreds

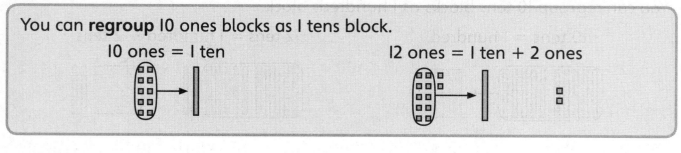

You can **regroup** 10 ones blocks as 1 tens block.

10 ones = 1 ten   12 ones = 1 ten + 2 ones

1. Circle each group of 10 ones blocks. How many ones are left?

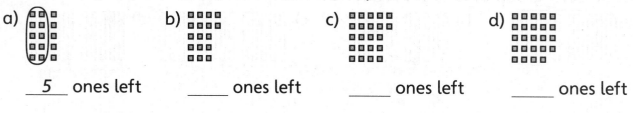

a)   b)   c)   d)

___5___ ones left   _____ ones left   _____ ones left   _____ ones left

2. Regroup each group of 10 ones as 1 tens block. Draw the new number.

	Before	After
a)		
c)		

	Before	After
b)		
d)		

3. Regroup 10 ones blocks as 1 tens block. Draw the new number.
   Then fill in the blanks.

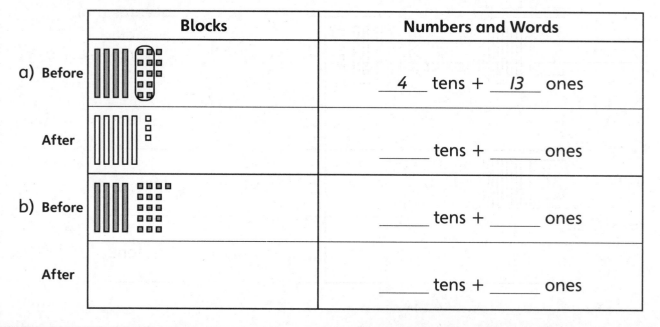

	Blocks	Numbers and Words
a) Before		___4___ tens + ___13___ ones
After		_____ tens + _____ ones
b) Before		_____ tens + _____ ones
After		_____ tens + _____ ones

COPYRIGHT © 2016 JUMP MATH: NOT TO BE COPIED.

You can regroup 10 tens blocks as 1 hundreds block.

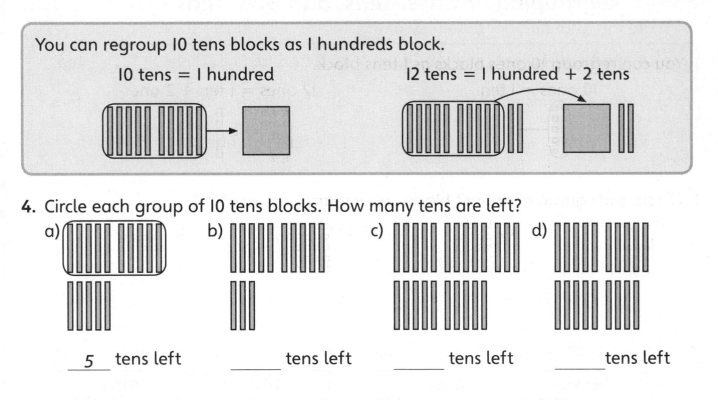

10 tens = 1 hundred   12 tens = 1 hundred + 2 tens

4. Circle each group of 10 tens blocks. How many tens are left?

a)   b)   c)   d)

___5___ tens left   _____ tens left   _____ tens left   _____tens left

5. Regroup 10 tens blocks as 1 hundreds block. Draw the new number.
Then fill in the blanks.

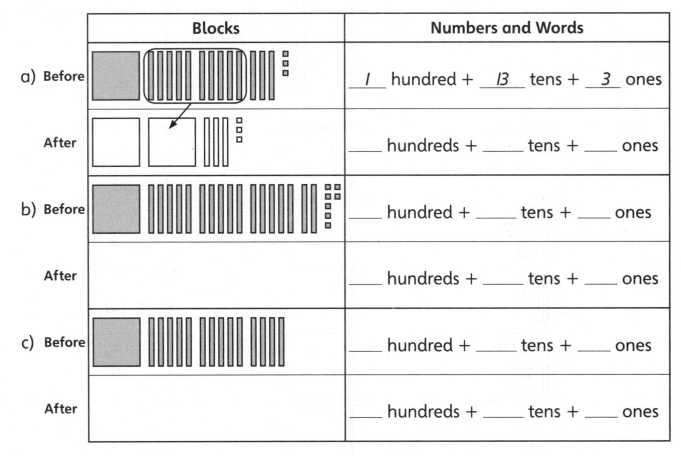

	Blocks	Numbers and Words
a) Before		___1___ hundred + __13__ tens + __3__ ones
After		____ hundreds + _____ tens + ____ ones
b) Before		____ hundred + _____ tens + ____ ones
After		____ hundreds + _____ tens + ____ ones
c) Before		____ hundred + _____ tens + ____ ones
After		____ hundreds + _____ tens + ____ ones

COPYRIGHT © 2016 JUMP MATH. NOT TO BE COPIED.

6. Write the total number of tens or ones.

a) 4 hundreds + 2 tens = __42__ tens   b) 2 hundreds + 7 tens = _____ tens

c) 5 tens + 7 ones = _____ ones   d) 3 hundreds + 0 tens = _____ tens

e) I hundred + I ten = _____ tens   f) 6 tens + 0 ones = _____ ones

7. Regroup. Then fill in the blank.

a) 3 tens + 12 ones = 4 tens + __2__ ones

b) 5 hundreds + 14 tens = 6 hundreds + _____ tens

c) 5 tens + 14 ones = _____ tens + 4 ones

d) 3 hundreds + II tens = 4 hundreds + _____ ten

e) 4 tens + _____ ones = 5 tens + 3 ones

f) _____ hundred + 18 tens = 2 hundreds + 8 tens

g) _____ tens + 17 ones = 4 tens + 7 ones

h) 7 hundreds + 19 tens = _____ hundreds + 9 ones

8. Regroup. Then fill in the blank.

a) 3 hundreds + 5 tens + 14 ones = 3 hundreds + _____ tens + 4 ones

b) 4 hundreds + 16 tens + 7 ones = _____ hundreds + 6 tens + 7 ones

c) I hundred + 13 tens + 4 ones = _____ hundreds + 3 tens + 4 ones

d) 5 hundreds + 2 tens + 19 ones = 5 hundreds + _____ tens + 9 ones

e) 2 hundreds + 3 tens + 15 ones = _____ hundreds + 4 tens + 5 ones

f) 7 hundreds + 8 tens + 13 ones = 7 hundreds + 9 tens + _____ ones

9. Draw base ten models to show the regrouping of ones, tens, and hundreds in Question 8.a).

COPYRIGHT © 2016 JUMP MATH: NOT TO BE COPIED

1. Find the **sum** by drawing the blocks and by adding the digits.

a) 24 + 15

	With Blocks		With Digits	
	Tens	Ones	Tens	Ones
24	‖	⬚⬚⬚⬚	2	4
15	|	⬚⬚⬚⬚⬚	1	5
Sum	‖‖	⬚⬚⬚⬚⬚⬚⬚⬚⬚	3	9

24 + 15 = _____

b) 62 + 21

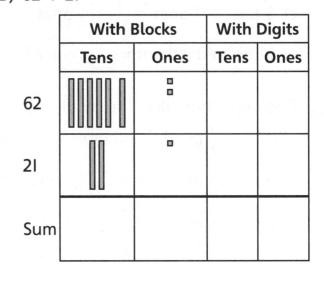

62 + 21 = _____

c) 29 + 50

d) 36 + 23

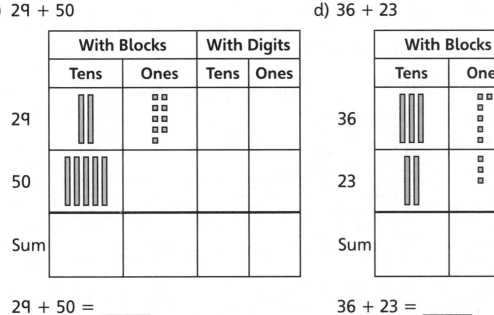

	With Blocks		With Digits	
	Tens	Ones	Tens	Ones
29	‖			
50	‖‖‖			
Sum				

29 + 50 = _____

36 + 23 = _____

2. Add the numbers by adding the digits. Start in the ones place.

a)
```
   2 3
 + 1 2
_____
```

b)
```
   4 8
 + 2 1
_____
```

c)
```
   6 3
 + 3 6
_____
```

d)
```
   4 3
 + 4 5
_____
```

e)
```
   8 7
 + 1 0
_____
```

COPYRIGHT © 2016 JUMP MATH: NOT TO BE COPIED.

3. Find the sum by drawing the blocks and by adding the digits. Then regroup.

a) 14 + 38

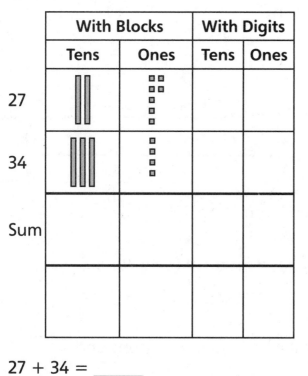

	With Blocks		With Digits	
	Tens	Ones	Tens	Ones
14			1	4
38			3	8
Sum			4	12
			5	2

14 + 38 = _____

b) 19 + 12

	With Blocks		With Digits	
	Tens	Ones	Tens	Ones
19				
12				
Sum				

19 + 12 = _____

c) 27 + 34

	With Blocks		With Digits	
	Tens	Ones	Tens	Ones
27				
34				
Sum				

27 + 34 = _____

d) 48 + 7

	With Blocks		With Digits	
	Tens	Ones	Tens	Ones
48				
7				
Sum				

48 + 7 = _____

COPYRIGHT © 2016 JUMP MATH: NOT TO BE COPIED.

4. Add the ones digits. Then fill in the blanks.

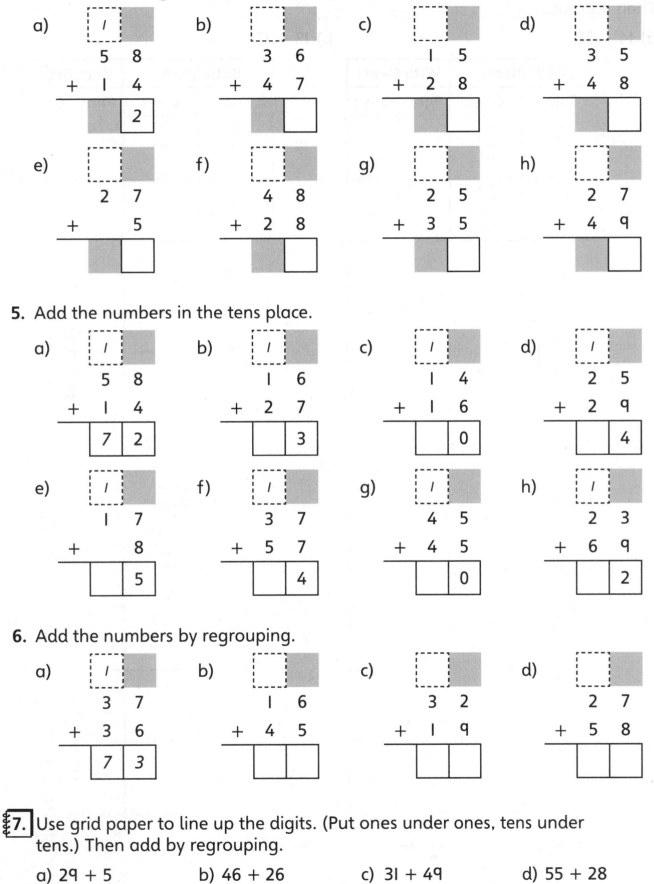

a)
```
  1
  5 8
+ 1 4
    2
```

b)
```
  3 6
+ 4 7
```

c)
```
  1 5
+ 2 8
```

d)
```
  3 5
+ 4 8
```

e)
```
  2 7
+   5
```

f)
```
  4 8
+ 2 8
```

g)
```
  2 5
+ 3 5
```

h)
```
  2 7
+ 4 9
```

5. Add the numbers in the tens place.

a)
```
  1
  5 8
+ 1 4
  7 2
```

b)
```
  1
  1 6
+ 2 7
    3
```

c)
```
  1
  1 4
+ 1 6
    0
```

d)
```
  1
  2 5
+ 2 9
    4
```

e)
```
  1
  1 7
+   8
    5
```

f)
```
  1
  3 7
+ 5 7
    4
```

g)
```
  1
  4 5
+ 4 5
    0
```

h)
```
  1
  2 3
+ 6 9
    2
```

6. Add the numbers by regrouping.

a)
```
  1
  3 7
+ 3 6
  7 3
```

b)
```
  1 6
+ 4 5
```

c)
```
  3 2
+ 1 9
```

d)
```
  2 7
+ 5 8
```

7. Use grid paper to line up the digits. (Put ones under ones, tens under tens.) Then add by regrouping.

a) 29 + 5   b) 46 + 26   c) 31 + 49   d) 55 + 28

COPYRIGHT © 2016 JUMP MATH: NOT TO BE COPIED.

1. Add by adding the ones, tens, and hundreds.

a)
```
    2  3  4
  + 3  5  2
  _____
```
____ hundreds + ____ tens + ____ ones

+ ____ hundreds + ____ tens + ____ ones

= ____ hundreds + ____ tens + ____ ones

b)
```
    4  7  2
  + 5  1  6
  _____
```
____ hundreds + ____ tens + ____ ones

+ ____ hundreds + ____ ten + ____ ones

= ____ hundreds + ____ tens + ____ ones

c)
```
    1  0  8
  + 5  2  1
  _____
```
____ hundred + ____ tens + ____ ones

+ ____ hundreds + ____ tens + ____ one

= ____ hundreds + ____ tens + ____ ones

2. Add the digits. Start in the ones place.

a)
```
    2  9  5
  + 3  0  2
  _____
```
b)
```
    4  2  3
  + 2  6  1
  _____
```
c)
```
    3  1  2
  +    5  7
  _____
```
d)
```
    5  5  5
  + 4  4  4
  _____
```

e)
```
    3  4  7
  + 5  0  2
  _____
```
f)
```
    1  2  5
  + 3  6  4
  _____
```
g)
```
    4  2  3
  + 2  3  5
  _____
```
h)
```
    6  3  1
  + 2  2  7
  _____
```

i)
```
    4  2  8
  +    6  1
  _____
```
j)
```
    2  3  5
  + 5  0  0
  _____
```
k)
```
    4  2  3
  + 3  3  6
  _____
```
l)
```
    1  1  5
  + 2  6  1
  _____
```

m)
```
    1  3  1
  + 1  3  1
  _____
```
n)
```
    3  2  8
  +    6  1
  _____
```
o)
```
    9  8  9
  +    1  0
  _____
```
p)
```
    4  7  3
  + 4  2  4
  _____
```

COPYRIGHT © 2016 JUMP MATH: NOT TO BE COPIED.

3. Add. You will need to regroup tens as hundreds.

a)
```
    2  3  4
  + 3  8  2
```
____ hundreds + ____ tens + ____ ones

\+ ____ hundreds + ____ tens + ____ ones

= ____ hundreds + ____ tens + ____ ones

after regrouping = ____ hundreds + ____ ten + ____ ones

b)
```
    5  8  7
  + 2  5  2
```
____ hundreds + ____ tens + ____ ones

\+ ____ hundreds + ____ tens + ____ ones

= ____ hundreds + ____ tens + ____ ones

after regrouping = ____ hundreds + ____ tens + ____ ones

4. Add. You will need to regroup tens as hundreds.

a)
```
   [ 1 ]
    3  7  5
  + 1  8  1
  ─────────
    5  5  6
```

b)
```
   [   ]
    1  9  6
  + 2  4  1
```

c)
```
   [   ]
    1  8  4
  + 1  8  5
```

d)
```
   [   ]
    2  4  5
  + 2  8  3
```

5. Add. You will need to regroup ones as tens.

a)
```
      [   ]
    1  4  7
  + 5  3  8
```

b)
```
      [   ]
    3  6  7
  + 5  1  7
```

c)
```
      [   ]
    4  3  5
  + 4  3  5
```

d)
```
      [   ]
    2  2  3
  + 6  4  9
```

6. Write the numbers in the grid. Then find the sum by regrouping.

a) 725 + 168   b) 250 + 450   c) 649 + 216   d) 491 + 323

	7	2	5												
+	1	6	8												

COPYRIGHT © 2016 JUMP MATH: NOT TO BE COPIED.

7. Add. You will need to regroup twice.

a) 745 + 187

	/	/	
	7	4	5
+	1	8	7
	9	3	2

b) 368 + 498

	3	6	8
+	4	9	8

c) 649 + 276

	6	4	9
+	2	7	6

d) 587 + 123

	5	8	7
+	1	2	3

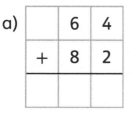

Sometimes the sum of two 2-digit numbers is a 3-digit number.

Example: 52 + 73

		5 tens	+	2 ones			5	2
+		7 tens	+	3 ones	or	+	7	3
		12 tens	+	5 ones		1	2	5

after regrouping = **1** hundred + **2** tens + **5** ones

8. Add the numbers. The answer will be a 3-digit number.

a)

	6	4
+	8	2

b)

	3	6
+	9	3

c)

	6	4
+	6	4

d)

	5	4
+	8	2

9. Add. You might need to regroup once or twice.

a)

	3	5	1
+	3	9	2

b)

	2	6	3
+		9	8

c)

	6	4	9
+	2	1	0

d)

	6	8	9
+	1	5	3

10. Add. Regroup where necessary.

a) 495 + 311　　b) 526 + 269　　c) 312 + 453　　d) 555 + 294

11. Blanca has 164 toy cars. Ed has 87.
How many toy cars do they have in total?

COPYRIGHT © 2016 JUMP MATH: NOT TO BE COPIED.

NS3-14 Subtraction without Regrouping

1. Subtract by crossing out tens and ones.

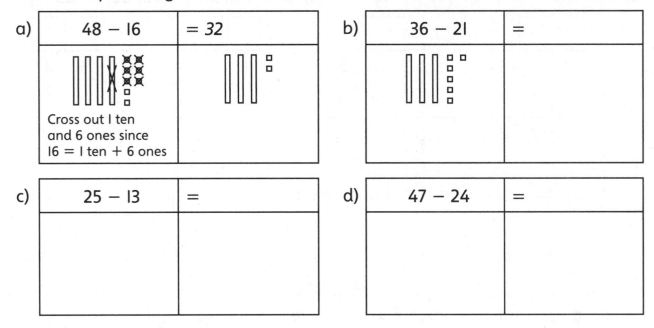

a)

48 − 16	= 32

Cross out 1 ten and 6 ones since 16 = 1 ten + 6 ones

b)

36 − 21	=

c)

25 − 13	=

d)

47 − 24	=

2. Write the number of tens and ones in each number. Then subtract.

a)
$$49 = \underline{4}\ tens + \underline{9}\ ones$$
$$- 26 = \underline{2}\ tens + \underline{6}\ ones$$
$$= \underline{2}\ tens + \underline{3}\ ones$$
$$= \underline{23}$$

b)
$$59 = \underline{}\ tens + \underline{}\ ones$$
$$- 23 = \underline{}\ tens + \underline{}\ ones$$
$$= \underline{}\ tens + \underline{}\ ones$$
$$= \underline{}$$

c)
$$67 = \underline{}\ tens + \underline{}\ ones$$
$$- 53 = \underline{}\ tens + \underline{}\ ones$$
$$= \underline{}\ ten + \underline{}\ ones$$
$$= \underline{}$$

d)
$$86 = \underline{}\ tens + \underline{}\ ones$$
$$- 54 = \underline{}\ tens + \underline{}\ ones$$
$$= \underline{}\ tens + \underline{}\ ones$$
$$= \underline{}$$

e)
$$97 = \underline{}\ tens + \underline{}\ ones$$
$$- 56 = \underline{}\ tens + \underline{}\ ones$$
$$= \underline{}\ tens + \underline{}\ one$$
$$= \underline{}$$

f)
$$81 = \underline{}\ tens + \underline{}\ one$$
$$- 61 = \underline{}\ tens + \underline{}\ one$$
$$= \underline{}\ tens + \underline{}\ ones$$
$$= \underline{}$$

COPYRIGHT © 2016 JUMP MATH: NOT TO BE COPIED.

3. Write in expanded form using numerals only. Then subtract.

a)
$$46 = 40 + 6$$
$$- 32 = 30 + 2$$
$$= 10 + 4$$
$$= 14$$

b)
$$95 =$$
$$- 62 =$$
$$=$$
$$=$$

c)
$$37 =$$
$$- 11 =$$
$$=$$
$$=$$

d)
$$63 =$$
$$- 20 =$$
$$=$$
$$=$$

e)
$$29 =$$
$$- 14 =$$
$$=$$
$$=$$

f)
$$58 =$$
$$- 41 =$$
$$=$$
$$=$$

4. Subtract the ones digits, then the tens digits.

a)
$$\begin{array}{rr} 2 & 8 \\ - 1 & 2 \\ \hline \end{array}$$

b)
$$\begin{array}{rr} 4 & 8 \\ - 2 & 7 \\ \hline \end{array}$$

c)
$$\begin{array}{rr} 6 & 9 \\ - 5 & 3 \\ \hline \end{array}$$

d)
$$\begin{array}{rr} 4 & 9 \\ - 4 & 5 \\ \hline \end{array}$$

e)
$$\begin{array}{rr} 8 & 7 \\ - 5 & 3 \\ \hline \end{array}$$

You can subtract 3-digit numbers by lining up the digits.

Example: 256 − 124

Write hundreds under hundreds. Write tens under tens. Write ones under ones.

Subtract ones. Subtract tens. Subtract hundreds.

	2	5	6
−	1	2	4
	1	3	2

---

5. Subtract. Start in the ones place.

a)
	7	2	9
−	3	1	6

b)
	8	9	5
−	2	5	4

c)
	5	2	4
−	4	0	1

d)
	3	9	8
−	1	6	3

e)
	5	2	3
−	3	1	0

f)
	9	5	8
−	4	2	3

g)
	4	6	4
−	2	6	1

h)
	3	7	8
−	3	6	1

COPYRIGHT © 2016 JUMP MATH: NOT TO BE COPIED.

NS3-15 Subtraction with Regrouping—Tens

1. Regroup 1 tens block as 10 ones blocks.

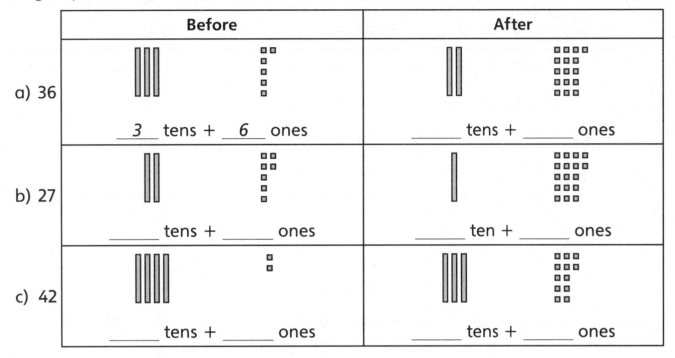

	Before	After
a) 36	___3___ tens + ___6___ ones	_____ tens + _____ ones
b) 27	_____ tens + _____ ones	_____ ten + _____ ones
c) 42	_____ tens + _____ ones	_____ tens + _____ ones

2. Regroup 1 ten as 10 ones.

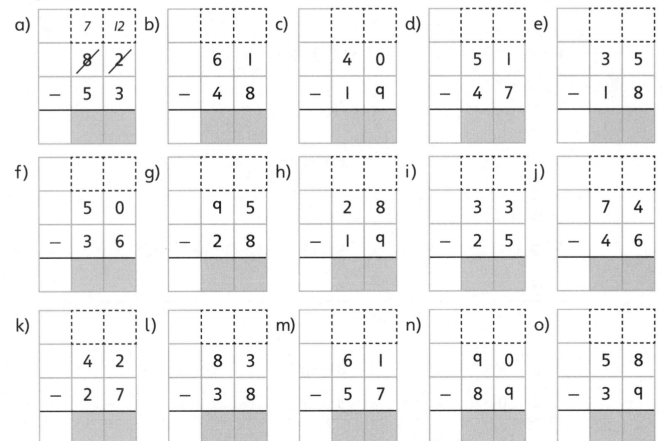

COPYRIGHT © 2016 JUMP MATH: NOT TO BE COPIED.

3. Regroup I ten as 10 ones. Then subtract. Start in the ones place.

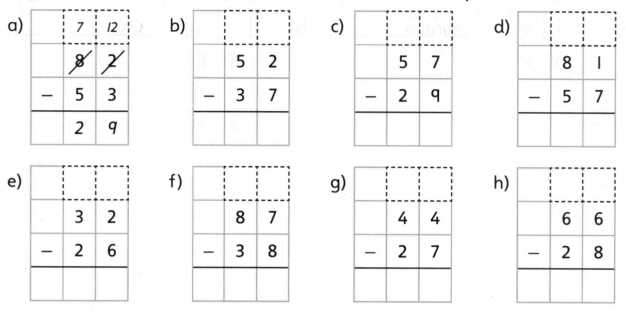

a)

	7	12
	8̷	2̷
−	5	3
	2	9

b)

	5	2
−	3	7

c)

	5	7
−	2	9

d)

	8	1
−	5	7

e)

	3	2
−	2	6

f)

	8	7
−	3	8

g)

	4	4
−	2	7

h)

	6	6
−	2	8

4. Circle the greater digit in the ones place. Regroup if you need to, and write "regroup." Otherwise, write "OK."

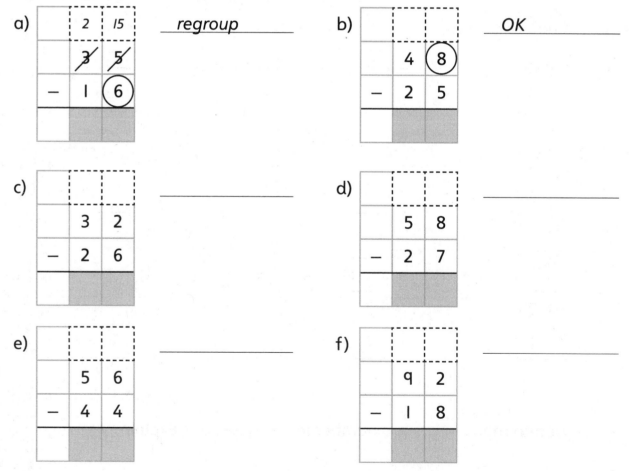

a)

	2	15
	3̷	5̷
−	1	⑥

____regroup____

b)

	4	⑧
−	2	5

____OK____

c)

	3	2
−	2	6

_____

d)

	5	8
−	2	7

_____

e)

	5	6
−	4	4

_____

f)

	9	2
−	1	8

_____

COPYRIGHT © 2016 JUMP MATH: NOT TO BE COPIED.

5. Write "regroup" or "OK." Then subtract, regrouping if needed.

a)

	2	15
	3̷	5̷
−	1	6
	1	9

regroup

b)

	6	8
−	2	5
	4	3

OK

c)

	3	2
−	2	6

_____

d)

	4	8
−	2	7

_____

6. Subtract. Regroup if needed.

a)

	3	12
	4̷	2̷
−	2	7
	1	5

b)

	5	2
−	3	1

c)

	6	6
−	2	9

d)

	8	1
−	5	0

e)

	4	4
−	3	7

f)

	9	7
−	3	9

g)

	4	4
−	2	4

h)

	5	6
−	1	5

i)

	9	2
−	8	1

j)

	8	7
−	3	7

k)

	5	0
−	1	7

l)

	9	2
−	2	6

7. Do you need to regroup the top number in this question? Explain.

$$\begin{array}{r} 62 \\ - 47 \\ \hline \end{array}$$

COPYRIGHT © 2016 JUMP MATH: NOT TO BE COPIED.

NS3-16 Subtraction with Regrouping—Hundreds

To subtract 327 − 182, regroup 1 hundreds block as 10 tens blocks.

Then subtract by crossing out ones, tens, and hundreds.

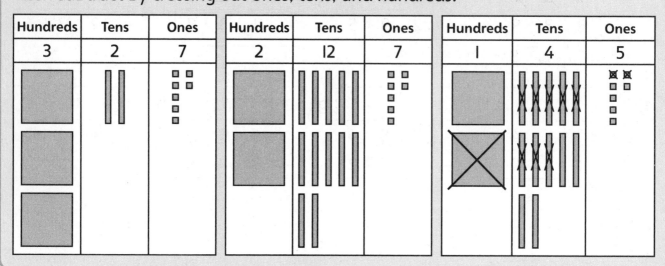

1. Regroup 1 hundred as 10 tens.

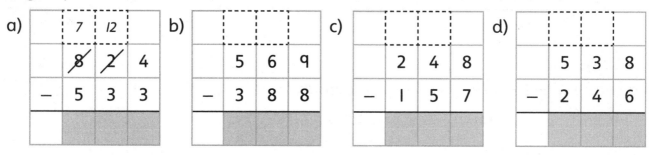

2. Regroup 1 hundred as 10 tens. Then subtract. Start in the ones place.

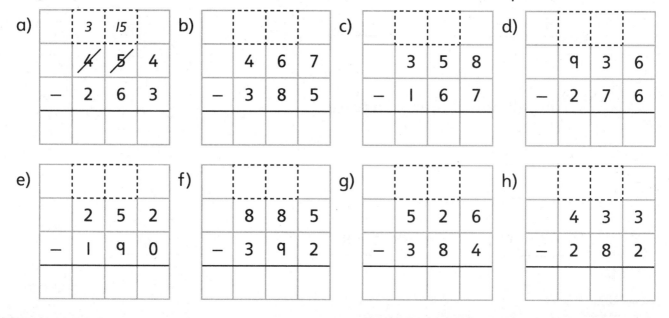

COPYRIGHT © 2016 JUMP MATH: NOT TO BE COPIED.

3. Subtract. Regroup I hundred as 10 tens, or I ten as 10 ones.

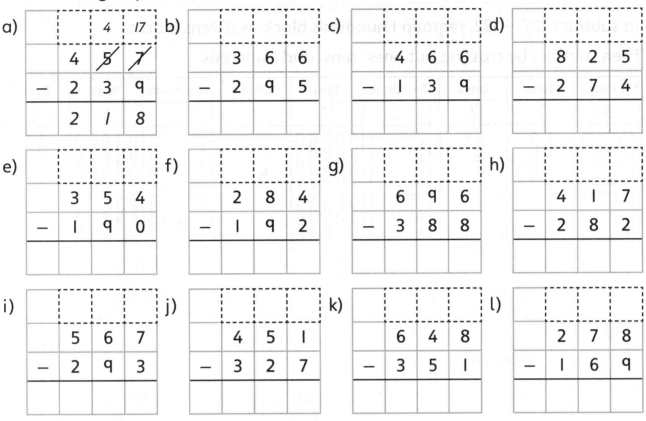

a)

		4	17
	4	5̶	7̶
−	2	3	9
	2	1	8

b)

	3	6	6
−	2	9	5

c)

	4	6	6
−	1	3	9

d)

	8	2	5
−	2	7	4

e)

	3	5	4
−	1	9	0

f)

	2	8	4
−	1	9	2

g)

	6	9	6
−	3	8	8

h)

	4	1	7
−	2	8	2

i)

	5	6	7
−	2	9	3

j)

	4	5	1
−	3	2	7

k)

	6	4	8
−	3	5	1

l)

	2	7	8
−	1	6	9

To subtract 642 − 279, you need to regroup twice.

Step 1: **Step 2:** **Step 3:** **Step 4:** **Step 5:**

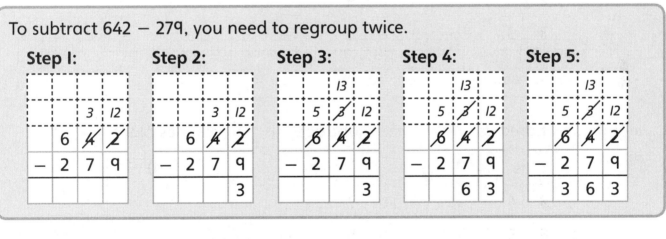

4. Subtract. You will need to regroup twice.

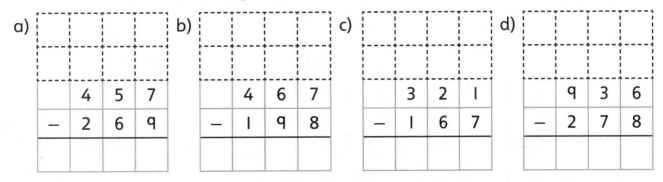

a)

	4	5	7
−	2	6	9

b)

	4	6	7
−	1	9	8

c)

	3	2	1
−	1	6	7

d)

	9	3	6
−	2	7	8

COPYRIGHT © 2016 JUMP MATH: NOT TO BE COPIED.

5. Subtract. You will need to regroup twice.

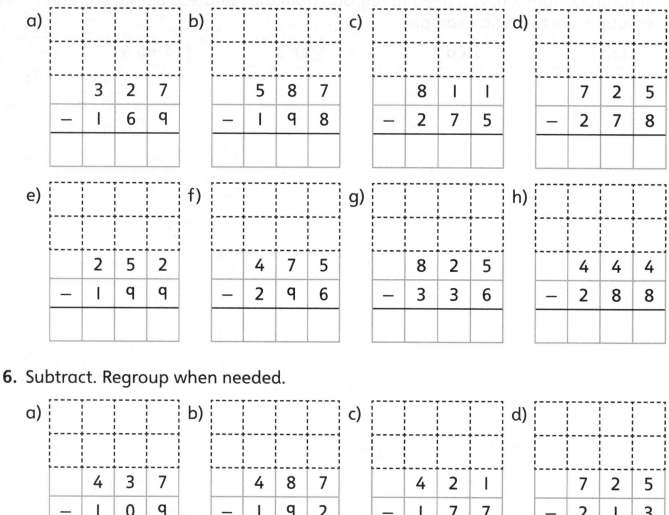

a)
```
    3  2  7
 -  1  6  9
```

b)
```
    5  8  7
 -  1  9  8
```

c)
```
    8  1  1
 -  2  7  5
```

d)
```
    7  2  5
 -  2  7  8
```

e)
```
    2  5  2
 -  1  9  9
```

f)
```
    4  7  5
 -  2  9  6
```

g)
```
    8  2  5
 -  3  3  6
```

h)
```
    4  4  4
 -  2  8  8
```

6. Subtract. Regroup when needed.

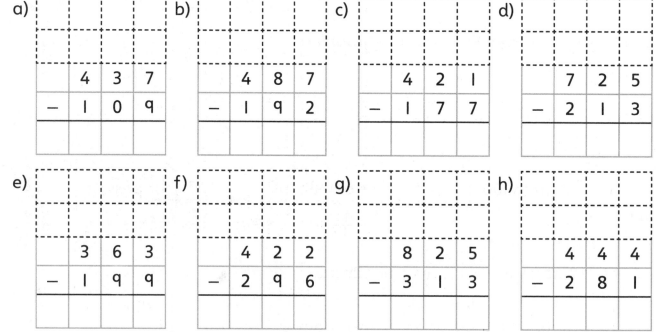

a)
```
    4  3  7
 -  1  0  9
```

b)
```
    4  8  7
 -  1  9  2
```

c)
```
    4  2  1
 -  1  7  7
```

d)
```
    7  2  5
 -  2  1  3
```

e)
```
    3  6  3
 -  1  9  9
```

f)
```
    4  2  2
 -  2  9  6
```

g)
```
    8  2  5
 -  3  1  3
```

h)
```
    4  4  4
 -  2  8  1
```

7. Sam has 346 dollars. He gives 175 dollars to a charity.
How much money does he have left? Show your work.

8. Clara has 562 stickers in her collection. She gives 384 stickers
to her sister. How many stickers does Clara have left?

COPYRIGHT © 2016 JUMP MATH: NOT TO BE COPIED.

To subtract from 100, you need to regroup from the hundreds before you can regroup from the tens. Example:

Step 1:

	1	0	0
−		4	8

Step 2:

		0	10
	1̸	0̸	0
−		4	8

Step 3:

		9	
	0	1̸0̸	10
	1̸	0̸	0̸
−		4	8
			2

Step 4:

		9	
	0	1̸0̸	10
	1̸	0̸	0̸
−		4	8
		5	2

9. Subtract by regrouping.

a)

	1	0	0
−		4	7

b)

	1	0	0
−		5	2

c)

	1	0	0
−		6	5

d)

	1	0	0
−		1	9

10. Now subtract from 99 without regrouping.

a)

	9	9
−	4	7

b)

	9	9
−	5	2

c)

	9	9
−	6	5

d)

	9	9
−	1	9

To subtract from 100, first subtract from 99. Then add 1 to your answer.

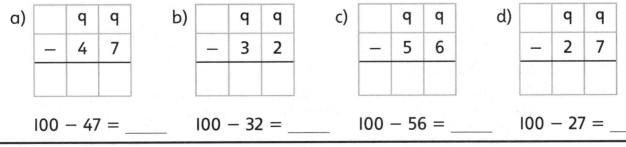

11. Subtract from 99. Use the answer to subtract from 100.

a)

	9	9
−	4	7

b)

	9	9
−	3	2

c)

	9	9
−	5	6

d)

	9	9
−	2	7

100 − 47 = _____   100 − 32 = _____   100 − 56 = _____   100 − 27 = _____

COPYRIGHT © 2016 JUMP MATH: NOT TO BE COPIED.

NS3-17 Problems and Puzzles

1. Tasha has 12 pencil crayons. 8 are at home and
the rest are at school.

a) How many pencil crayons are at school?

b) How did you solve the problem? (Did you use a calculation?
Make a model? Draw a picture?)

2. Takakkaw Falls in British Columbia is 302 m tall.
The Canadian Horseshoe Falls in Ontario
is 57 m tall.

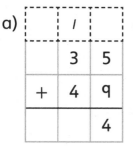

a) Which waterfall is taller? How do you know?

b) How much taller is the taller waterfall?

3. Rani wants to add the numbers. She starts by adding the
ones digits. Explain why Rani wrote the number 1 above the 3.

a)

	1	
	3	5
+	4	9
		4

b)

	1		
	3	6	7
+	2	4	1
		0	8

4. Find the mistake in Ben's work.

a)

	2	
	4	7
+	2	5
	8	1

b)

	3	9
+	5	
	8	9

c)

	1		
	5	8	
+	2	6	0
	8	4	0

5. Jin has 17 books. Tina has 35 books.

a) How many more books does Tina have than Jin?

b) How many books do they have altogether?

COPYRIGHT © 2016 JUMP MATH: NOT TO BE COPIED.

6. Sandy has 243 marbles. Tony has 178 marbles.

   a) How many marbles do they have in total?

   b) How do you know that Sandy has more marbles than Tony?

   c) How many more marbles does Sandy have? Show your work.

7. Find the mistake in Glen's work.

a)
			16
	5	6	
−	4	8	
	1	8	

b)
	5	6	3
−	2	4	
	3	2	3

c)
		3	14
		4̶	3̶
−		2	8
		1	6

8. A ferry between Prince Edward Island and Nova Scotia holds 200 cars. By 8:00 a.m., 73 cars arrive. By 9:00 a.m., 84 more cars arrive.

   a) How many cars in total arrive by 9:00 a.m.?

   b) How many more cars can be loaded before the ferry is full?

9. Place the numbers 1, 2, 3, 4, 5, 6 in the top six boxes to make the largest possible sum.

10. Place the numbers 1, 2, 3, 4 in the top four boxes to make the largest possible difference.

11. Here are the maximum depths of the Great Lakes.

   a) Write the depths in order from least to greatest.

   b) How much deeper is Lake Superior than Lake Michigan?

   c) How much deeper is Lake Huron than Lake Erie?

Maximum Depths of the Great Lakes	
Lake Superior	406 m
Lake Michigan	281 m
Lake Huron	229 m
Lake Erie	64 m
Lake Ontario	244 m

COPYRIGHT © 2016 JUMP MATH: NOT TO BE COPIED.

The parts of an addition sentence have special names.

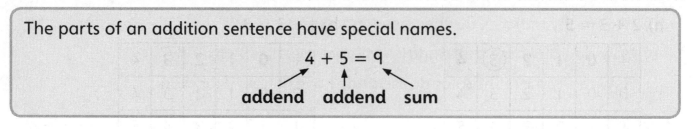

$$4 + 5 = 9$$

addend   addend   sum

I. Circle the addends. Draw a box around the sum.

a) $\boxed{15} = \bigcirc{5} + \bigcirc{10}$

b) $5 + 7 = 12$

c) $17 + 3 = 20$

d) $8 = 5 + 3$

e) $2 + 57 = 59$

f) $4 + 2 + 1 = 7$

g) $25 = 10 + 15$

h) $47 = 18 + 29$

i) $32 + 30 = 62$

j) $15 + 2 = 17$

k) $100 = 60 + 40$

l) $64 = 32 + 15 + 17$

An **addition chart** shows the sum of two addends.

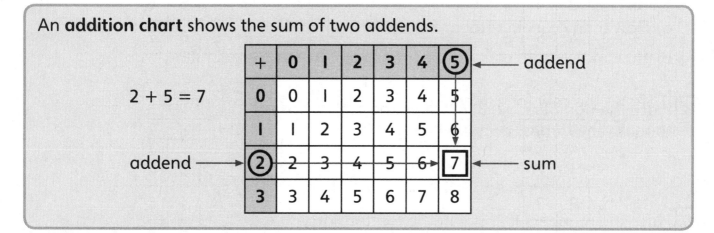

$2 + 5 = 7$

addend ⟶ sum

2. Complete the addition chart.

a)

+	0	1	2	3
0	0	1		
1		2		
2				
3			5	

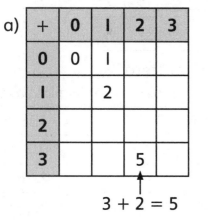

$3 + 2 = 5$

b)

+	4	5	6	7	8
4	8	9			
5					
6			12		
7			13		
8					

COPYRIGHT © 2016 JUMP MATH: NOT TO BE COPIED.

3. Circle the addends in the addition chart. Draw a box around the sum.

a) $2 + 3 = 5$

+	0	I	2	③	4
0	0	I	2	3	4
I	I	2	3	4	5
②	2	3	4	〔5〕	6

b) $I + 2 = 3$

+	0	I	2	3	4
0	0	I	2	3	4
I	I	2	3	4	5
2	2	3	4	5	6

c) $I + 3 = 4$

+	0	I	2	3	4
0	0	I	2	3	4
I	I	2	3	4	5
2	2	3	4	5	6
3	3	4	5	6	7

d) $0 + 4 = 4$

+	0	I	2	3	4
0	0	I	2	3	4
I	I	2	3	4	5
2	2	3	4	5	6
3	3	4	5	6	7

4. a) Shade the **row** for addend 3.

+	0	I	2	3	4
0	0	I	2	3	4
I	I	2	3	4	5
2	2	3	4	5	6
3	3	4	5	6	7
4	4	5	6	7	8

Describe the pattern.

Start at _____

and add _____ .

b) Shade the **column** for addend 2.

+	0	I	2	3	4
0	0	I	2	3	4
I	I	2	3	4	5
2	2	3	4	5	6
3	3	4	5	6	7
4	4	5	6	7	8

Describe the pattern.

Start at _____

and add _____ .

COPYRIGHT © 2016 JUMP MATH: NOT TO BE COPIED.

5. Draw a box around the sum for $3 + 4$.
Draw a box around the sum for $4 + 3$.

a) What do you notice?

_____

b) What property of addition does this show?

_____

_____

+	0	1	2	3	4
0	0	1	2	3	4
1	1	2	3	4	5
2	2	3	4	5	6
3	3	4	5	6	7
4	4	5	6	7	8

6.

+	0	1	2	3	4	5	6	7	8	9
0	0	1	2	3	4	5	6	7	8	9
1	1	2	3	4	5	6	7	8	9	10
2	2	3	4	5	6	7	8	9	10	11
3	3	4	5	6	7	8	9	10	11	12
4	4	5	6	7	8	9	10	11	12	13
5	5	6	7	8	9	10	11	12	13	14
6	6	7	8	9	10	11	12	13	14	15
7	7	8	9	10	11	12	13	14	15	16
8	8	9	10	11	12	13	14	15	16	17
9	9	10	11	12	13	14	15	16	17	18

a) Describe the pattern in the light shaded squares.

Start at _____ and add _____ .

b) Describe the pattern in the dark shaded squares.

_____

c) Shade a pattern of your own. Describe the pattern you shaded.

_____

COPYRIGHT © 2016 JUMP MATH: NOT TO BE COPIED.

7. Alex shaded all the squares for the sum 7 in the addition chart.

+	0	1	2	3	4	5	6	7	8	9
0	0	1	2	3	4	5	6	7	8	9
1	1	2	3	4	5	6	7	8	9	10
2	2	3	4	5	6	7	8	9	10	11
3	3	4	5	6	7	8	9	10	11	12
4	4	5	6	7	8	9	10	11	12	13
5	5	6	7	8	9	10	11	12	13	14
6	6	7	8	9	10	11	12	13	14	15
7	7	8	9	10	11	12	13	14	15	16
8	8	9	10	11	12	13	14	15	16	17
9	9	10	11	12	13	14	15	16	17	18

a) Fill in the blanks to complete the addition sentences.

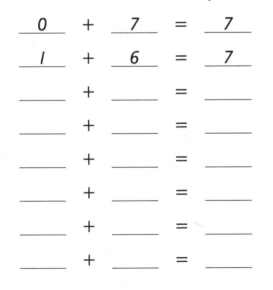

$$\underline{\quad 0 \quad} + \underline{\quad 7 \quad} = \underline{\quad 7 \quad}$$

$$\underline{\quad 1 \quad} + \underline{\quad 6 \quad} = \underline{\quad 7 \quad}$$

$$\underline{\quad\quad} + \underline{\quad\quad} = \underline{\quad\quad}$$

$$\underline{\quad\quad} + \underline{\quad\quad} = \underline{\quad\quad}$$

$$\underline{\quad\quad} + \underline{\quad\quad} = \underline{\quad\quad}$$

$$\underline{\quad\quad} + \underline{\quad\quad} = \underline{\quad\quad}$$

$$\underline{\quad\quad} + \underline{\quad\quad} = \underline{\quad\quad}$$

$$\underline{\quad\quad} + \underline{\quad\quad} = \underline{\quad\quad}$$

b) Shade the column for addend zero. Then find the sums.

$2 + 0 = \underline{\quad\quad}$　　　$5 + 0 = \underline{\quad\quad}$　　　$7 + 0 = \underline{\quad\quad}$　　　$8 + 0 = \underline{\quad\quad}$

c) When you add zero to a number, what is the result?

_____

COPYRIGHT © 2016 JUMP MATH: NOT TO BE COPIED.

NS3-19 Making 10 to Add

1. Fill in the missing numbers.

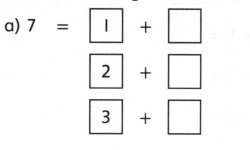

a) $7 = \boxed{1} + \boxed{}$
$ \boxed{2} + \boxed{}$
$ \boxed{3} + \boxed{}$

b) $6 = \boxed{1} + \boxed{}$
$ \boxed{2} + \boxed{}$
$ \boxed{3} + \boxed{}$

2. Fill in the missing numbers.

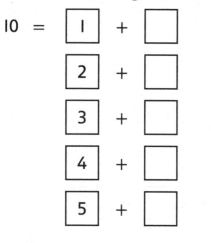

$10 = \boxed{1} + \boxed{}$
$ \boxed{2} + \boxed{}$
$ \boxed{3} + \boxed{}$
$ \boxed{4} + \boxed{}$
$ \boxed{5} + \boxed{}$

3. Circle the pair that adds to 10.

a) ②　7　⑧

b) 3　7　4

c) 5　3　5

d) 6　4　5

e) 1　8　9

4. Circle the pair that adds to 10. Write the number that is left over in the box.

a) ④ + 5 + ⑥ = 10 + $\boxed{5}$

b) $7 + 3 + 4 = 10 + \boxed{}$

c) $8 + 3 + 2 = 10 + \boxed{}$

d) $6 + 9 + 4 = 10 + \boxed{}$

e) $9 + 1 + 7 = 10 + \boxed{}$

f) $5 + 8 + 2 = 10 + \boxed{}$

g) $5 + 3 + 5 = 10 + \boxed{}$

h) $3 + 9 + 1 = 10 + \boxed{}$

i) $3 + 7 + 4 = 10 + \boxed{}$

j) $6 + 5 + 4 = 10 + \boxed{}$

k) $5 + 7 + 5 = 10 + \boxed{}$

l) $5 + 7 + 3 = 10 + \boxed{}$

m) $3 + 7 + 8 = 10 + \boxed{}$

n) $4 + 8 + 6 = 10 + \boxed{}$

COPYRIGHT © 2016 JUMP MATH: NOT TO BE COPIED.

5. Add mentally.

a) 10 + 5 = _____   b) 10 + 7 = _____

c) 40 + 8 = _____   d) 50 + 9 = _____

e) 60 + 1 = _____   f) 20 + 3 = _____

g) 40 + 4 = _____   h) 30 + 6 = _____

i) 90 + 9 = _____   j) 120 + 5 = _____

k) 460 + 7 = _____   l) 980 + 6 = _____

m) 800 + 3 = _____   n) 670 + 5 = _____

BONUS ▶

o) 400 + 12 = _____   p) 300 + 25 = _____

6. Fill in the boxes.

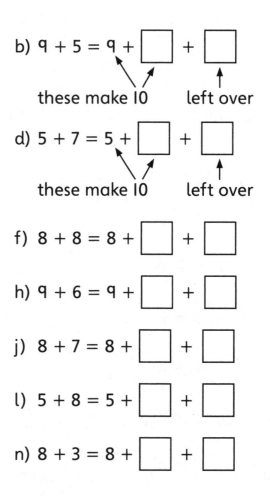

a) 8 + 6 = 8 + ⬚2⬚ + ⬚4⬚

these make 10   left over

b) 9 + 5 = 9 + ⬚ + ⬚

these make 10   left over

c) 6 + 5 = 6 + ⬚ + ⬚

these make 10   left over

d) 5 + 7 = 5 + ⬚ + ⬚

these make 10   left over

e) 9 + 4 = 9 + ⬚ + ⬚

f) 8 + 8 = 8 + ⬚ + ⬚

g) 7 + 6 = 7 + ⬚ + ⬚

h) 9 + 6 = 9 + ⬚ + ⬚

i) 6 + 6 = 6 + ⬚ + ⬚

j) 8 + 7 = 8 + ⬚ + ⬚

k) 7 + 8 = 7 + ⬚ + ⬚

l) 5 + 8 = 5 + ⬚ + ⬚

m) 6 + 9 = 6 + ⬚ + ⬚

n) 8 + 3 = 8 + ⬚ + ⬚

COPYRIGHT © 2016 JUMP MATH: NOT TO BE COPIED.

7. Add by following the steps.

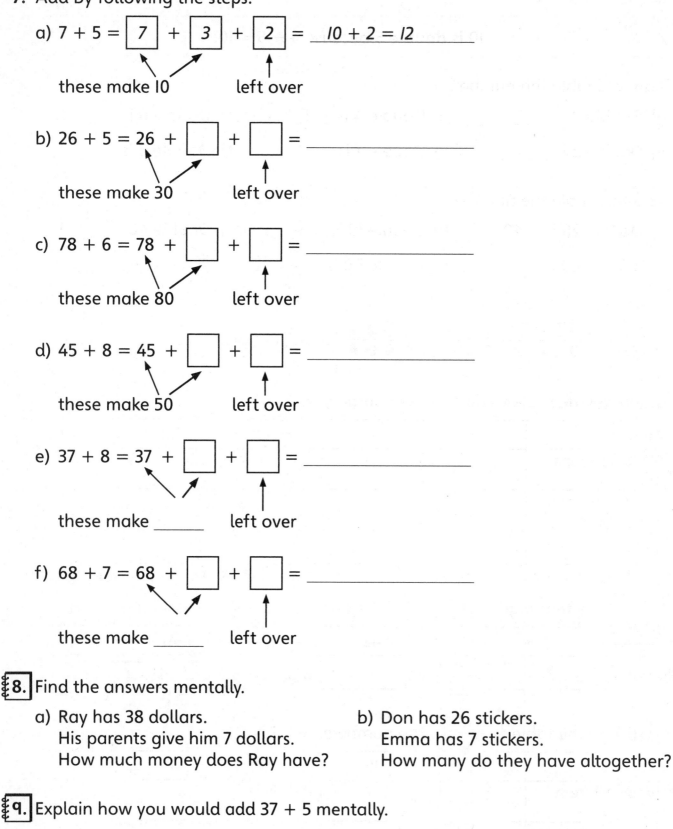

a) $7 + 5 = \boxed{7} + \boxed{3} + \boxed{2} = \underline{\;10 + 2 = 12\;}$

these make 10   left over

b) $26 + 5 = 26 + \boxed{} + \boxed{} = \underline{\hspace{3cm}}$

these make 30   left over

c) $78 + 6 = 78 + \boxed{} + \boxed{} = \underline{\hspace{3cm}}$

these make 80   left over

d) $45 + 8 = 45 + \boxed{} + \boxed{} = \underline{\hspace{3cm}}$

these make 50   left over

e) $37 + 8 = 37 + \boxed{} + \boxed{} = \underline{\hspace{3cm}}$

these make _____   left over

f) $68 + 7 = 68 + \boxed{} + \boxed{} = \underline{\hspace{3cm}}$

these make _____   left over

8. Find the answers mentally.

a) Ray has 38 dollars.
His parents give him 7 dollars.
How much money does Ray have?

b) Don has 26 stickers.
Emma has 7 stickers.
How many do they have altogether?

9. Explain how you would add $37 + 5$ mentally.

10. Add $48 + 5$ mentally. Then use your answer to add $480 + 50$ mentally.

COPYRIGHT © 2016 JUMP MATH: NOT TO BE COPIED.

NS3-20 Doubles

10 is **double** 5 because 5 + 5 = 10.

1. Add to double the number.
   a) Double 3 is __6__.   b) Double 4 is __8__.   c) Double 6 is _____.
   d) Double 2 is _____.   e) Double 7 is _____.   f) Double 8 is _____.

2. Add to double the number.
   a) Double 20 is __40__.   b) Double 10 is _____.   c) Double 40 is _____.
   d) Double 60 is _____.   e) Double 90 is _____.   f) Double 50 is _____.

16 = 10 + 6

double 10 ⌐   ⌐ double 6

So double 16 is 20 + 12.

3. Complete the table to double the numbers.

Number	24	14	12	32	22
Write the tens and ones	20 + 4				
Double the tens and ones	40 + 8				
Double	48				

4. Double the tens digit. Then double the ones digit to double the number.

Number	31	43	32	41	13
Double	62				

5. Complete the table to double the numbers.

Number	27	16	38	46	78
Write the tens and ones	20 + 7				
Double the tens and ones	40 + 14				
Double	54				

> You can add **near-doubles** by doubling the smaller number and adding 1.

6. Show how you can add by doubling the smaller number and adding 1.

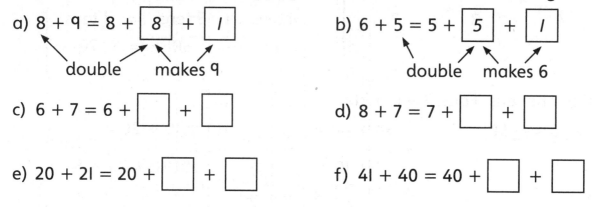

a) $8 + 9 = 8 + \boxed{8} + \boxed{1}$ double   makes 9

b) $6 + 5 = 5 + \boxed{5} + \boxed{1}$ double   makes 6

c) $6 + 7 = 6 + \boxed{} + \boxed{}$

d) $8 + 7 = 7 + \boxed{} + \boxed{}$

e) $20 + 21 = 20 + \boxed{} + \boxed{}$

f) $41 + 40 = 40 + \boxed{} + \boxed{}$

> You can add near-doubles by doubling the larger number and subtracting 1.

7. Show how you can add by doubling the larger number and subtracting 1.

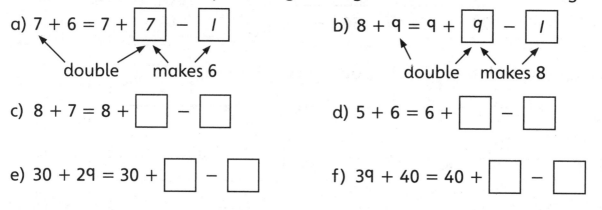

a) $7 + 6 = 7 + \boxed{7} - \boxed{1}$ double   makes 6

b) $8 + 9 = 9 + \boxed{9} - \boxed{1}$ double   makes 8

c) $8 + 7 = 8 + \boxed{} - \boxed{}$

d) $5 + 6 = 6 + \boxed{} - \boxed{}$

e) $30 + 29 = 30 + \boxed{} - \boxed{}$

f) $39 + 40 = 40 + \boxed{} - \boxed{}$

> You can add numbers that differ by 2 by doubling the number between them.

8. Add by doubling the middle number.

a) $7 + 9 = \underline{\quad 8 + 8 \quad} = \underline{\quad 16 \quad}$

b) $3 + 5 = \underline{} = \underline{}$

c) $8 + 6 = \underline{} = \underline{}$

d) $13 + 15 = \underline{} = \underline{}$

e) $29 + 31 = \underline{} = \underline{}$

f) $62 + 64 = \underline{} = \underline{}$

9. Abella adds $8 + 9$ by adding $8 + 8 - 1$. Is she correct? Explain.

_____

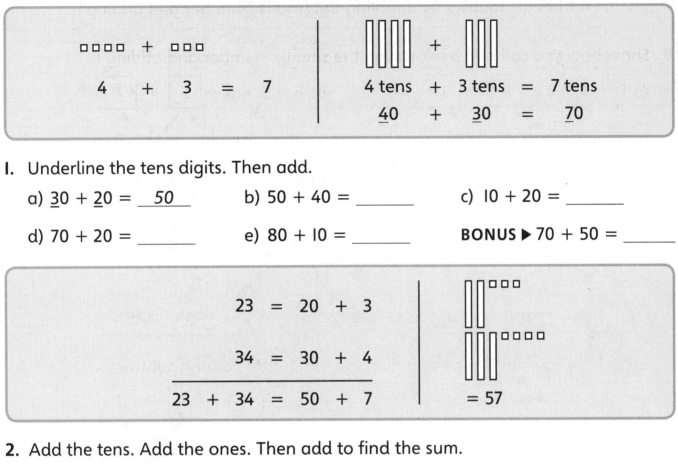

1. Underline the tens digits. Then add.

a) $\underline{3}0 + \underline{2}0 =$ __50__

b) $50 + 40 =$ _____

c) $10 + 20 =$ _____

d) $70 + 20 =$ _____

e) $80 + 10 =$ _____

BONUS ▶ $70 + 50 =$ _____

2. Add the tens. Add the ones. Then add to find the sum.

a)
$21 =$ __20__ $+$ __1__
$32 =$ __30__ $+$ __2__
$21 + 32 =$ __50__ $+$ __3__ $=$ __53__

b)
$43 =$ __40__ $+$ ____
$35 =$ __30__ $+$ ____
$43 + 35 =$ ____ $+$ ____ $=$ ____

c)
$54 =$ ____ $+$ ____
$13 =$ ____ $+$ ____
$54 + 13 =$ ____ $+$ ____ $=$ ____

d)
$63 =$ ____ $+$ ____
$26 =$ ____ $+$ ____
$63 + 26 =$ ____ $+$ ____ $=$ ____

3. Underline the tens digits. Circle the ones digits. Then add mentally.

a) $\underline{4}② + \underline{2}③ =$ __65__

b) $17 + 31 =$ _____

c) $63 + 24 =$ _____

d) $56 + 23 =$ _____

e) $21 + 64 =$ _____

f) $44 + 22 =$ _____

COPYRIGHT © 2018 JUMP MATH. NOT TO BE COPIED.

$$28 = 20 + 8$$
$$34 = 30 + 4$$
$$28 + 34 = 50 + 12$$

$$= 50 + 10 + 2 = 62$$

4. Regroup the second number.

a) $40 + 13 = 40 +$ __10__ $+$ __3__

b) $50 + 16 = 50 +$ _____ $+$ _____

c) $70 + 18 = 70 +$ _____ $+$ _____

d) $90 + 14 = 90 +$ _____ $+$ _____

5. Add the tens and ones. Regroup, then find the sum.

a)
$$37 = \underline{\ 30\ } + \underline{\ 7\ }$$
$$16 = \underline{\ 10\ } + \underline{\ 6\ }$$
$$37 + 16 = \underline{\ 40\ } + \underline{\ 13\ }$$
$$= \underline{\ 53\ }$$

b)
$$24 = \underline{\ 20\ } + \underline{\quad}$$
$$59 = \underline{\ 50\ } + \underline{\quad}$$
$$24 + 59 = \underline{\quad} + \underline{\quad}$$
$$= \underline{\quad}$$

c)
$$59 = \underline{\quad} + \underline{\quad}$$
$$43 = \underline{\quad} + \underline{\quad}$$
$$59 + 43 = \underline{\quad} + \underline{\quad}$$
$$= \underline{\quad}$$

d)
$$42 = \underline{\quad} + \underline{\quad}$$
$$28 = \underline{\quad} + \underline{\quad}$$
$$42 + 28 = \underline{\quad} + \underline{\quad}$$
$$= \underline{\quad}$$

6. Underline the tens digits. Circle the ones digits. Then add.

a) $4\underline{5} + 2\underline{7} = $ __$60 + 12 = 72$__

b) $45 + 29 = $ _____

c) $27 + 68 = $ _____

d) $36 + 86 = $ _____

7. Simon's dog needs to eat 95 g of dog food each day.
This morning it ate 69 g of food. In the afternoon it ate 37 g.

a) How many grams of food did the dog eat today?

b) Did Simon's dog eat enough food? Explain.

WOOF

8. Jane's sister worked 17 hours at a restaurant this week and 24 hours the week before. How many hours did she work altogether the past two weeks?

COPYRIGHT © 2016 JUMP MATH: NOT TO BE COPIED.

NS3-22 Subtraction Fluency

□□□ + □□
3 + 2 = 5   ⟵   read backwards for subtraction   □□□☒☒
5 − 2 = 3

1. Write a subtraction sentence for the addition sentence.

   a) 4 + 3 = 7

   __7__ − __3__ = __4__

   b) 3 + 6 = 9

   _____ − _____ = __3__

   c) 7 + 3 = 10

   _____ − _____ = _____

   d) 5 + 5 = 10

   _____ − _____ = _____

   | 4 + 3 = 7 | so | 40 + 30 = 70 |
   | 7 − 3 = 4 | so | 70 − 30 = 40 |

2. Write a subtraction sentence for the addition sentence

   a) 20 + 40 = 60

   __60__ − __40__ = __20__

   b) 30 + 20 = 50

   _____ − _____ = __30__

   c) 50 + 30 = 80

   _____ − _____ = _____

   d) 60 + 40 = 100

   _____ − _____ = _____

   □□□□☒☒☒
   7 − 3 = 4   ⟵   read backwards for addition   □□□□ + □□□
   4 + 3 = 7

3. Write an addition sentence for the subtraction sentence.

   a) 9 − 3 = 6

   __6__ + __3__ = __9__

   b) 8 − 5 = 3

   _____ + _____ = __8__

   c) 6 − 2 = 4

   _____ + _____ = _____

   d) 7 − 1 = 6

   _____ + _____ = _____

COPYRIGHT © 2016 JUMP MATH: NOT TO BE COPIED.

$$7 - 3 = 4 \quad \text{so} \quad 70 - 30 = 40$$
$$4 + 3 = 7 \quad \text{so} \quad 40 + 30 = 70$$

4. Write an addition sentence for the subtraction sentence.

a) $70 - 10 = 60$

   $\underline{\ 60\ } + \underline{\ 10\ } = \underline{\ 70\ }$

b) $50 - 20 = 30$

   $\underline{\hspace{1cm}} + \underline{\hspace{1cm}} = \underline{\ 50\ }$

c) $60 - 40 = 20$

   $\underline{\hspace{1cm}} + \underline{\hspace{1cm}} = \underline{\hspace{1cm}}$

d) $80 - 10 = 70$

   $\underline{\hspace{1cm}} + \underline{\hspace{1cm}} = \underline{\hspace{1cm}}$

5. Fill in the addend. Then subtract.

a) $\underline{\ 4\ } + 3 = 7$

   so $7 - 3 = \underline{\ 4\ }$

b) $\underline{\hspace{1cm}} + 2 = 8$

   so $8 - 2 = \underline{\hspace{1cm}}$

c) $\underline{\hspace{1cm}} + 4 = 6$

   so $\underline{\hspace{1cm}} - \underline{\hspace{1cm}} = \underline{\hspace{1cm}}$

d) $\underline{\hspace{1cm}} + 4 = 9$

   so $\underline{\hspace{1cm}} - \underline{\hspace{1cm}} = \underline{\hspace{1cm}}$

6. Fill in the addend. Then subtract.

a) $\underline{\ 20\ } + 30 = 50$

   so $50 - 30 = \underline{\ 20\ }$

b) $\underline{\hspace{1cm}} + 50 = 60$

   so $60 - 50 = \underline{\hspace{1cm}}$

c) $\underline{\hspace{1cm}} + 40 = 90$

   so $\underline{\hspace{1cm}} - \underline{\hspace{1cm}} = \underline{\hspace{1cm}}$

d) $\underline{\hspace{1cm}} + 10 = 80$

   so $\underline{\hspace{1cm}} - \underline{\hspace{1cm}} = \underline{\hspace{1cm}}$

7. Think of the addition sentence. Then subtract.

a) $9 - 4 = \underline{\hspace{1cm}}$

b) $70 - 50 = \underline{\hspace{1cm}}$

c) $8 - 1 = \underline{\hspace{1cm}}$

d) $60 - 20 = \underline{\hspace{1cm}}$

e) $8 - 2 = \underline{\hspace{1cm}}$

f) $90 - 70 = \underline{\hspace{1cm}}$

g) $7 - 5 = \underline{\hspace{1cm}}$

h) $50 - 30 = \underline{\hspace{1cm}}$

i) $9 - 6 = \underline{\hspace{1cm}}$

BONUS ▶

j) $12 - 5 = \underline{\hspace{1cm}}$

k) $14 - 9 = \underline{\hspace{1cm}}$

l) $120 - 70 = \underline{\hspace{1cm}}$

COPYRIGHT © 2016 JUMP MATH: NOT TO BE COPIED.

NS3-23 Subtracting Mentally

REMINDER ▶ You can count up to subtract.

$9 - 5 = 4$ 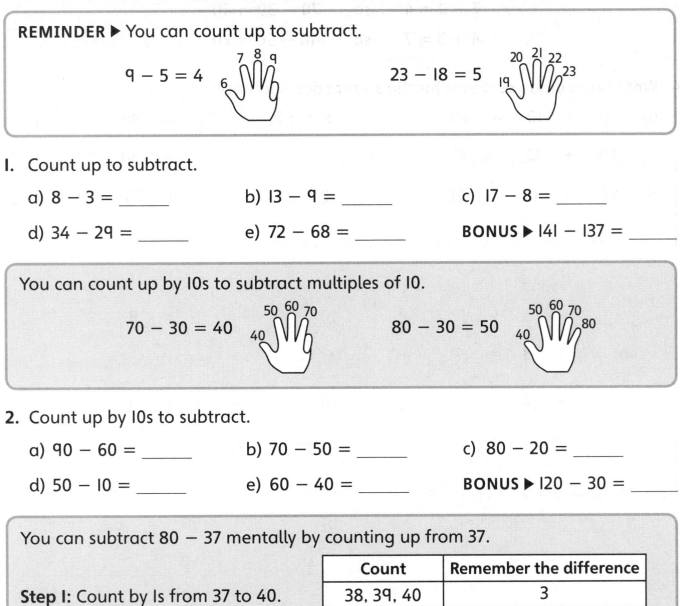 $23 - 18 = 5$

1. Count up to subtract.

a) $8 - 3 =$ _____

b) $13 - 9 =$ _____

c) $17 - 8 =$ _____

d) $34 - 29 =$ _____

e) $72 - 68 =$ _____

BONUS ▶ $141 - 137 =$ _____

You can count up by 10s to subtract multiples of 10.

$70 - 30 = 40$ $80 - 30 = 50$

2. Count up by 10s to subtract.

a) $90 - 60 =$ _____

b) $70 - 50 =$ _____

c) $80 - 20 =$ _____

d) $50 - 10 =$ _____

e) $60 - 40 =$ _____

BONUS ▶ $120 - 30 =$ _____

You can subtract $80 - 37$ mentally by counting up from 37.

	Count	Remember the difference
Step 1: Count by 1s from 37 to 40.	38, 39, 40	3
Step 2: Count by 10s from 40 to 80.	50, 60, 70, 80	40
Step 3: Add.		$3 + 40 = 43$

3. Subtract mentally by counting up.

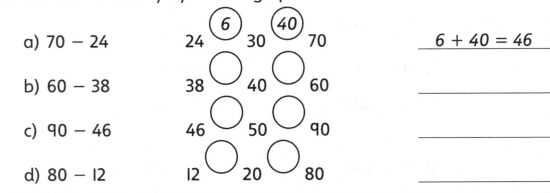

a) $70 - 24$ 24 6 30 40 70 $6 + 40 = 46$

b) $60 - 38$ 38 40 60   _____

c) $90 - 46$ 46 50 90   _____

d) $80 - 12$ 12 20 80   _____

You can subtract 73 − 28 mentally by counting up from 28.

	Count	Remember the difference
Step I: Count by Is from 28 to 30.	29, 30	2
Step 2: Count by I0s from 30 to 70.	40, 50, 60, 70	40
Step 3: Count by Is from 70 to 73.	71, 72, 73	3
Step 4: Add.		2 + 40 + 3 = 45

4. Subtract mentally by counting up.

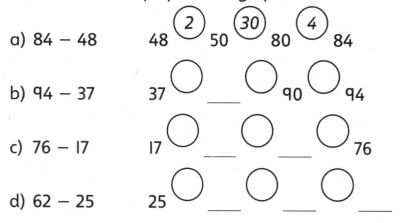

a) 84 − 48   48 ②50 ㉚80 ④84   <u>2 + 30 + 4 = 36</u>

b) 94 − 37   37 ○ __ ○ 90 ○ 94   _____

c) 76 − 17   17 ○ __ ○ __ ○ 76   _____

d) 62 − 25   25 ○ __ ○ __ ○ __   _____

5. Subtract mentally by counting up.

a) 112 − 77   77 ○ 80 ○ 110 ○ 112   _____

b) 134 − 68   68 ○ __ ○ 130 ○ __   _____

c) 143 − 89   89 ○ __ ○ __ ○ __   _____

6. Eric has room for 72 stamps in his book. He collected 35 stamps. How many more stamps can he put in his book?

_____

7. A plane can seat I34 people. 76 people are already seated. How many more people can the plane seat?

_____

_____

COPYRIGHT © 2016 JUMP MATH: NOT TO BE COPIED

NS3-24 Parts and Totals

I. Shade boxes to show the number of marbles. Then find the total and the difference.

a) 5 green marbles
3 blue marbles

difference _2 marbles_

green

total _8 marbles_

blue

b) 4 green marbles
6 blue marbles

difference _____

green

total _____

blue

c) 8 green marbles
4 blue marbles

difference _____

green

total _____

blue

d) 9 green marbles
4 blue marbles

difference _____

green

total _____

blue

e) 3 green marbles
8 blue marbles

difference _____

green

total _____

blue

COPYRIGHT © 2016 JUMP MATH: NOT TO BE COPIED.

4 green marbles
3 more blue marbles than green

You can draw the diagram using these steps.

Step I: Shade the amount you know.

green

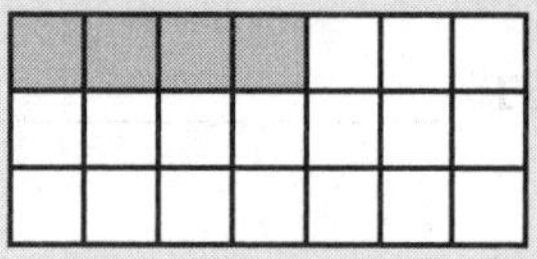

Step 2: Find the other amount.

green

blue

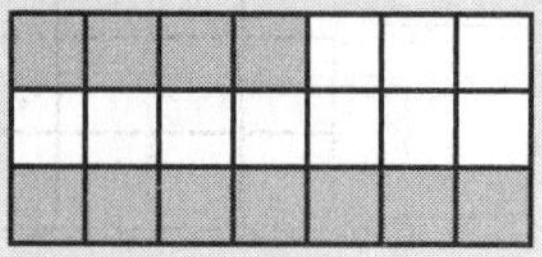

2. Draw the diagram. Then fill in the blanks.

a) 5 green marbles
2 more blue marbles than green marbles

green

blue

difference _____

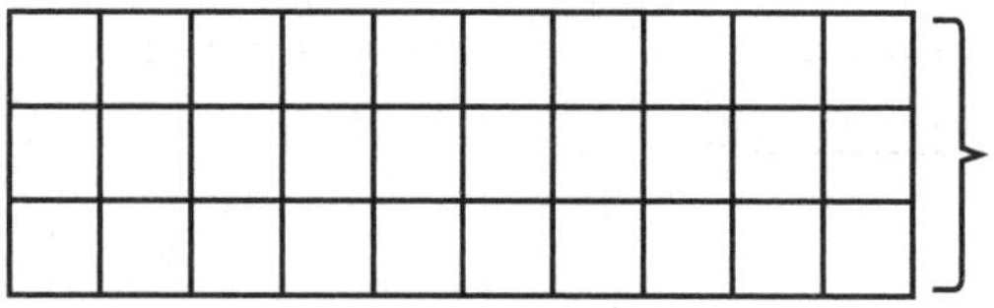

total _____

b) 4 blue marbles
3 more green marbles than blue marbles

green

blue

difference _____

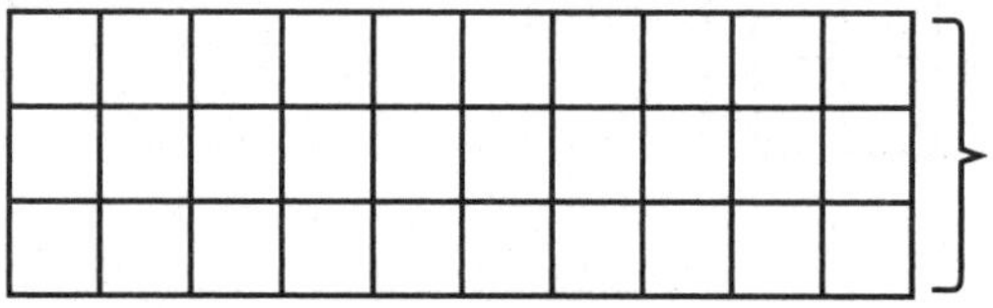

total _____

Sometimes you know the larger amount.

6 green marbles

green

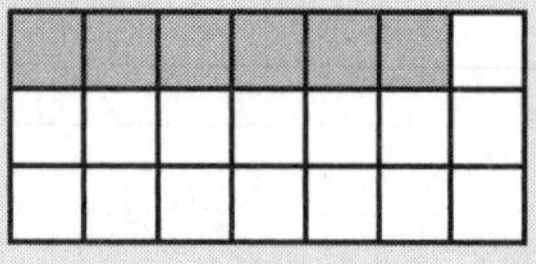

4 more green marbles than blue marbles

green

blue

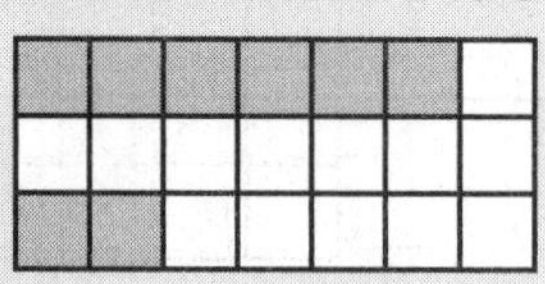

3. Draw the diagram. Then fill in the blanks.

7 green marbles
3 more green marbles than blue marbles

green

blue

difference _____

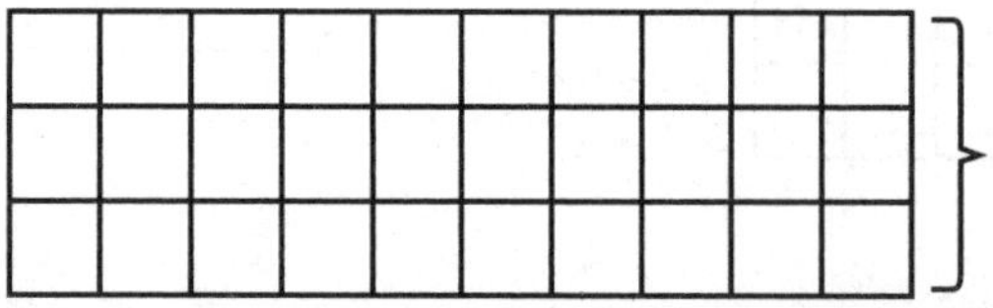

total _____

COPYRIGHT © 2016 JUMP MATH: NOT TO BE COPIED.

4. Draw the diagram. Then fill in the blanks.

a) 9 green marbles
   5 blue marbles

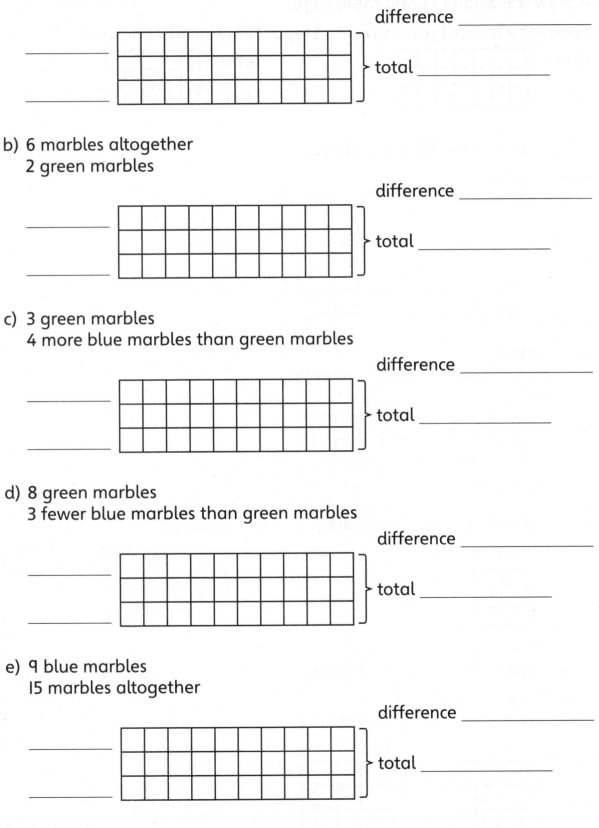

difference _____

total _____

b) 6 marbles altogether
   2 green marbles

difference _____

total _____

c) 3 green marbles
   4 more blue marbles than green marbles

difference _____

total _____

d) 8 green marbles
   3 fewer blue marbles than green marbles

difference _____

total _____

e) 9 blue marbles
   15 marbles altogether

difference _____

total _____

COPYRIGHT © 2016 JUMP MATH: NOT TO BE COPIED.

I. Fill in the table.

	Green Marbles	Blue Marbles	Total	Difference
a)	3	5	8	2 more blue marbles than green
b)	2	9		
c)	4		6	
d)		2	7	
e)	6		10	
f)	3			I more blue marble than green
g)		2		I more green marble than blue
h)		4		I more blue marble than green
i)	7			5 more green marbles than blue
j)		5		4 more green marbles than blue
k)		12		6 more blue marbles than green
l)	12	35		
m)	35			20 more green marbles than blue

COPYRIGHT © 2016 JUMP MATH: NOT TO BE COPIED.

2. Write + or −.

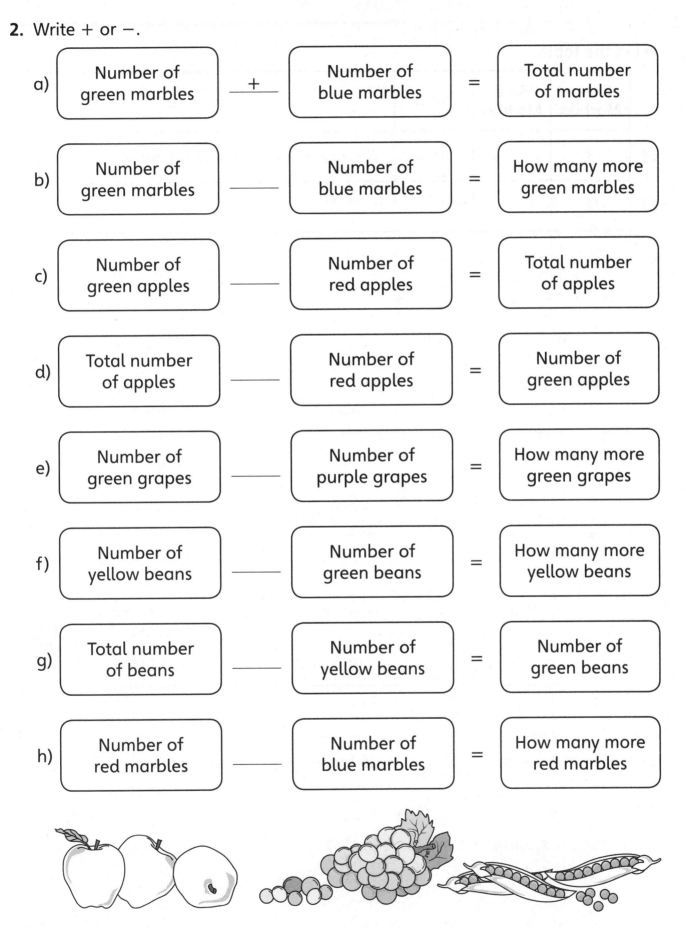

a)
| Number of green marbles | **+** | Number of blue marbles | **=** | Total number of marbles |

b)
| Number of green marbles | ——— | Number of blue marbles | **=** | How many more green marbles |

c)
| Number of green apples | ——— | Number of red apples | **=** | Total number of apples |

d)
| Total number of apples | ——— | Number of red apples | **=** | Number of green apples |

e)
| Number of green grapes | ——— | Number of purple grapes | **=** | How many more green grapes |

f)
| Number of yellow beans | ——— | Number of green beans | **=** | How many more yellow beans |

g)
| Total number of beans | ——— | Number of yellow beans | **=** | Number of green beans |

h)
| Number of red marbles | ——— | Number of blue marbles | **=** | How many more red marbles |

COPYRIGHT © 2016 JUMP MATH: NOT TO BE COPIED.

3. Fill in the table. Circle the number in the table that answers the question.

		Red	Green	Total	Difference
a)	Kate has 3 green fish and 4 red fish. How many fish does she have altogether?	4	3	⑦	1
b)	Bill has 4 green fish and 6 red fish. How many fish does he have altogether?				
c)	Mary has 8 green fish and 2 more green fish than red fish. How many fish does she have?				
d)	Jun has 19 fish. He has 15 green fish. How many red fish does he have?				
e)	Hanna has 8 green fish and 3 fewer red fish than green fish. How many fish does she have?				
f)	Ken has 22 red fish and 33 green fish. How many more green fish does he have?				

4. Alice has 3 science books and 4 art books. How many books does she have?

5. Marko has 5 pets. 3 are cats. The rest are dogs. How many dogs does he have?

6. Ed has 25 red apples. He has 14 more green apples than red apples. How many apples does he have?

7. There are 25 students in a class. 16 of the students have pets.

   a) How many students do not have pets?

   b) How many more students have pets than don't have pets?

COPYRIGHT © 2016 JUMP MATH: NOT TO BE COPIED.

NS3-26 Sums and Differences

Solve the problems mentally.

1. Luc has 7 dollars and Amy has 15 dollars.
How much money do they have altogether?

2. Anne is 12 years old. Her sister is 23. How much
older is her sister?

3. A library has 520 books. 150 were borrowed.
How many books are left?

4. 52 students went on a school trip. 27 of the students
are wearing hats. How many are not wearing hats?

5. Jayden paid 75 cents for a goldfish that costs 62 cents.
How much change did he get back?

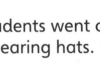

6. Clara's mother is 47. Her aunt is 33. How much older is Clara's
mother than Clara's aunt?

7. The Calgary Tower in Calgary, Alberta, is about 190 metres tall.
The CN Tower in Toronto, Ontario, is about 460 metres tall.
About how much taller is the CN Tower?

8. Ethan sold 27 raffle tickets altogether on Wednesday
and Thursday. On Thursday, he sold 13 tickets.
How many tickets did he sell on Wednesday?

9. Sara had 35 pencil crayons. She lost 4.
How many does she have left?

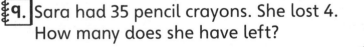

COPYRIGHT © 2016 JUMP MATH: NOT TO BE COPIED.

10. A one-year-old elephant at a zoo weights about 300 kg. How much would two elephants of this size weigh?

11. Alex biked 24 kilometres on Monday and 13 kilometres on Tuesday.

   a) How much farther did she bike on Monday than on Tuesday?

   b) How far did she bike altogether?

12. Tristan drove 90 kilometres on Tuesday. He drove 40 more kilometres on Wednesday than on Tuesday.

   a) How far did he drive on Wednesday?

   b) How far did he drive altogether?

13. Amir has 85 cents. Liz has 30 cents. Count up to find how much more money Amir has than Liz.

14. Josh read two books by Roald Dahl. *The BFG* is 208 pages long. *Charlie and the Chocolate Factory* is 53 pages shorter than *The BFG*. How many pages did he read altogether?

15. Marla has 61 baseball cards. She gives away 29 cards and gets 32 cards in return.

   a) Count up to find how many cards Marla has after she gives away the 29 cards

   b) How many cards does she have altogether after she receives the 32 cards in the trade.
   Hint: Use doubling.

COPYRIGHT © 2016 JUMP MATH: NOT TO BE COPIED.

ME3-1 Measuring in Centimetres

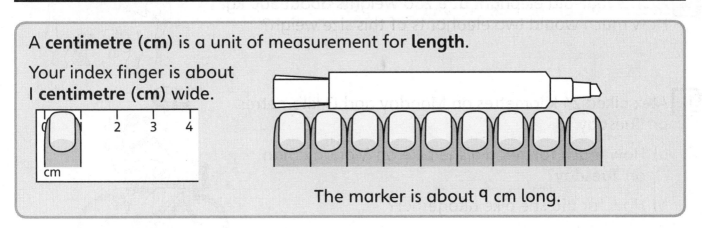

A **centimetre (cm)** is a unit of measurement for **length**.

Your index finger is about
1 **centimetre (cm)** wide.

The marker is about 9 cm long.

1. Use your index finger to estimate the length to the closest centimetre.

   a) My pen is about _____ cm long.

   b) My pencil is about _____ cm long.

   c) My crayon is about _____ cm long.

   d) My eraser is about _____ cm long.

   e) My JUMP Math book is about _____ cm wide.

   f) My desk is about _____ cm wide.

2. Your hand is about 10 cm wide. Use your spread-out hand to estimate the length.

   a) My JUMP Math book is about _____ cm long.

   b) My desk is about _____ cm long.

   c) My arm is about _____ cm long.

   d) My leg is about _____ cm long.

   e) My shoe is about _____ cm long.

   BONUS ▶ My desk is about _____ cm tall.

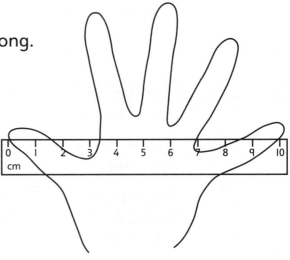

COPYRIGHT © 2016 JUMP MATH: NOT TO BE COPIED.

3. How far apart are the arrows?

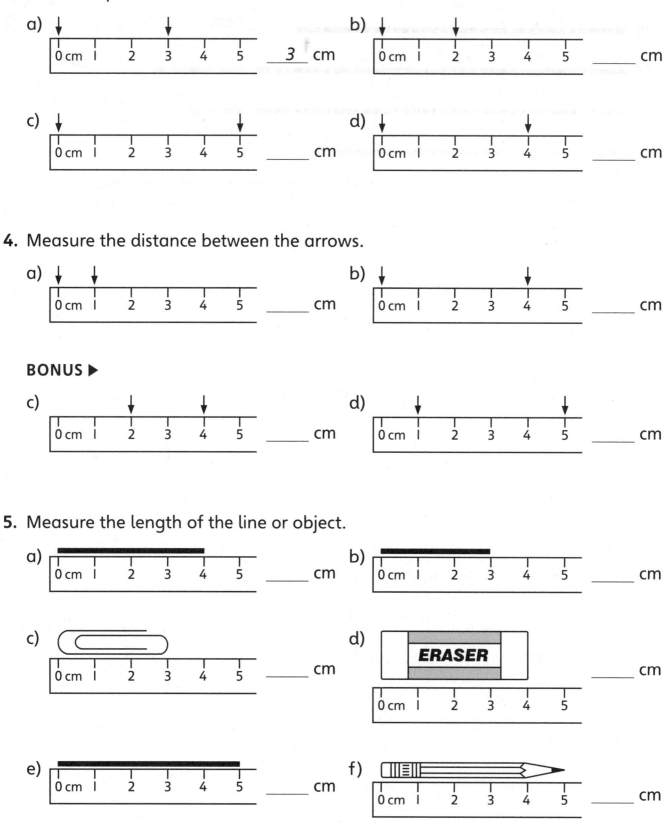

a) 0 cm 1 2 3 4 5 ___3___ cm

b) 0 cm 1 2 3 4 5 _____ cm

c) 0 cm 1 2 3 4 5 _____ cm

d) 0 cm 1 2 3 4 5 _____ cm

4. Measure the distance between the arrows.

a) 0 cm 1 2 3 4 5 _____ cm

b) 0 cm 1 2 3 4 5 _____ cm

BONUS ▶

c) 0 cm 1 2 3 4 5 _____ cm

d) 0 cm 1 2 3 4 5 _____ cm

5. Measure the length of the line or object.

a) 0 cm 1 2 3 4 5 _____ cm

b) 0 cm 1 2 3 4 5 _____ cm

c) 0 cm 1 2 3 4 5 _____ cm

d) **ERASER** 0 cm 1 2 3 4 5 _____ cm

e) 0 cm 1 2 3 4 5 _____ cm

f) 0 cm 1 2 3 4 5 _____ cm

COPYRIGHT © 2016 JUMP MATH: NOT TO BE COPIED

Measurement 3-1

6. Measure the length of the line or object.

a) _____ _____ cm

b) _____ _____ cm

c) _____ _____ cm

d) _____ _____ cm

e) 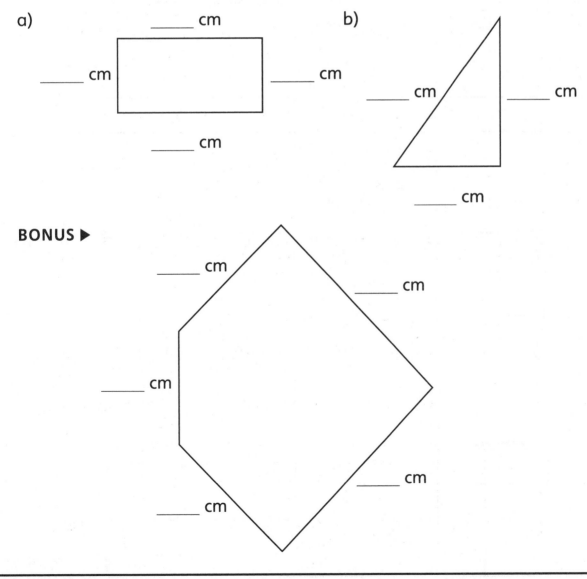 _____ cm

f) _____ cm

7. Measure all the sides of the shape.

a) _____ cm

_____ cm   _____ cm

_____ cm

b) _____ cm   _____ cm

_____ cm

BONUS ▶

_____ cm

_____ cm

_____ cm

_____ cm

_____ cm

COPYRIGHT © 2016 JUMP MATH: NOT TO BE COPIED.

ME3-2 Measuring and Drawing in Centimetres

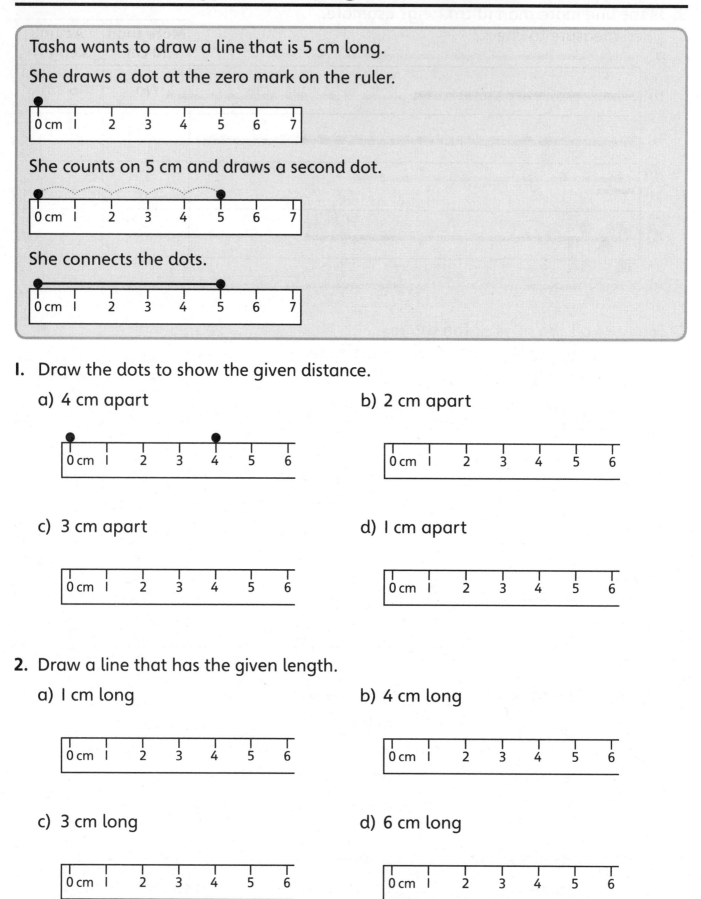

Tasha wants to draw a line that is 5 cm long.

She draws a dot at the zero mark on the ruler.

She counts on 5 cm and draws a second dot.

She connects the dots.

1. Draw the dots to show the given distance.

   a) 4 cm apart

   b) 2 cm apart

   c) 3 cm apart

   d) 1 cm apart

2. Draw a line that has the given length.

   a) 1 cm long

   b) 4 cm long

   c) 3 cm long

   d) 6 cm long

COPYRIGHT © 2016 JUMP MATH: NOT TO BE COPIED.

3. Is the line more than 10 cm long? Estimate.
Then measure to check.

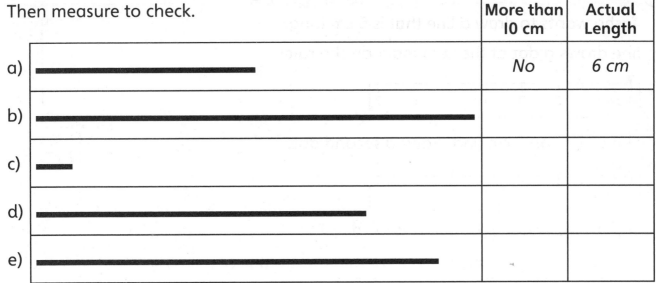

	More than 10 cm	Actual Length
a)	No	6 cm
b)		
c)		
d)		
e)		

4. Are the dots less than 10 cm apart? Estimate.
Then measure to check.

	Less than 10 cm	Distance (cm)
a)		
b)		
c)		
d)		
e)		

5. Draw a line that has the given length. Use a ruler.

    a) 5 cm long   b) 10 cm long   c) 13 cm long

6. Sketch a line that has the given length. Do not use a ruler.

    a) 7 cm long   b) 9 cm long   c) 14 cm long

7. Draw the object to the exact measurement.

    a) a worm, 5 cm long   b) a leaf, 11 cm long   c) a spoon, 9 cm long

COPYRIGHT © 2016 JUMP MATH: NOT TO BE COPIED.

ME3-3 Metres

A baseball bat is about I **metre** long.

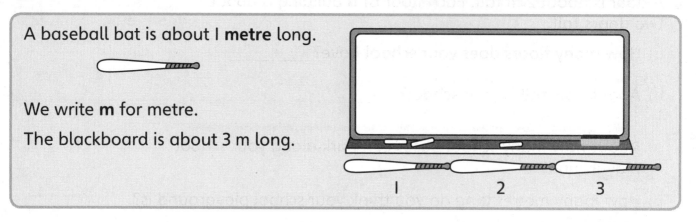

We write **m** for metre.

The blackboard is about 3 m long.

I. Estimate. Then measure to the closest metre.

	Object	Estimate (m)	Measurement (m)
a)	Length of a board		
b)	Height of a board		
c)	Width of a cupboard		
d)	Height of a cupboard		
e)	Width of a classroom window		
f)	Length of the classroom		

Use these lengths to estimate.

  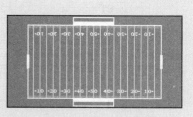 

A door is about 2 m tall.　　A bike is about 2 m long.　　A school bus is about 10 m long.　　A football field is about 100 m long.

2. a) A car is about 2 bikes long. How long is the car? _____

　 b) A large truck is as long as 2 school buses. How long is the truck? _____

　 c) Kim runs 6 lengths of a football field. How far does she run? _____

COPYRIGHT © 2016 JUMP MATH: NOT TO BE COPIED.

3. A door is about 2 m tall. Each floor of a building is about two doors tall.

    a) How many floors does your school have? _____

    b) About how tall is your school? _____

4. a) About how many school buses can park along your school playground?

    b) How many metres long do you think your school playground is? Explain.

5. a) Tina runs 250 m, then walks 450 m. How far does she travel?

    b) Cam walks 125 m, runs 350 m, then walks 125 m. How far does he travel?

    c) Who travels farther, Tina or Cam?

6. Ren has 120 m of white yarn, 325 m of red yarn, and 45 m of blue yarn. He needs a total of 450 m of yarn to make a pair of socks.

    a) Does Ren have enough yarn for white and red socks?

    b) Does Ren have enough yarn for blue and red socks?

7. The table shows the heights of some tall towers in Canada.

Tower	Location	Height (m)
CN Tower	Toronto, ON	553
Ryan Tower	Chelsea, QC	229
Calgary Tower	Calgary, AB	191
Bell Aliant Tower	Moncton, NB	127

    a) How much taller is the CN Tower than the Ryan Tower?

    b) How much shorter is the Bell Aliant Tower than the Calgary Tower?

    c) How much taller is the Ryan Tower than the Bell Aliant Tower?

    d) Make your own question about the height of towers. Share your question and ask a classmate to solve it.

COPYRIGHT © 2016 JUMP MATH: NOT TO BE COPIED.

ME3-4 Metres and Centimetres

A metre stick is about 100 cm long.
1 m = 100 cm

| 0 cm | 10 | 20 | 30 | 40 | 50 | 60 | 70 | 80 | 90 | 100 |

1. a) Stretch your arms out. The distance in the picture is called your **arm span**.

   Ask a classmate to measure your arm span with a piece of string.

   Arm span = _____ cm

   Is your arm span more or less than a metre? _____

   b) Stretch your arms out. Bend one elbow as shown. The distance in the picture is called your **arm-and-elbow span**.

   Ask a classmate to measure your arm-and-elbow span with a piece of string.

   Arm-and-elbow span = _____ cm

   Is your arm-and-elbow span more or less than 1 m? _____

   c) Which distance is closest to 1 m? _____

Ed uses a metre stick to measure the length of the board. The board is more than 2 m long.

Ed measures the leftover length in centimetres. The board is 2 m 70 cm long.

A measurement in metres and centimetres is called a **mixed measurement**.

2 m   70 cm

2. Measure in metres and centimetres.

   a) Width of a cupboard = _____ m _____ cm

   b) Height of the back of a chair = _____ m _____ cm

   c) Width of a window = _____ m _____ cm

   d) Length of a board = _____ m _____ cm

   e) Length of a carpet = _____ m _____ cm

COPYRIGHT © 2016 JUMP MATH: NOT TO BE COPIED

3. Write the measurements in centimetres.

Metres	1 m	2 m	3 m	4 m	5 m	6 m	7 m	8 m
Centimetres	100 cm	200 cm						

4. Change the metres to centimetres. Change the mixed measurement to centimetres.

a) 3 m = ___300___ cm,

    so 3 m 5 cm

      = ___300 + 5___ cm

      = ___305___ cm

b) 5 m = _____ cm,

    so 5 m 15 cm

      = _____ cm

      = _____ cm

c) 2 m = _____ cm,

    so 2 m 73 cm

      = _____ cm

      = _____ cm

d) 4 m = _____ cm,

    so 4 m 8 cm

      = _____ cm

      = _____ cm

e) 6 m = _____ cm,

    so 6 m 20 cm

      = _____ cm

      = _____ cm

f) 1 m = _____ cm,

    so 1 m 3 cm

      = _____ cm

      = _____ cm

5. Change the mixed measurement to centimetres.

a) 7 m 70 cm

      = ___700 + 70___ cm

      = _____ cm

b) 9 m 99 cm

      = _____ cm

      = _____ cm

c) 8 m 1 cm

      = _____ cm

      = _____ cm

d) 3 m 25 cm

      = _____ cm

e) 7 m 76 cm

      = _____ cm

f) 2 m 2 cm

      = _____ cm

6. Circle the digit that shows the metres.

a) ③05 cm   b) 516 cm   c) 283 cm   d) 402 cm   e) 650 cm   f) 107 cm

BONUS ▶ Change the metres to centimetres. Write the lengths of the animals from shortest to longest.

Animal	Bengal tiger	Canadian lynx	Cougar	Snow leopard
Length	2 m 90 cm	90 cm	2 m 20 cm	2 m

COPYRIGHT © 2016 JUMP MATH: NOT TO BE COPIED.

ME3-5 Kilometres

> A **kilometre (km)** is a unit of measurement for long distances. I km = 1000 m

1. a) 1000 = _____ hundreds = _____ tens = _____ ones

   b) A football field is about 100 m long. How many football fields
      long is I km? _____

   c) A school bus is about 10 m long. How many school buses can
      park end to end along a I km distance? _____

2. You can walk I km in about 15 minutes. Name a place that is about
   I km from your home or school. _____

3. a) What is longer, 999 m or I km? How do you know? _____

   _____

   b) Emma thinks that 5 km is shorter than 850 m, because 5 is less
      than 850. Is she correct? Explain.

   _____

   _____

4. a) Is the object less than I m long, about I m long, or more than I m long?

   a paper clip _____   a bicycle _____

   a book _____   a baseball bat _____

   b) Suppose the objects are lined up end to end. Is the line less than I km long,
      about I km long, or more than I km long?

   1000 paper clips   1000 bicycles

   _____   _____

   1000 books   1000 baseball bats

   _____   _____

   BONUS ▶ 500 bicycles _____

COPYRIGHT © 2016 JUMP MATH: NOT TO BE COPIED.

5. Use the map to write the distances between the cities.

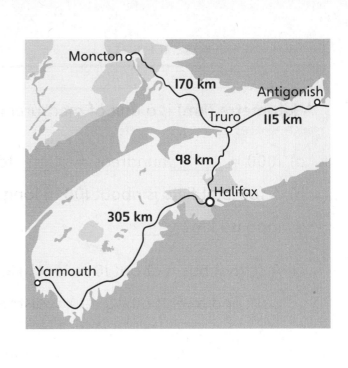

a) Moncton and Truro _____ km

b) Yarmouth and Halifax _____ km

c) Truro and Antigonish _____ km

d) Halifax and Truro _____ km

6. Use the map to answer the questions.

a) Jin travels from Moncton to Truro and then to Antigonish. How far does he travel?

b) Rani travels from Yarmouth to Halifax and then to Truro. How far does she travel?

c) David travels from Halifax to Truro, then to Moncton. How far does he travel?

d) Order the distances Jin, Rani, and David travel from longest to shortest.

e) How much farther is it from Halifax to Yarmouth than from Halifax to Moncton?

f) Make your own question using the distances on the map. Solve it.

7. The map shows part of Yukon Territory.

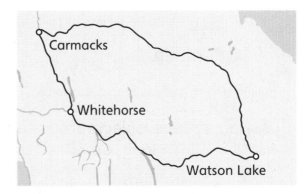

a) The distance from Carmacks to Whitehorse is 177 km. The distance from Watson Lake to Whitehorse is 261 km longer.

How far is Carmacks from Watson Lake?

b) Liz drives from Carmacks to Whitehorse and then to Watson Lake. How far does she drive?

c) There is another road from Carmacks to Watson Lake. This road is 584 km long.

Which road from Carmacks to Watson Lake is longer, the road through Whitehorse, or the other road? How much longer?

COPYRIGHT © 2016 JUMP MATH: NOT TO BE COPIED.

ME3-6 Choosing Units

A finger is about 1 cm wide.	A giant step is about 1 m long.	A door handle is about 1 m above the floor.	You can walk 1 km in about 15 minutes.

1. Draw a line to match the object to the best unit to measure it.

   a) length of a beetle   m   b) height of an adult   m

       height of a door   cm   distance to the moon   km

   c) height of a drum   km   d) width of a book   m

       distance across an ocean   cm   length of a river   km

       height of a teepee   m   height of a house   cm

2. Order the lengths from shortest to longest. Write "1st" for the shortest, "2nd" for the middle length, and "3rd" for the longest.

   a) length of a beetle _____   b) length of a carrot _____

       distance an airplane flies _____   length of a bus _____

       length of a classroom _____   distance across a bridge _____

3. Order the lengths from shortest "1st" to longest "3rd." Write the best unit to measure each length. Choose from centimetres, metres, and kilometres.

   a)   b)

       _3rd_   _____   _____   _____   _____   _____

       Unit _m_   Unit ____   Unit ____   Unit ____   Unit ____   Unit ____

4. Circle the best unit to measure the length.

   a) length of a plane   cm   m   km   b) height of a building   cm   m   km

   c) width of a coin   cm   m   km   d) height a plane flies   cm   m   km

   e) height of a cup   cm   m   km   f) length of a pen   cm   m   km

   g) width of a paddle   cm   m   km   h) distance to North Pole   cm   m   km

COPYRIGHT © 2016 JUMP MATH: NOT TO BE COPIED.

REMINDER ▶ 1 m = 100 cm

5. Change the measurement from metres to centimetres.

a) 5 m = __500__ cm   b) 3 m = _____ cm   c) 7 m = _____ cm

6. Change the measurement from metres to centimetres. Circle the greater measurement.

a) 3 m   5 cm   b) 5 m   45 cm   c) 780 cm   6 m

= _____ cm   = _____ cm   = _____ cm

7. Change metres to centimetres. Add the leftover centimetres.

a) 3 m 45 cm   b) 5 m 80 cm   c) 1 m 4 cm

= __300__ cm + __45__ cm   = _____ cm + ____ cm   = _____ cm + ____ cm

= __345__ cm   = _____ cm   = _____ cm

d) 6 m 54 cm   e) 7 m 30 cm   f) 2 m 9 cm

= _____ cm + ____ cm   = _____ cm + ____ cm   = _____ cm + ____ cm

= _____ cm   = _____ cm   = _____ cm

8. Change the mixed measurement to centimetres. Circle the greater measurement.

a) 3 m 2 cm   5 cm   b) 6 m 5 cm   65 cm   c) 280 cm   2 m 90 cm

= _____ cm   = _____ cm   = _____ cm

BONUS ▶ Order the lengths in Question 8 from shortest to longest.

_____

9. Change all measurements to centimetres. Show the measurements on the number line.

A. 50 cm   **B.** 1 m = _____   **C.** 2 m 50 cm = _____

0 cm   50 cm   100 cm   150 cm   200 cm   250 cm

10. The table shows the lengths of snakes at a zoo.

    a) Change all measurements to centimetres.

    b) Order the snakes from longest to shortest.

    _____

    _____

    _____

    _____

Snake	Length	Length (cm)
Coral snake	73 cm	
Fox snake	1 m 23 cm	
Yellow-bellied Racer	2 m	
Rattlesnake	1 m 30 cm	

11. Circle the correct length of the object.

    a) length of a bed

       195 cm or 195 m

    b) length of a bus

       10 m or 10 km

    c) length of a toothbrush

       16 cm or 16 m

    d) length of a driveway

       9 cm or 9 m

    e) height of a school

       14 cm or 14 m

    f) width of a street

       40 m or 40 km

12. Fill in the best unit for the measurement. Choose from cm, m, and km.

    a) The Canadian Horseshoe Falls at Niagara Falls, ON, is as tall as a 12 floor building.

       The falls are about 57 _____ tall.

    b) A raccoon can grow up to 70 _____ long.

    c) A black bear is about 2 _____ long.

    d) A maple leaf is about 16 _____ wide.

13. Would you measure the distance in metres or in kilometres? Explain your choice.

    a) from your classroom to the school office

    b) from your home to the airport

    c) from Ottawa, ON, to Edmonton, AB

    d) around the schoolyard

COPYRIGHT © 2016 JUMP MATH: NOT TO BE COPIED

ME3-7 Measuring Around a Shape—Perimeter

> The distance around the outside of a shape is the **perimeter** of the shape.
> The perimeter of this shape is 6 toothpicks.

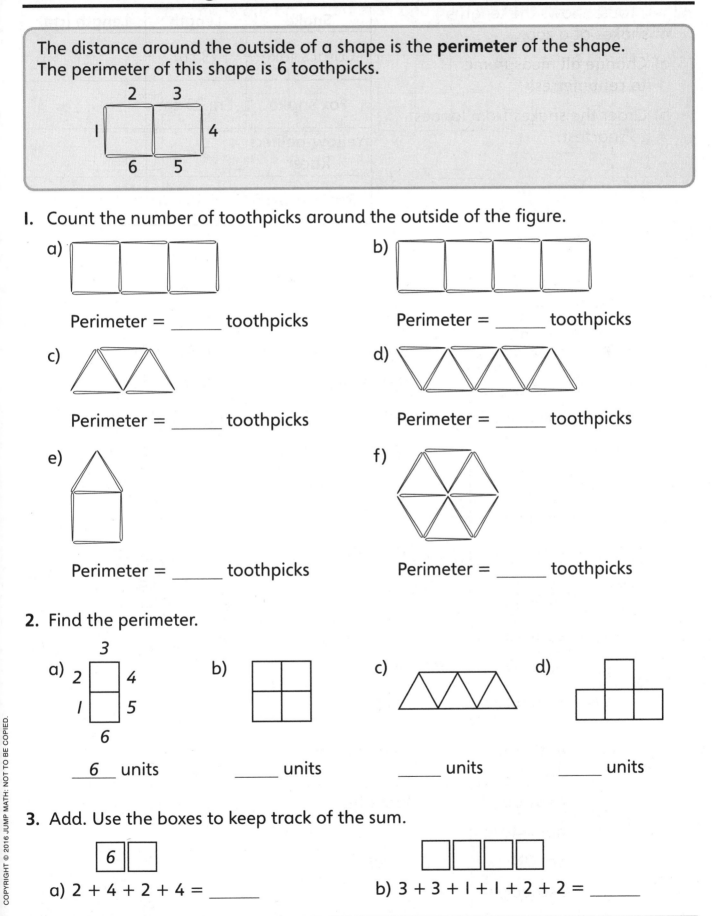

1. Count the number of toothpicks around the outside of the figure.

a)

Perimeter = _____ toothpicks

b)

Perimeter = _____ toothpicks

c)

Perimeter = _____ toothpicks

d)

Perimeter = _____ toothpicks

e)

Perimeter = _____ toothpicks

f)

Perimeter = _____ toothpicks

2. Find the perimeter.

a)

__6__ units

b)

_____ units

c)

_____ units

d)

_____ units

3. Add. Use the boxes to keep track of the sum.

a) 2 + 4 + 2 + 4 = _____

b) 3 + 3 + 1 + 1 + 2 + 2 = _____

COPYRIGHT © 2016 JUMP MATH: NOT TO BE COPIED.

4. Each small square is I cm long and I cm wide. Find the perimeter of the figure.

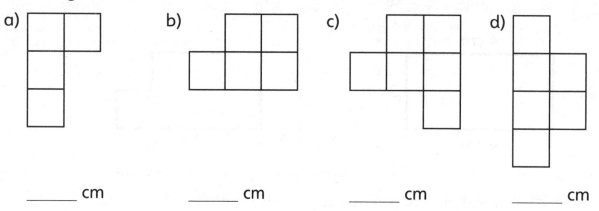

a)

b)

c)

d)

_____ cm   _____ cm   _____ cm   _____ cm

5. The length of each side of the figure is given. Add the lengths to find the perimeter.

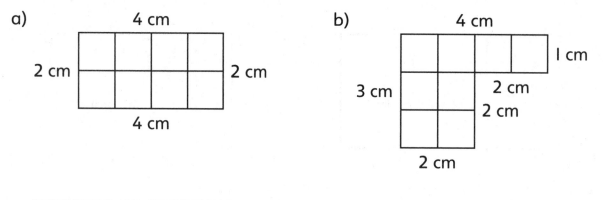

a)

4 cm

2 cm   2 cm

4 cm

b)

4 cm

3 cm   1 cm

2 cm

2 cm

2 cm

_____   _____

6. Find the perimeters of the figures in Question 5 by counting centimetres along the outside. Did you get the same answers as before? _____

7. Each small square is I cm long and I cm wide. Find the length of each side of the figure. Then write an addition sentence for the perimeter.

a)

2 cm

b)

COPYRIGHT © 2016 JUMP MATH: NOT TO BE COPIED.

Measurement 3-7

8. Each grid square is I cm long and I cm wide. Write the length of each side. Use the side lengths to find the perimeter.

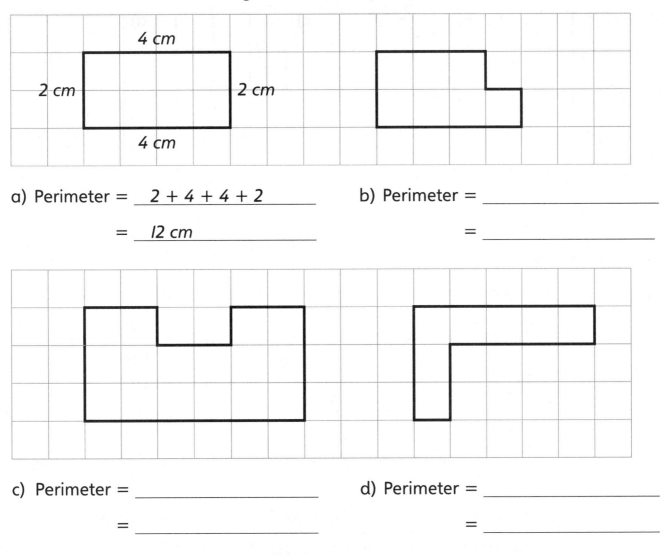

a) Perimeter = _2 + 4 + 4 + 2_

= _12 cm_

b) Perimeter = _____

= _____

c) Perimeter = _____

= _____

d) Perimeter = _____

= _____

9. Write an addition sentence for the perimeter of the swimming pool. Then find the perimeter.

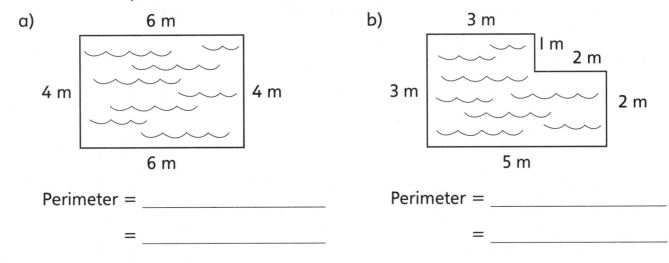

a)

Perimeter = _____

= _____

b)

Perimeter = _____

= _____

COPYRIGHT © 2016 JUMP MATH: NOT TO BE COPIED.

ME3-8 Exploring Perimeter

1. a) Estimate the lengths of the sides of the shape.

   b) Add the lengths to estimate the perimeter of the shape.

   c) Measure the sides to the closest centimetre. Find the perimeter.

Shape	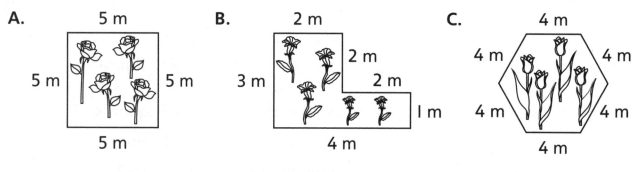		
Estimated Perimeter			
Measured Perimeter			

2. a) Find the perimeter of the flowerbeds.

   A.
   5 m
   5 m   5 m
   5 m

   B.
   2 m
   2 m
   3 m   2 m
   1 m
   4 m

   C.
   4 m
   4 m   4 m
   4 m   4 m
   4 m

   _____   _____   _____

   b) Order the flowerbeds from longest perimeter to shortest

   perimeter. _____

3. a) Perimeter of the shape you see _____

   Add one square so that the perimeter of the shape
   goes up by 2.

   New perimeter _____

   b) Perimeter of the shape you see _____

   Add one square so that the perimeter of the shape
   stays the same.

   New perimeter _____

COPYRIGHT © 2016 JUMP MATH: NOT TO BE COPIED.

4. a) All sides of the triangles are 1 unit long. Write the perimeter of each figure in the shape pattern.

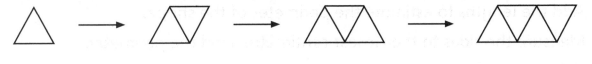

—————   —————   —————   —————

b) The perimeters make a number pattern. Describe the number pattern.

_____

c) Continue the number pattern.

What is the perimeter of the 5th figure? _____

What is the perimeter of the 6th figure? _____

BONUS ▶ Draw the 5th and 6th figures in the shape pattern. Check your answers from part c).

5th figure   6th figure

5. The picture shows two ways to make a rectangle using 4 squares.

a) Which rectangle, A or B, has the smaller perimeter? Explain.

b) Are there other ways to make a rectangle using 4 squares? Show your work.

c) On grid paper, draw two different shapes, rectangles or not rectangles, with a perimeter of 10 units.

6. On grid paper, draw the object with the given perimeter.

a) a square with a perimeter of 8 units

b) a square with a perimeter of 20 units

c) two different rectangles that each have a perimeter of 12 units

7. Ivan makes a poster from 6 squares with 1 m sides. He arranges the squares as shown. He puts a ribbon around the outside of the poster. How much ribbon does he need?

COPYRIGHT © 2016 JUMP MATH: NOT TO BE COPIED.

G3-1 Introduction to Classifying Data

> **Data** are facts or information you can use for calculating, answering questions, or planning. Your age, name, and hair colour are all pieces of data, called **data values**.
>
> A **category** is a group of data values that share an attribute, such as eye colour.

1. Mammals, birds, and fish are categories of animals.

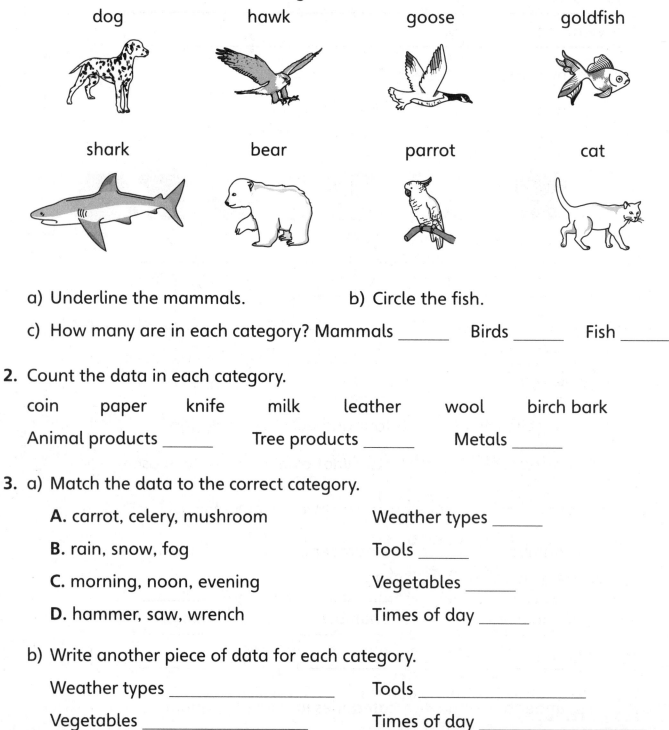

dog   hawk   goose   goldfish

shark   bear   parrot   cat

a) Underline the mammals.   b) Circle the fish.

c) How many are in each category? Mammals _____ Birds _____ Fish _____

2. Count the data in each category.

coin   paper   knife   milk   leather   wool   birch bark

Animal products _____   Tree products _____   Metals _____

3. a) Match the data to the correct category.

   A. carrot, celery, mushroom   Weather types _____

   B. rain, snow, fog   Tools _____

   C. morning, noon, evening   Vegetables _____

   D. hammer, saw, wrench   Times of day _____

   b) Write another piece of data for each category.

   Weather types _____   Tools _____

   Vegetables _____   Times of day _____

COPYRIGHT © 2016 JUMP MATH: NOT TO BE COPIED.

4. a) Write the letter for the shirt in the correct row of the table.

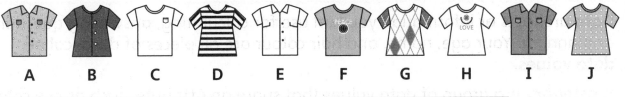

A B C D E F G H I J

Category	Shirts
Have a design	A,
Have no design	B,

How many shirts have a design? _____

How many shirts have no design? _____

b) Use the table to sort the shirts.

K L M N O P Q R S T

Shirt	K	L	M	N	O	P	Q	R	S	T
Dark colour		✓								
Light colour	✓									
Have a design	✓									

How many shirts are a dark colour and also have a design? _____

c) Think of other ways to sort shirts. What categories can you use?

_____

5. a) Sort the numbers. Cross out the number as you write it in the table.

2, 67, 903, 4, 9, 10, 38, 123, 560, 35

1-digit number	2-digit number	3-digit number

b) Can a number belong to two categories in part a)? Explain.

COPYRIGHT © 2016 JUMP MATH: NOT TO BE COPIED.

G3-2 Venn Diagrams

You can use ovals to sort objects by properties or attributes. Objects inside the oval have the property. Objects outside the oval do not have the property.

Use these shapes for Questions I and 2.

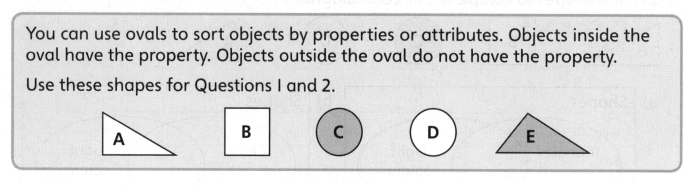

I. Write the letter of the shape inside or outside the oval.

a) B, C, D

Triangles

A, E

b)

Light colour

c)

Circles

A **Venn diagram** has overlapping ovals. Each oval is a category. Data can be in more than one category.

2. Shade the region. Write the correct letters in that region.

a) inside both ovals

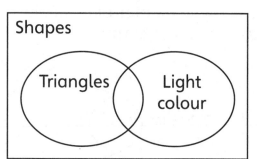

Shapes

Triangles   Light colour

b) outside both ovals

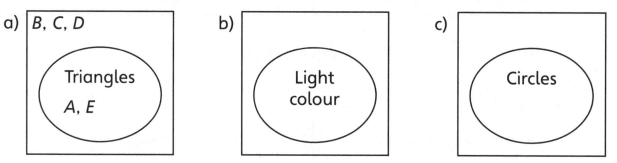

Shapes

Triangles   Light colour

c) light colour, but not triangle

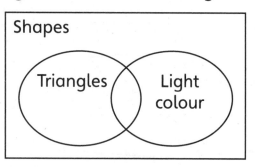

Shapes

Triangles   Light colour

d) triangle, but not light colour

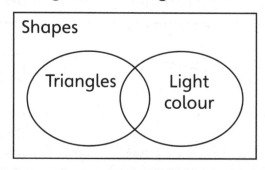

Shapes

Triangles   Light colour

COPYRIGHT © 2016 JUMP MATH: NOT TO BE COPIED.

3. Use the shapes to complete the Venn diagram.

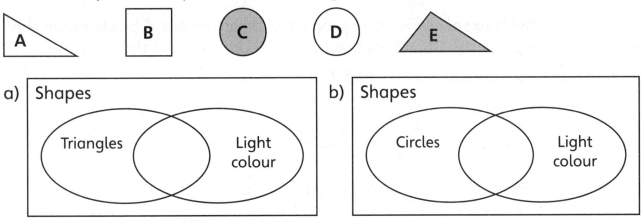

a)
Shapes

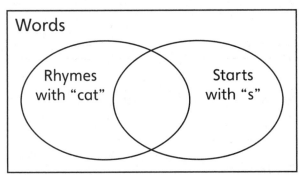

Triangles | Light colour

b)
Shapes

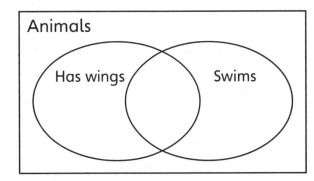

Circles | Light colour

4. Complete the Venn diagram. Some regions might stay empty.

a) rice, hat, sit, sat

Words

Rhymes with "cat" | Starts with "s"

b) dog, fish, robin, duck

Animals

Has wings | Swims

c) rat, rain, pot, sand

Words

Has 4 letters | Starts with "r"

d) Alberta, Canada, France, Ottawa
Use the first letter of each place to fill in the diagram.

Places

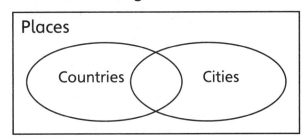

Countries | Cities

e) cat, dog, fish, gerbil, lizard, snake, turtle

Pets

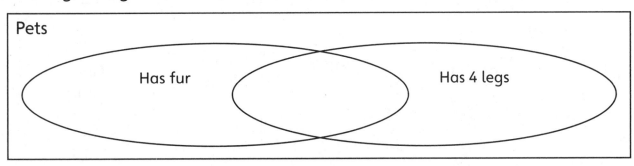

Has fur | Has 4 legs

COPYRIGHT © 2016 JUMP MATH: NOT TO BE COPIED.

5. a) Write the letter for the place in the correct region of the Venn diagram.

A. Canada   **B.** Ontario   **C.** Vancouver   **D.** Nova Scotia   **E.** USA

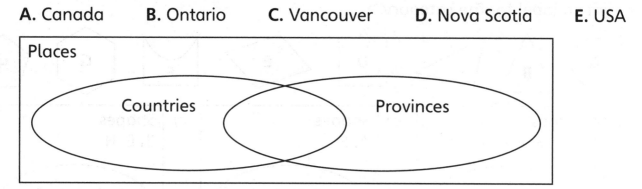

b) One region of the Venn diagram is empty. Explain what this means.

_____

_____

6. a) Complete the table using the shapes below.

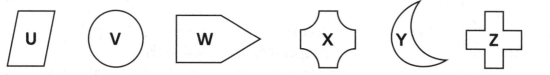

Shape	Only straight sides	Only curved sides	Both straight and curved sides
U	✓		
V			
W			
X			
Y			
Z			

b) Use the table to complete the Venn diagram.

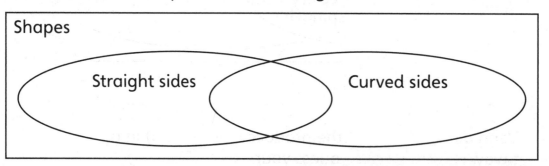

COPYRIGHT © 2016 JUMP MATH: NOT TO BE COPIED.

7. Alex sorted the shapes, but he forgot to label the category.
Write a label for the category.

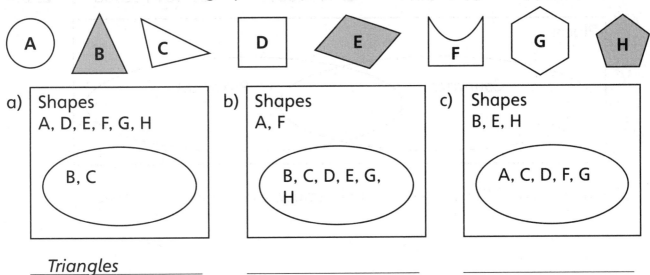

a) | Shapes
A, D, E, F, G, H

    B, C

_____ *Triangles* _____

b) | Shapes
A, F

    B, C, D, E, G, H

_____

c) | Shapes
B, E, H

    A, C, D, F, G

_____

8. **a)** Write the first letter of the fruit or vegetable in the correct region
of the Venn diagram.

| apple | blueberry | celery | lime |
| mushroom | pea | raspberry | spinach |

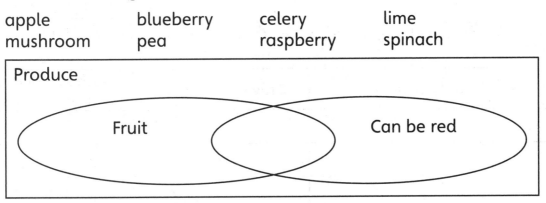

b) Emily sorted the produce differently, but she forgot to label
the categories. Write a label for each category.

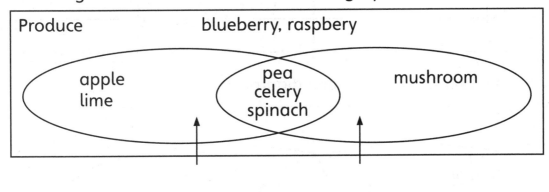

_____   _____

c) Draw a Venn diagram to sort the produce from part b) in a
different way. Have a partner guess your categories.

COPYRIGHT © 2016 JUMP MATH: NOT TO BE COPIED.

G3-3 Sides and Vertices of Shapes

> Triangles and squares are flat shapes. Flat shapes have **sides** and **vertices**.
> A **vertex** is where two sides meet.

1. Draw ✓ on each side. Write the number of sides.

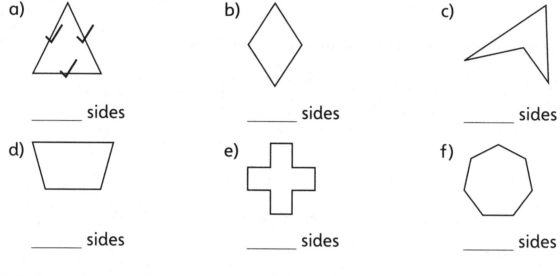

a) _____ sides

b) _____ sides

c) _____ sides

d) _____ sides

e) _____ sides

f) _____ sides

2. Circle each vertex. Write the number of vertices.

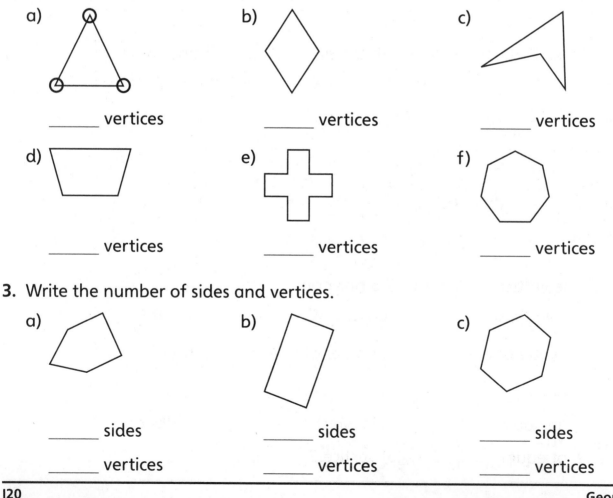

a) _____ vertices

b) _____ vertices

c) _____ vertices

d) _____ vertices

e) _____ vertices

f) _____ vertices

3. Write the number of sides and vertices.

a) _____ sides

_____ vertices

b) _____ sides

_____ vertices

c) _____ sides

_____ vertices

COPYRIGHT © 2016 JUMP MATH: NOT TO BE COPIED.

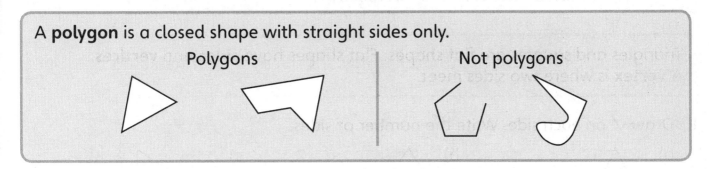

A **polygon** is a closed shape with straight sides only.

Polygons | Not polygons

4. Is the shape a polygon? Hint: Look at the examples above.

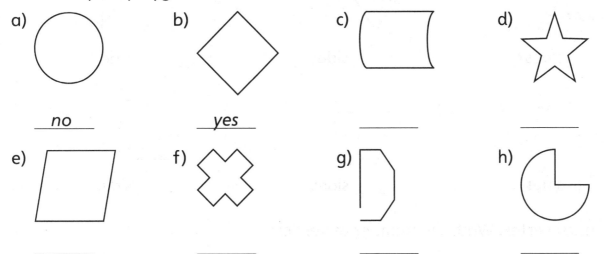

a)   _no_

b)   _yes_

c) _____

d) _____

e) _____

f) _____

g) _____

h) _____

5. a) Use a ruler. Draw a polygon with the given number of sides or vertices.

     A. 3 sides   **B.** 5 sides   **C.** 4 vertices   **D.** 8 vertices

b) Count the vertices or sides of the polygon you drew.

     A. _____ vertices   **B.** _____ vertices   **C.** _____ sides   **D.** _____ sides

c) What do you notice about the number of sides and vertices in polygons?

     _____

     BONUS ▶ Can you draw a polygon in which the number of sides does

              not equal the number of vertices? _____

COPYRIGHT © 2016 JUMP MATH: NOT TO BE COPIED.

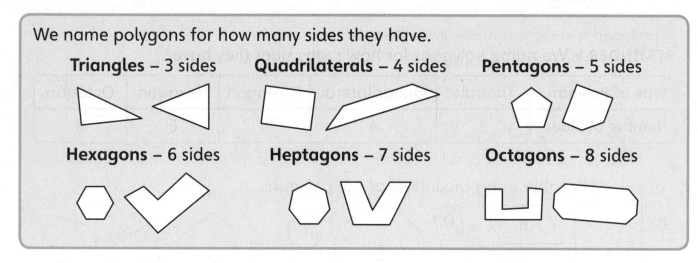

We name polygons for how many sides they have.

Triangles – 3 sides   **Quadrilaterals** – 4 sides   **Pentagons** – 5 sides

Hexagons – 6 sides   **Heptagons** – 7 sides   **Octagons** – 8 sides

6. a) How many sides does a stop sign have? _____

   b) Is this shape a polygon? _____

   c) What is it called? _____

7. a) Complete the table using the shapes on the right.

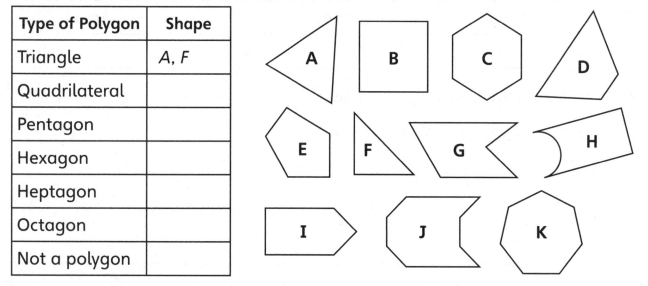

Type of Polygon	Shape
Triangle	A, F
Quadrilateral	
Pentagon	
Hexagon	
Heptagon	
Octagon	
Not a polygon	

b) Complete the Venn diagram.

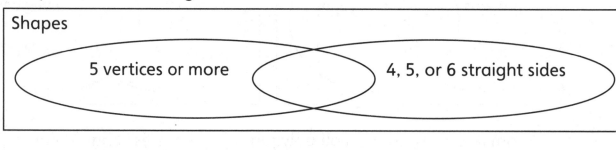

Shapes

5 vertices or more   4, 5, or 6 straight sides

8. a) Draw a shape with 4 sides that is not a polygon.

   b) Is your shape a quadrilateral? Explain.

Geometry 3-3

COPYRIGHT © 2016 JUMP MATH: NOT TO BE COPIED.

G3-4 Sorting Polygons

COPYRIGHT © 2016 JUMP MATH: NOT TO BE COPIED.

> **REMINDER ▶** We name polygons for how many sides they have.
>
> | Type of Polygon | Triangle | Quadrilateral | Pentagon | Hexagon | Octagon |
> |---|---|---|---|---|---|
> | **Number of Sides** | 3 | 4 | 5 | 6 | 8 |

I. a) Fill in the table using the letters of the polygons.

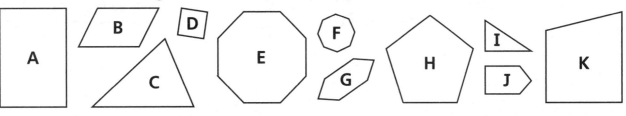

Type of Polygon	Triangle	Quadrilateral	Pentagon	Hexagon	Octagon
Shape					

Size of Polygon	Large	Small
Shape		

b) Which shapes are small triangles? _____

Which shapes are small pentagons? _____

c) Fill in the Venn diagrams.

Diagram A   Diagram B

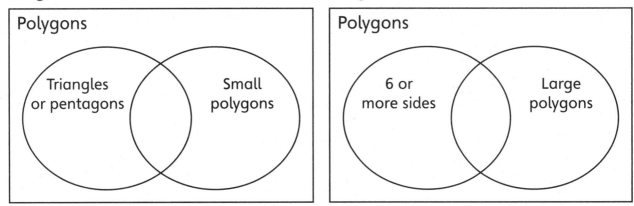

d) In Diagram A, where is the small polygon with 5 vertices? Shade that region.

e) In Diagram B, where is the small octagon? Shade that region.

---

2. a) Sort the polygons using the table.

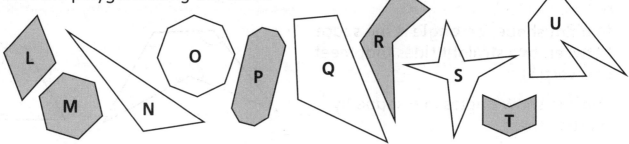

Type of Polygon	Triangle	Quadrilateral	Pentagon	Hexagon	Octagon
Shape					

b) Fill in the Venn diagrams.

Diagram A

Polygons

Hexagons   Shaded polygons

Diagram B

Polygons

4 vertices   Octagons

c) A region in Diagram B is empty. Explain why this happened.

_____

_____

d) Ava sorts the polygons. Write a label for each category.

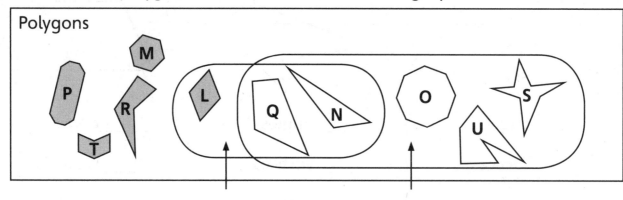

_____   _____

COPYRIGHT © 2016 JUMP MATH: NOT TO BE COPIED.

e) Choose 2 categories and make your own Venn diagram.
Fill in your Venn diagram.

In a flat shape, an **angle** is the space between two straight sides that meet at a vertex.

You can show angles in a shape by shading them.

I. Shade in all the angles in the shape. Write the number of angles inside the shape.

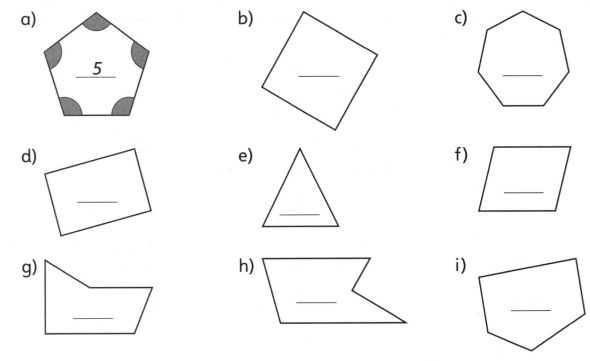

a) _5_

b) ____

c) ____

d) ____

e) ____

f) ____

g) ____

h) ____

i) ____

2. Count the angles inside the shape. Then count the vertices.

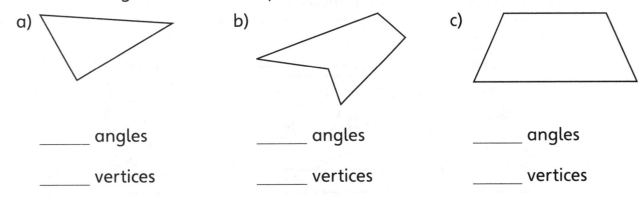

a) _____ angles

_____ vertices

b) _____ angles

_____ vertices

c) _____ angles

_____ vertices

3. Clara says that polygons have the same number of angles as vertices.

Is she correct? _____

COPYRIGHT © 2016 JUMP MATH: NOT TO BE COPIED.

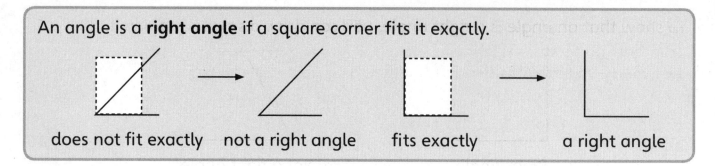

An angle is a **right angle** if a square corner fits it exactly.

does not fit exactly   not a right angle   fits exactly   a right angle

4. Use a square corner to find the right angles. Circle the right angles.

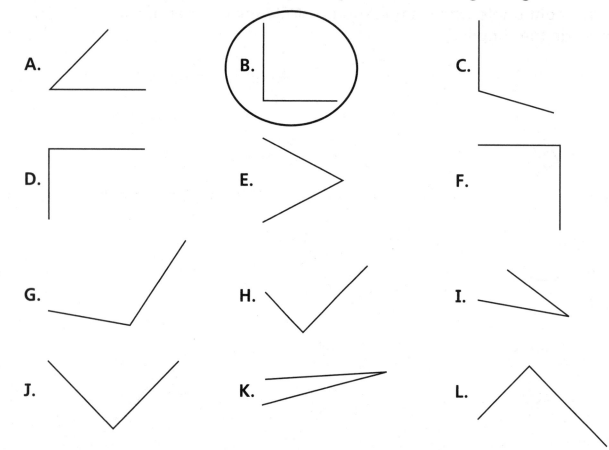

A.

B.

C.

D.

E.

F.

G.

H.

I.

J.

K.

L.

5. Use a ruler to draw the given angle.

a) a right angle

b) not a right angle

COPYRIGHT © 2016 JUMP MATH: NOT TO BE COPIED.

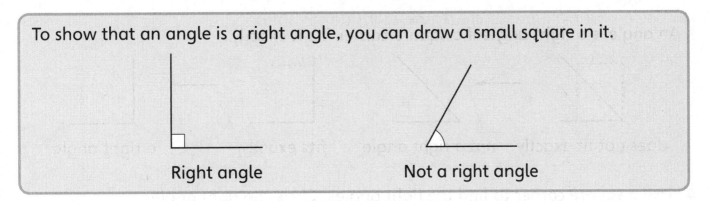

To show that an angle is a right angle, you can draw a small square in it.

Right angle   Not a right angle

6. Mark each right angle with a small square. Write the number of right angles inside the shape.

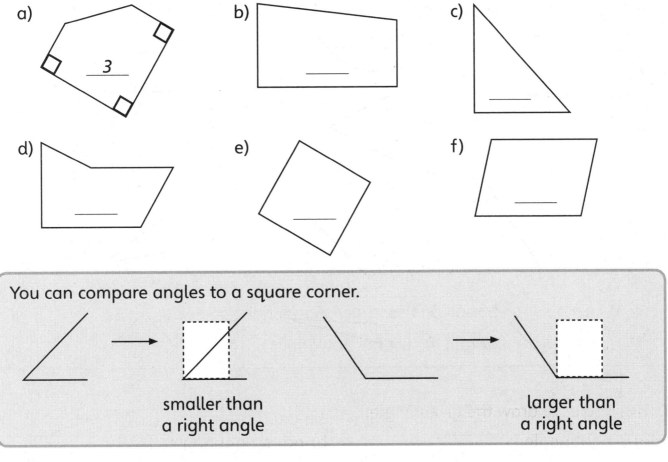

a)   _3_

b)   ___

c)   ___

d)   ___

e)   ___

f)   ___

You can compare angles to a square corner.

smaller than
a right angle

larger than
a right angle

7. Circle the angles that are smaller than a right angle. Write "L" on angles that are larger than a right angle.

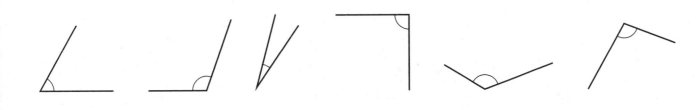

COPYRIGHT © 2016 JUMP MATH: NOT TO BE COPIED.

8. Use a square corner to check angles inside the shape.

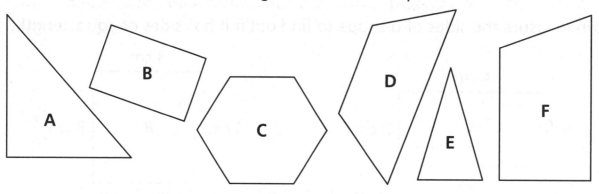

a) Mark all the right angles with a small square.

b) Write "S" in all angles smaller than a right angle.

c) Write "L" in all angles larger than a right angle.

d) Use the table to sort the polygons.

Has I or more angles smaller than a right angle	A
Has I or more right angles	A
Has I or more angles larger than a right angle	

e) Which polygon has all angles smaller than a right angle? _____

Which polygon has all angles larger than a right angle? _____

f) Use the Venn diagram to sort the polygons.

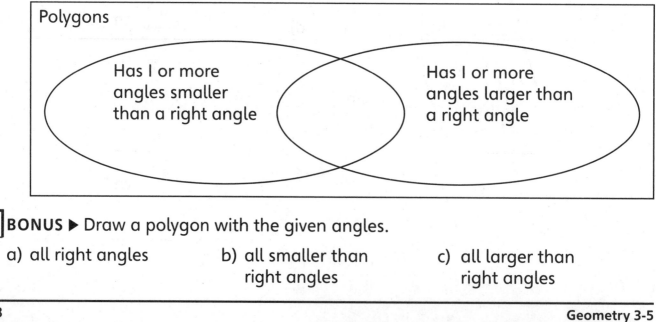

COPYRIGHT © 2016 JUMP MATH: NOT TO BE COPIED

BONUS ▶ Draw a polygon with the given angles.

a) all right angles

b) all smaller than right angles

c) all larger than right angles

G3-6 Shapes with Equal Sides

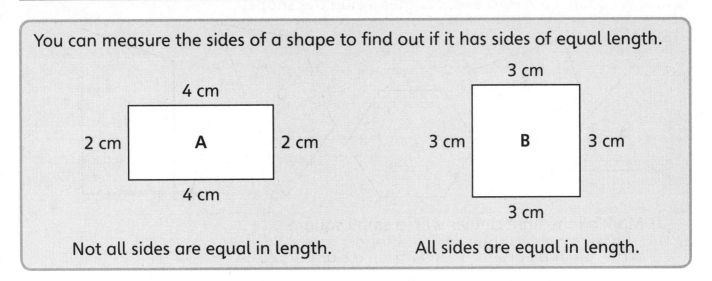

You can measure the sides of a shape to find out if it has sides of equal length.

4 cm

2 cm | A | 2 cm

4 cm

3 cm

3 cm | B | 3 cm

3 cm

Not all sides are equal in length.

All sides are equal in length.

I. Use a ruler to measure the sides in centimetres. Are the sides equal or not equal in length?

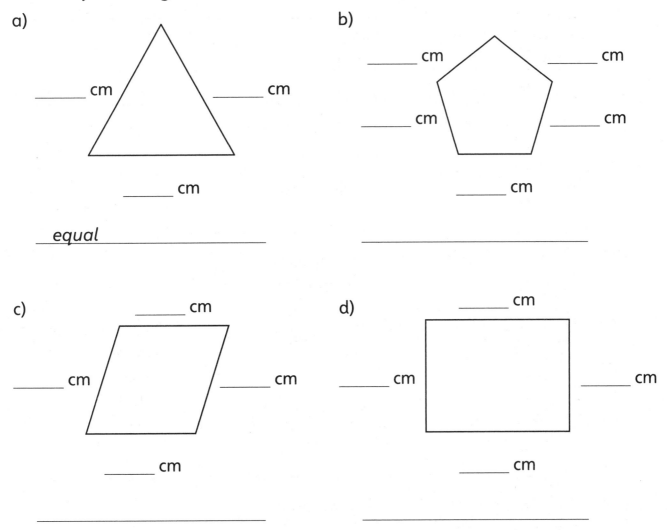

a)

_____ cm   _____ cm

_____ cm

equal

b)

_____ cm   _____ cm

_____ cm   _____ cm

_____ cm

c)

_____ cm

_____ cm   _____ cm

_____ cm

d)

_____ cm

_____ cm   _____ cm

_____ cm

COPYRIGHT © 2016 JUMP MATH: NOT TO BE COPIED.

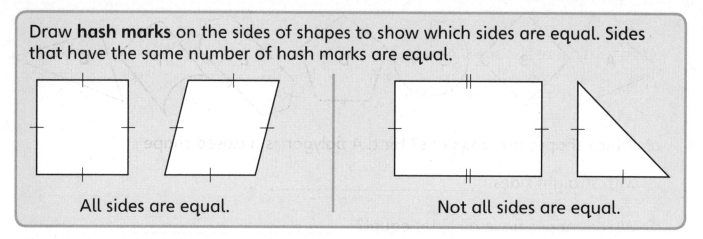

Draw **hash marks** on the sides of shapes to show which sides are equal. Sides that have the same number of hash marks are equal.

All sides are equal.   Not all sides are equal.

2. Draw hash marks to show which sides are equal.

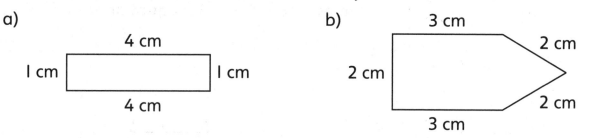

a)

4 cm

I cm   I cm

4 cm

b)

3 cm

2 cm   2 cm

2 cm

3 cm

3. a) Measure the sides of each shape in centimetres. Draw hash marks to show which sides are equal.

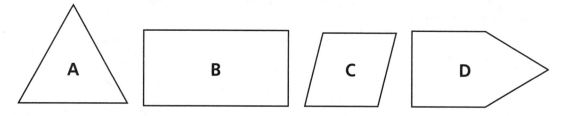

A   B   C   D

b) Complete the table for the shapes in part a).

All sides are equal	
Not all sides are equal	

4. Draw a shape with the given number of sides. Each shape must have not all equal sides.

a) 3 sides   b) 4 sides

BONUS ▶ Draw a shape that has 4 equal sides and is not a square.

Geometry 3-6

COPYRIGHT © 2016 JUMP MATH: NOT TO BE COPIED.

5.

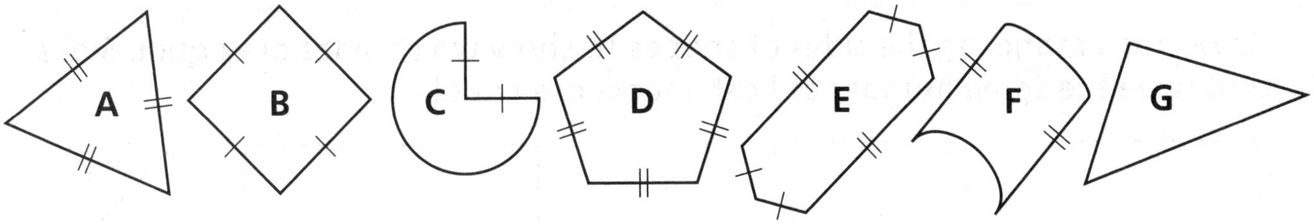

a) Which shapes are polygons? Hint: A polygon is a closed shape

with straight sides. _____

b) Which shapes have all sides equal? _____

You can describe shapes by their names, and by **all sides equal** or **not all sides equal**.

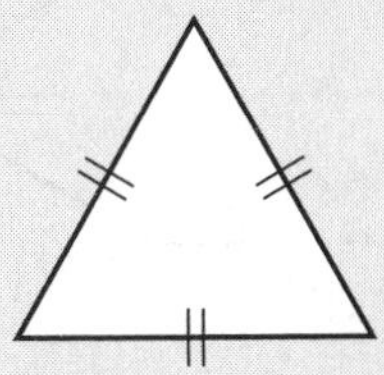

Triangle with all sides equal   Quadrilateral with not all sides equal

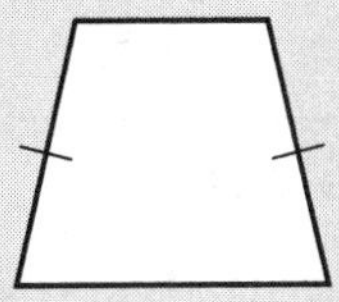

6. Does the polygon have all sides equal or not all sides equal?
Write the name of the polygon.

a)

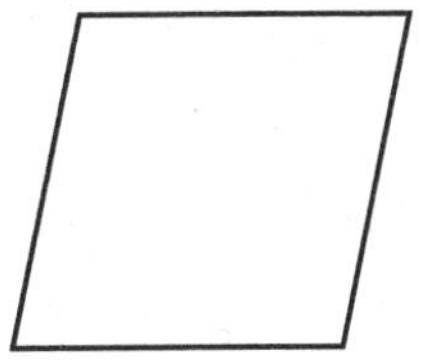

___All sides equal___

___Quadrilateral___

b)

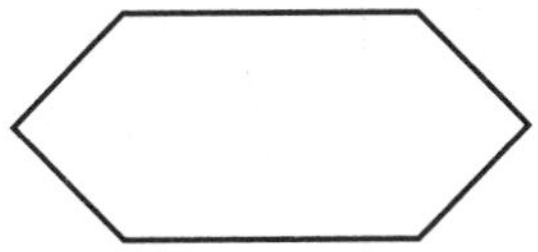

_____

_____

c)

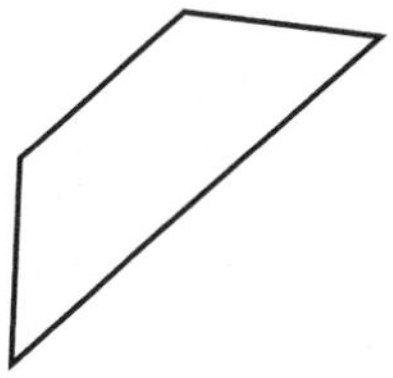

_____

_____

d)

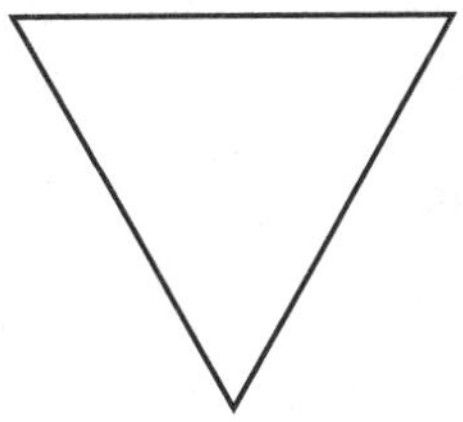

_____

_____

e)

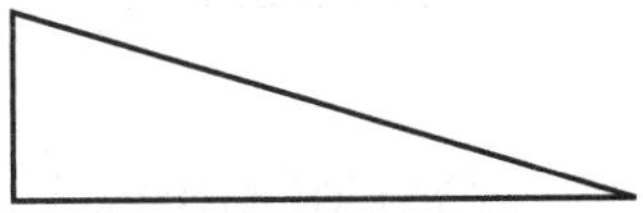

_____

_____

f)

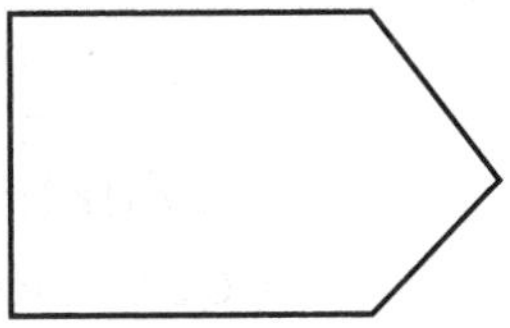

_____

_____

COPYRIGHT © 2016 JUMP MATH: NOT TO BE COPIED.

G3-7 Quadrilaterals

1. Count the number of sides for each shape. Then write the letter for each shape where it belongs in the table.

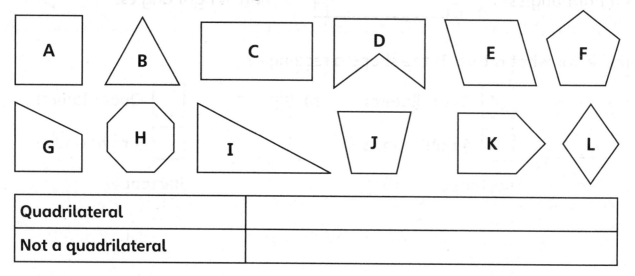

Quadrilateral	
Not a quadrilateral	

REMINDER ▶ Sides in a shape marked with the same number of hash marks are equal. Angles marked with a small square are right angles.

2.

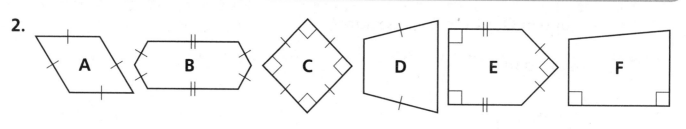

a) Which shapes are quadrilaterals? _____

b) Which shapes have all sides equal? _____

c) Which shapes have right angles? _____

d) Complete the Venn diagram.

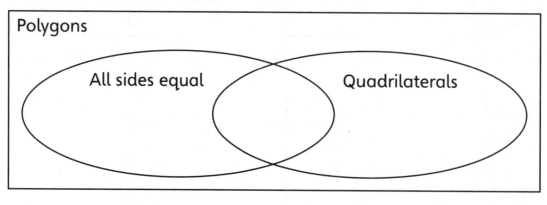

COPYRIGHT © 2016 JUMP MATH: NOT TO BE COPIED.

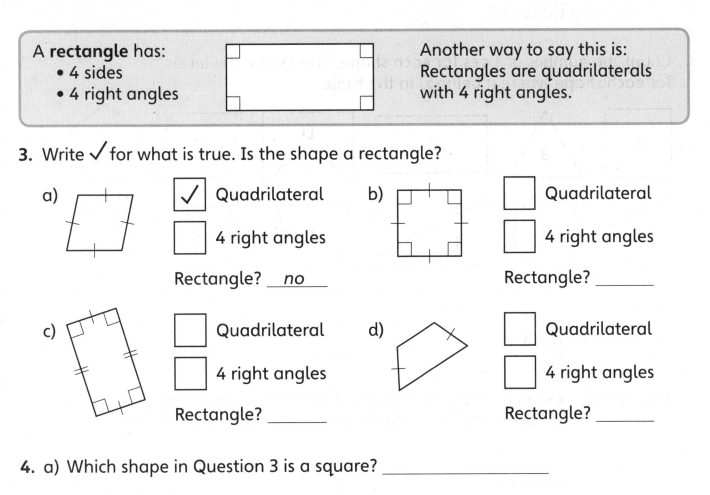

A **rectangle** has:
- 4 sides
- 4 right angles

Another way to say this is:
Rectangles are quadrilaterals with 4 right angles.

3. Write ✓ for what is true. Is the shape a rectangle?

a) ✓ Quadrilateral

☐ 4 right angles

Rectangle? __no__

b) ☐ Quadrilateral

☐ 4 right angles

Rectangle? _____

c) ☐ Quadrilateral

☐ 4 right angles

Rectangle? _____

d) ☐ Quadrilateral

☐ 4 right angles

Rectangle? _____

4. a) Which shape in Question 3 is a square? _____

b) Is the square a rectangle? _____

5. Complete the table.

		Quadrilateral? 4 sides	Rectangle? 4 sides 4 right angles	Square? 4 sides 4 right angles All sides equal
a)		yes	yes	no
b)				
c)				

6. Write ✓ if the shape is a rectangle. Write ✗ if the shape is not a rectangle.

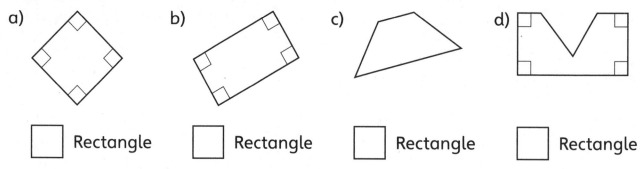

a)

☐ Rectangle

b)

☐ Rectangle

c)

☐ Rectangle

d)

☐ Rectangle

7. Use a ruler to draw the quadrilateral.

a) a rectangle that is not a square   b) not a rectangle

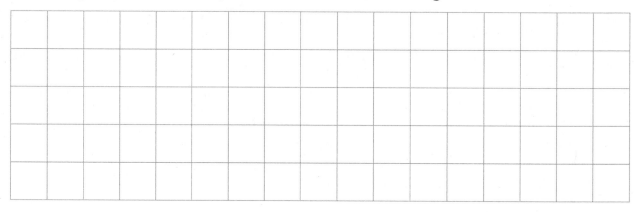

8. Complete the Venn diagram.

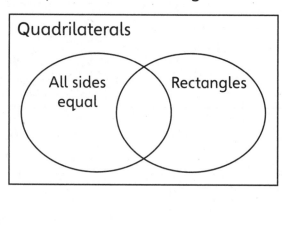

Quadrilaterals

All sides equal   Rectangles

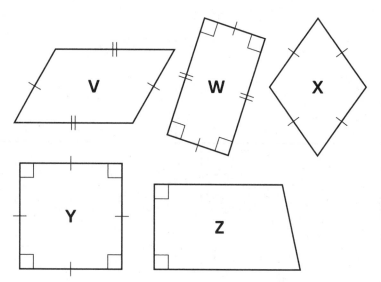

V   W   X

Y   Z

9. Are all squares rectangles? Explain how you know.

G3-8 More Quadrilaterals

A **rhombus** has:
- 4 sides
- all sides equal

Another way to say this is:
Rhombuses are quadrilaterals with all sides equal.

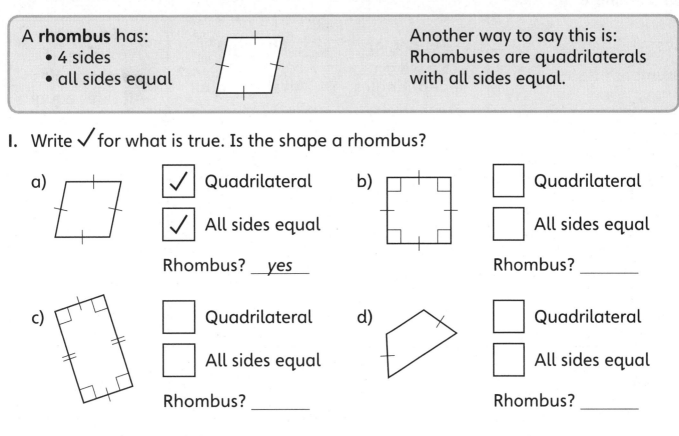

1. Write ✓ for what is true. Is the shape a rhombus?

a) ✓ Quadrilateral

✓ All sides equal

Rhombus? __yes__

b) ☐ Quadrilateral

☐ All sides equal

Rhombus? _____

c) ☐ Quadrilateral

☐ All sides equal

Rhombus? _____

d) ☐ Quadrilateral

☐ All sides equal

Rhombus? _____

2. a) Which shape in Question I is a square? _____

b) Is the square a rhombus? _____

3. Complete the table.

	Quadrilateral? 4 sides	Rhombus? 4 sides All sides equal	Square? 4 sides 4 right angles All sides equal
a)	yes	no	no
b)			
c)			

4. Are all squares rhombuses? Explain how you know.

COPYRIGHT © 2016 JUMP MATH: NOT TO BE COPIED.

5. Complete the table.

	Rectangle? 4 sides 4 right angles	Rhombus? 4 sides All sides equal	Square? 4 sides 4 right angles All sides equal
a) 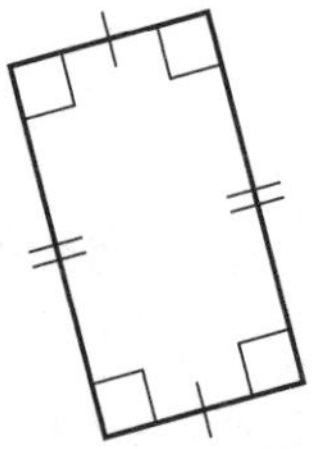			
b) 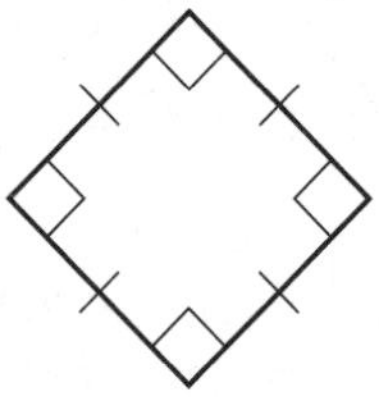			
c) 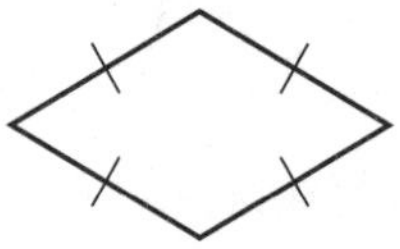			
d) 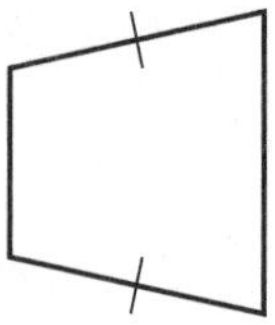			
e) 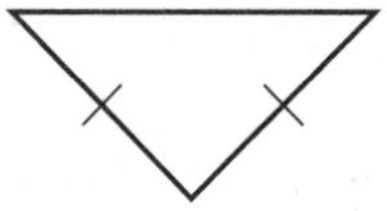			

BONUS ▶ Write all the names that describe the shape.

a)

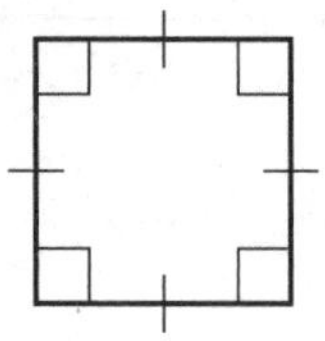

b)

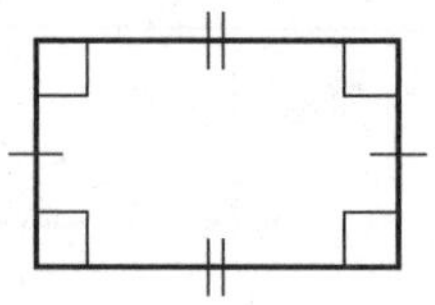

c)

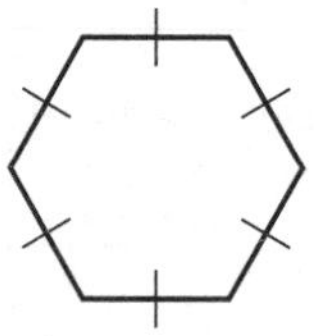

_____ _____ _____

_____ _____ _____

_____ _____ _____

_____ _____ _____

COPYRIGHT © 2016 JUMP MATH: NOT TO BE COPIED.

6. Use a ruler to draw a quadrilateral with the given angles or sides.

a) only 1 right angle

b) 2 angles larger than a right angle

c) no sides equal

d) only 2 sides equal

7. Use a ruler to draw a rectangle with the given sides.

a) 2 short sides and 2 long sides

b) all sides equal

BONUS ▶ Bo drew two quadrilaterals.

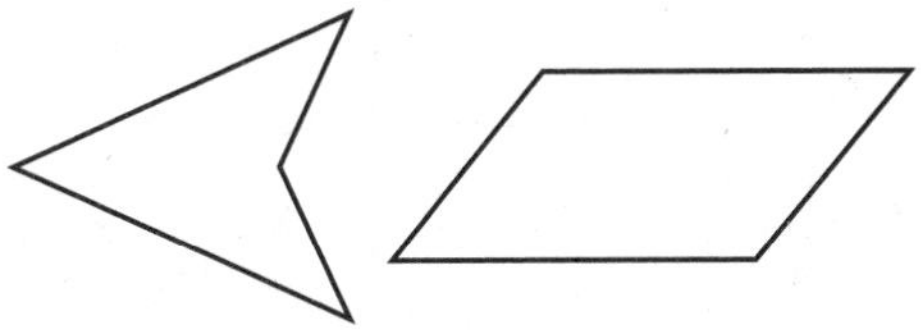

They have 2 equal long sides, 2 equal short sides, and are not rectangles.

Draw another shape like this in the grid.

COPYRIGHT © 2016 JUMP MATH: NOT TO BE COPIED.

G3-9 Parallel Sides

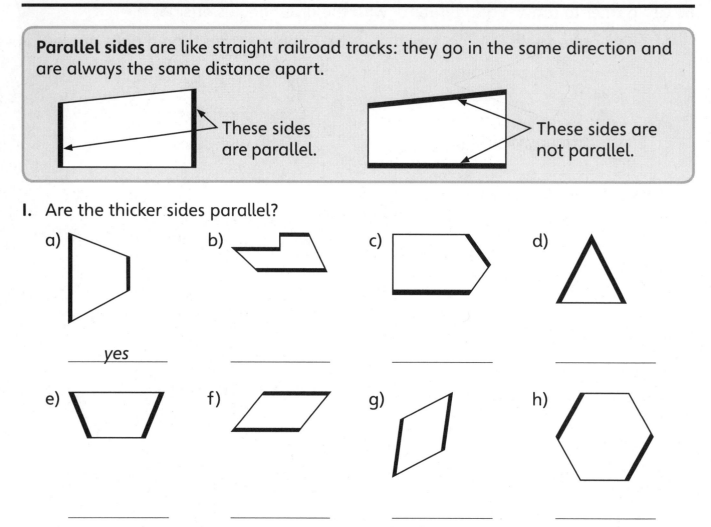

Parallel sides are like straight railroad tracks: they go in the same direction and are always the same distance apart.

These sides are parallel.

These sides are not parallel.

1. Are the thicker sides parallel?

a) _____yes_____   b) _____   c) _____   d) _____

e) _____   f) _____   g) _____   h) _____

2. The picture shows 2 parallel sides. Join the dots to make a quadrilateral.

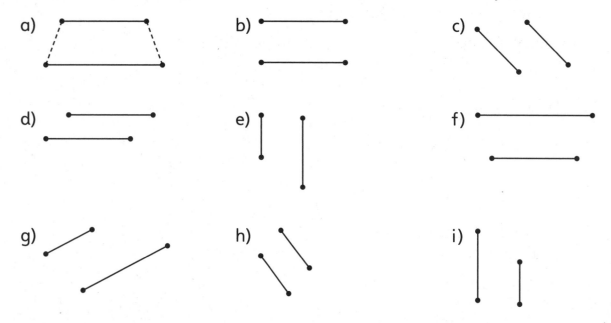

a)   b)   c)

d)   e)   f)

g)   h)   i)

COPYRIGHT © 2016 JUMP MATH: NOT TO BE COPIED.

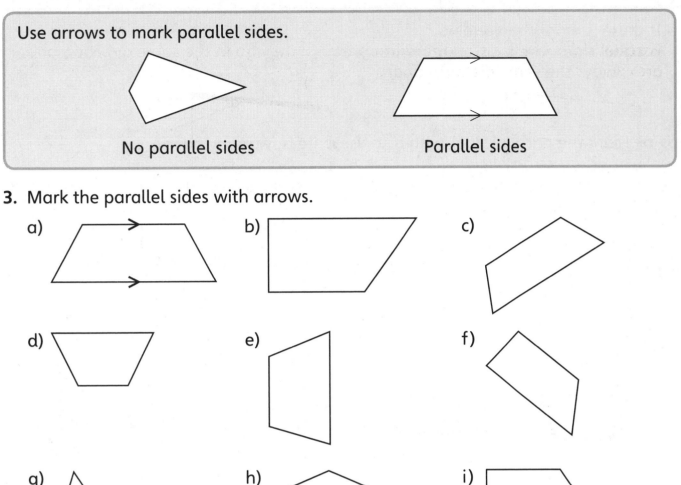

Use arrows to mark parallel sides.

No parallel sides

Parallel sides

3. Mark the parallel sides with arrows.

a)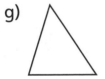

b)

c)

d)

e)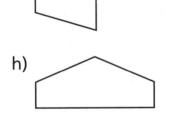

f)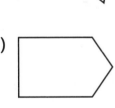

g)

h)

i)

4. Draw a quadrilateral with the given sides.

a) I pair of parallel sides

b) no parallel sides

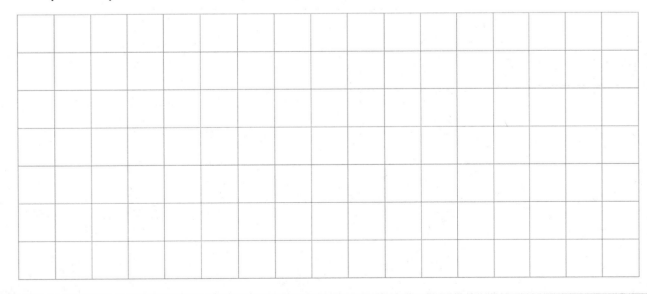

COPYRIGHT © 2016 JUMP MATH: NOT TO BE COPIED.

> If there is more than one pair of parallel sides, use a different number of arrows for each pair.

5. a) Mark the parallel sides with arrows. Write how many pairs of sides are parallel.

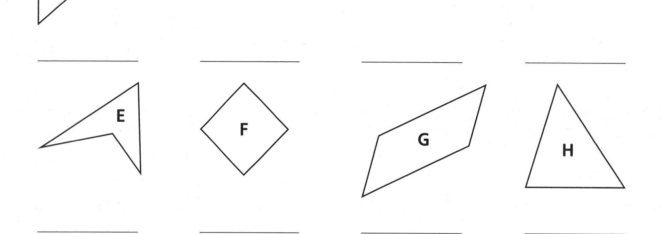

b) Complete the table for the shapes in part a).

No parallel sides	
I pair of parallel sides	
2 pairs of parallel sides	

> Parallel sides must be straight.

6. Are the thicker sides parallel?

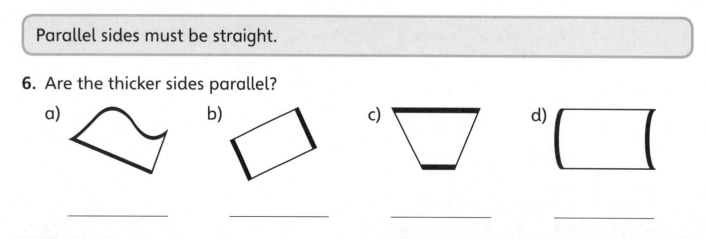

a) b) c) d)

COPYRIGHT © 2016 JUMP MATH: NOT TO BE COPIED.

Geometry 3-9

G3-10 Special Quadrilaterals

> A **parallelogram** is a quadrilateral with 2 pairs of parallel sides.
>
> A **trapezoid** is a quadrilateral with only 1 pair of parallel sides.

1. Write ✓ beside the name that matches the shape.

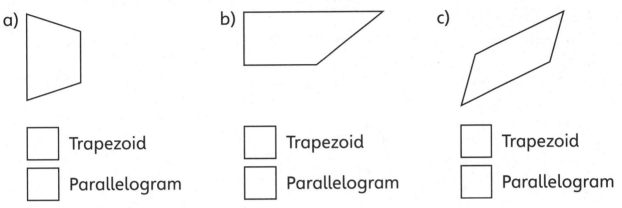

a)

☐ Trapezoid

☐ Parallelogram

b)

☐ Trapezoid

☐ Parallelogram

c)

☐ Trapezoid

☐ Parallelogram

2. Mark parallel sides with arrows. Label the shape as "trapezoid,"
   "parallelogram," or "neither."

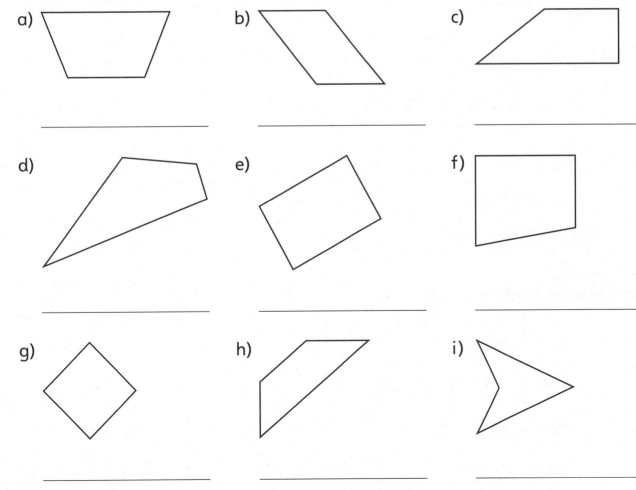

a)

_____

b)

_____

c)

_____

d)

_____

e)

_____

f)

_____

g)

_____

h)

_____

i)

_____

COPYRIGHT © 2016 JUMP MATH: NOT TO BE COPIED.

A rectangle is a quadrilateral with 4 right angles.

REMINDER ▶ A rectangle is a quadrilateral with 4 right angles.

3. Does the name match the shape? Write ✓ or ✗.

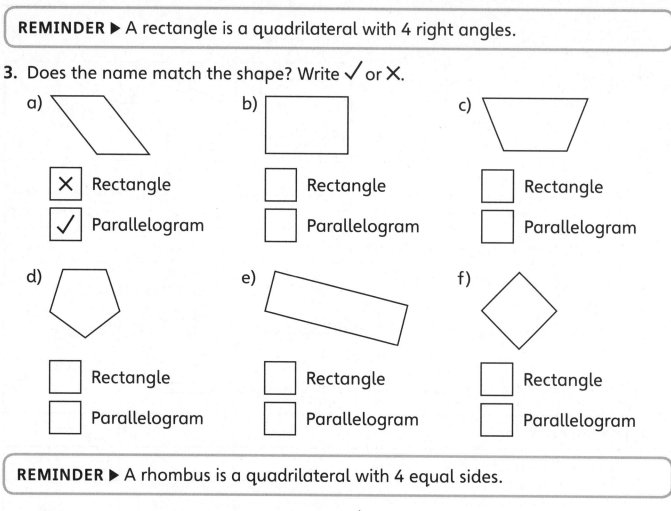

a)
- ✗ Rectangle
- ✓ Parallelogram

b)
- ☐ Rectangle
- ☐ Parallelogram

c)
- ☐ Rectangle
- ☐ Parallelogram

d)
- ☐ Rectangle
- ☐ Parallelogram

e)
- ☐ Rectangle
- ☐ Parallelogram

f)
- ☐ Rectangle
- ☐ Parallelogram

REMINDER ▶ A rhombus is a quadrilateral with 4 equal sides.

4. Does the name match the shape? Write ✓ or ✗.

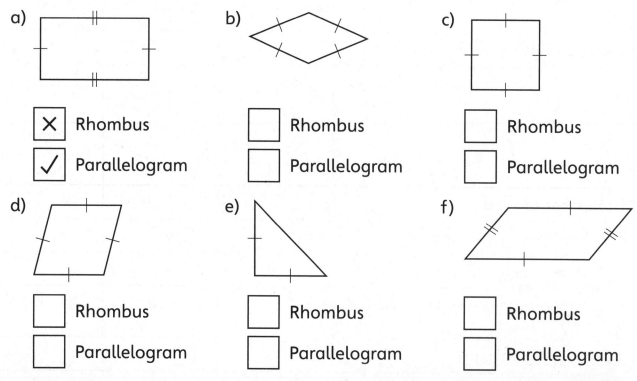

a)
- ✗ Rhombus
- ✓ Parallelogram

b)
- ☐ Rhombus
- ☐ Parallelogram

c)
- ☐ Rhombus
- ☐ Parallelogram

d)
- ☐ Rhombus
- ☐ Parallelogram

e)
- ☐ Rhombus
- ☐ Parallelogram

f)
- ☐ Rhombus
- ☐ Parallelogram

COPYRIGHT © 2016 JUMP MATH: NOT TO BE COPIED.

G3-II Comparing Special Quadrilaterals

1. Compare the two shapes by completing the table.

a)

	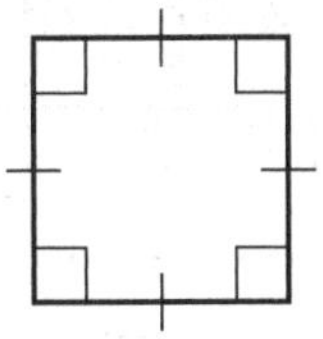	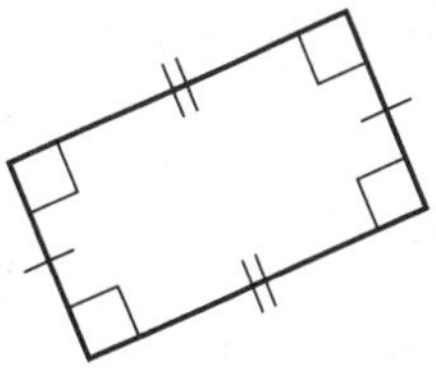	Same?
Number of sides	4	4	yes
Number of right angles	4	4	
Number of pairs of parallel sides	2	2	
Are all sides equal?	yes	no	

b)

	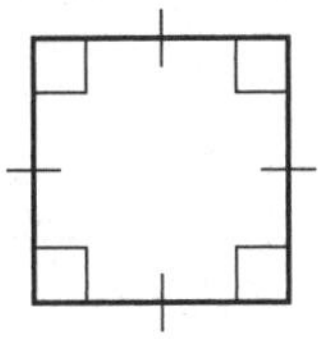	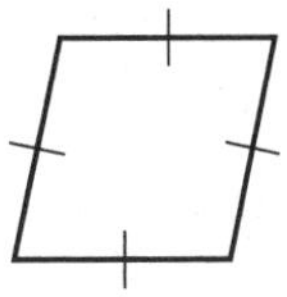	Same?
Number of sides			
Number of right angles			
Number of pairs of parallel sides			
Number of angles larger than a right angle			
Are all sides equal?			

c)

	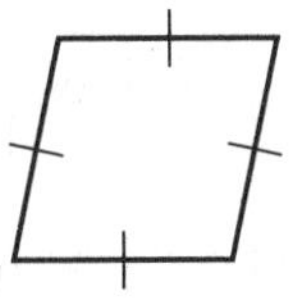	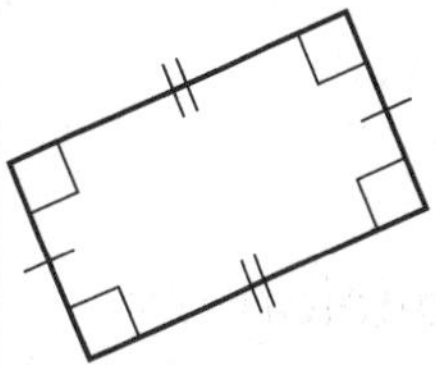	Same?
Number of sides			
Number of right angles			
Number of pairs of parallel sides			
Number of angles smaller than a right angle			
Are all sides equal?			

COPYRIGHT © 2016 JUMP MATH: NOT TO BE COPIED.

2. Compare the two shapes by completing the table.

   a)

	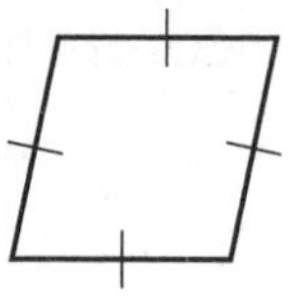	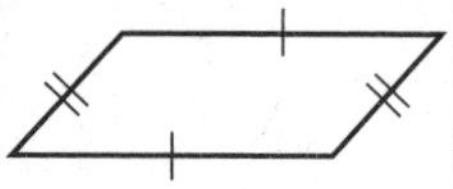	Same?
Number of sides			
Number of vertices			
Number of right angles			
Number of pairs of parallel sides			
Are all sides equal?			

   b)

	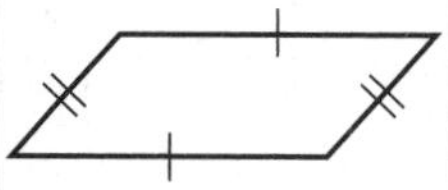	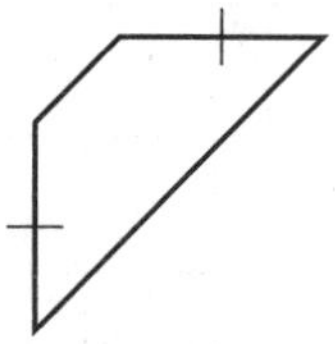	Same?
Number of sides			
Number of vertices			
Number of right angles			
Number of pairs of parallel sides			
Number of angles larger than a right angle			
Number of angles smaller than a right angle			
Are all sides equal?			

3. The shapes in Question I have the same number of sides.

   Do they have the same number of vertices? _____

   📓 BONUS ▶ Make a table to compare the two shapes.

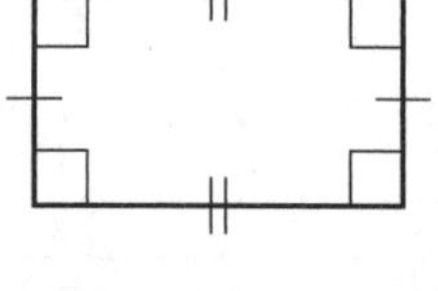

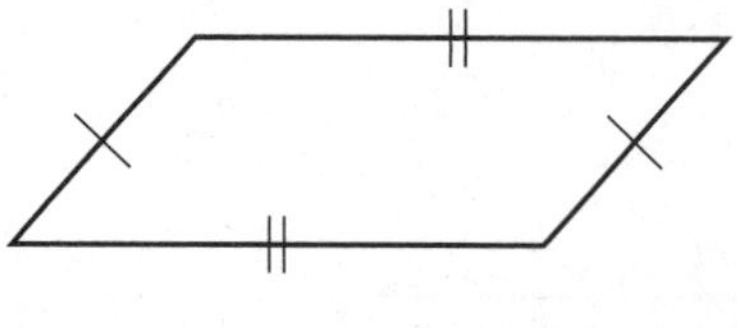

COPYRIGHT © 2016 JUMP MATH: NOT TO BE COPIED.

G3-I2 Polygons (Advanced)

I. a) Complete the table using the shapes below.
   Write "yes" or "no" in each column.

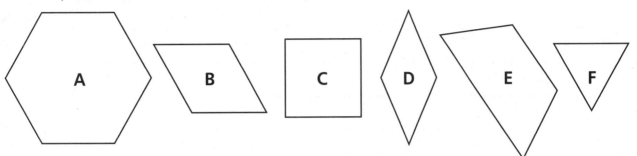

Shape	Quadrilateral	All sides equal	Has right angles	Has exactly 2 pairs of parallel sides
A				
B				
C				
D				
E				
F				

b) What 3 shapes in part a) are rhombuses? _____

c) What quadrilateral is not a parallelogram? _____

2. Use pattern blocks to build a shape that matches the description.
   Draw a picture that shows the blocks you used to build your shape.

   a) Use some of I type of rhombus to make a hexagon.

   b) Use 2 different types of blocks together to make a trapezoid.

   c) Use a trapezoid and another type of block to make a parallelogram.

   d) Use 2 blocks to make a rhombus.

   BONUS ▶ Use a hexagon and some other blocks to make a quadrilateral.

COPYRIGHT © 2016 JUMP MATH: NOT TO BE COPIED.

3. Describe how the shapes are the same and how they are different. You should include:

- the number of sides and the number of vertices

- the number of right angles, angles larger than a right angle, and angles smaller than a right angle

- the number of pairs of parallel sides

- if all sides are equal

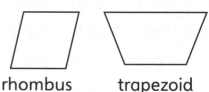

rhombus   trapezoid

4. Describe the shape. You should include:

- the number of sides and the number of vertices

- the number of pairs of parallel sides

- if all sides are equal

- the number of right angles, angles larger than a right angle, and angles smaller than a right angle

- the best possible name for the shape

a)

b)

c)

5. Name the polygon based on the description.

a) I have 4 equal sides. All of my angles are right angles.

b) I have 5 sides and 5 vertices.

c) I am a quadrilateral with 1 pair of parallel sides.

d) I am a quadrilateral with 4 equal sides. I have no right angles.

e) I have 6 sides and 6 vertices.

f) I am a quadrilateral. I have 2 short equal sides and 2 long equal sides. I have no right angles.

6. a) Which pattern block has the largest angle?

b) Which pattern block has the smallest angle?

c) Which pattern blocks have all angles the same size?

COPYRIGHT © 2016 JUMP MATH: NOT TO BE COPIED.

G3-13 Congruent Shapes

Karen places shapes one on top of the other. She tries to make the shapes match.

If they match exactly, the shapes are **congruent**.

Congruent shapes have the same size and shape.

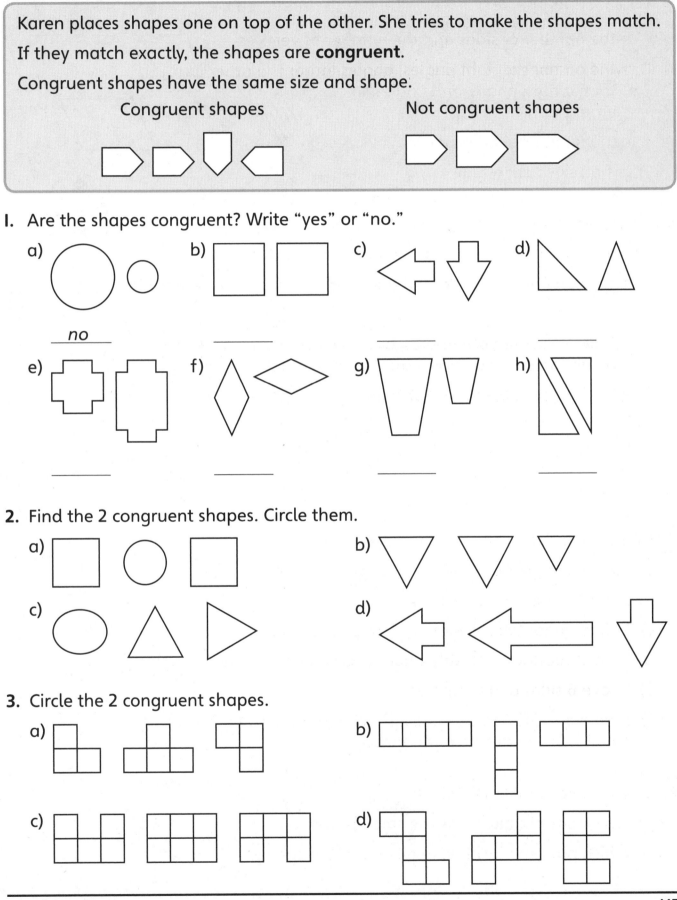

Congruent shapes   Not congruent shapes

1. Are the shapes congruent? Write "yes" or "no."

   a)   b)   c)   d)

   _no_   _____   _____   _____

   e)   f)   g)   h)

   _____   _____   _____   _____

2. Find the 2 congruent shapes. Circle them.

   a)   b)

   c)   d)

3. Circle the 2 congruent shapes.

   a)   b)

   c)   d)

COPYRIGHT © 2016 JUMP MATH: NOT TO BE COPIED.

Congruent shapes have the same size and shape. They can have different colours, designs, or directions.

4. Draw **X** on the shape that is not congruent to the other two.

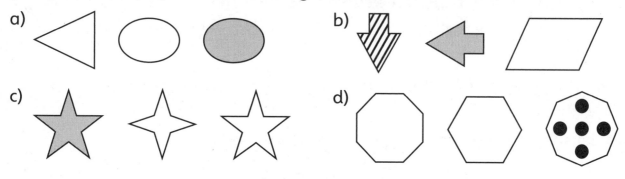

a)   b)

c)   d)

5. Find the dark shape that is congruent to the light shape. Fill in the letter of the dark shape.

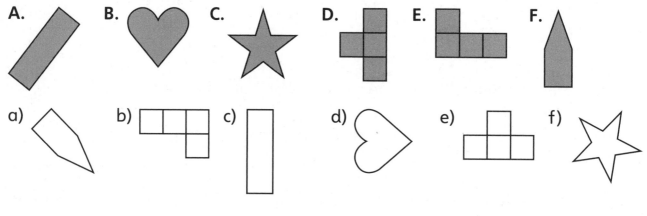

A.   B.   C.   D.   E.   F.

a)   b)   c)   d)   e)   f)

___   ___   ___   ___   ___   ___

6. Circle the 2 shapes that are congruent.

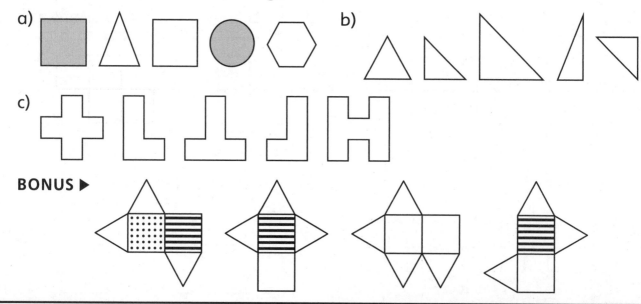

a)   b)

c)

BONUS ▶

COPYRIGHT © 2016 JUMP MATH: NOT TO BE COPIED.

7. Draw a shape congruent to the shaded shape.

a)
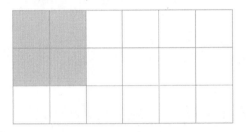

b)
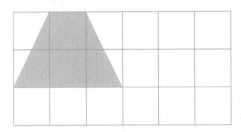

8. Draw a special quadrilateral of the given type that is not congruent to the shaded shape.

a) a square

b) a trapezoid

9. Colour the congruent shapes the same colour. You will need 4 different colours.

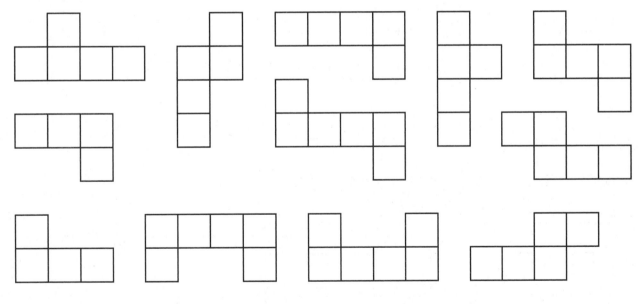

10. Draw 2 triangles that are not congruent.

11. Are the shapes congruent? Explain.

a)

b)

COPYRIGHT © 2016 JUMP MATH: NOT TO BE COPIED.

I. Luc draws a line to break the shape into 2 parts. Are the parts of the shape congruent?

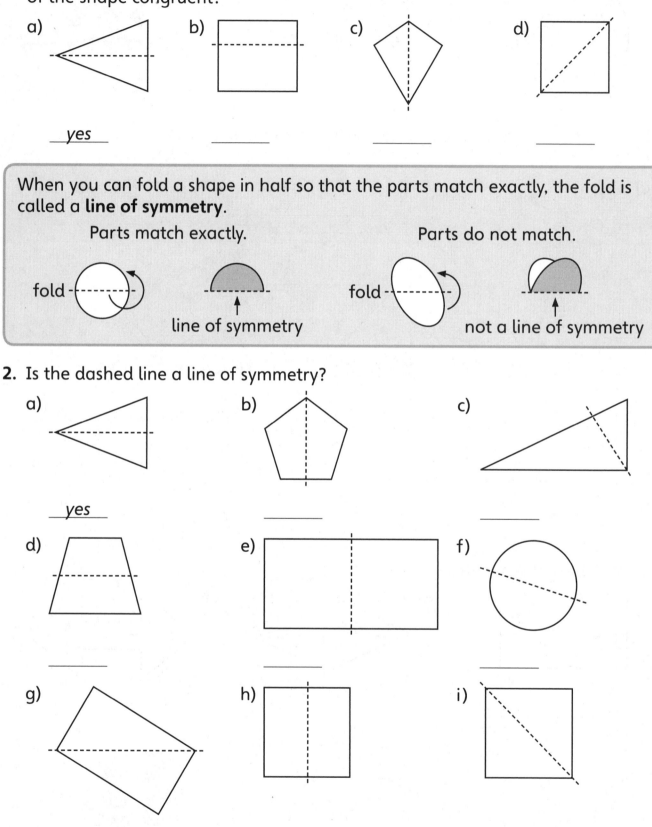

a)

b)

c)

d)

yes   _____   _____   _____

When you can fold a shape in half so that the parts match exactly, the fold is called a **line of symmetry**.

Parts match exactly.   Parts do not match.

fold   line of symmetry   fold   not a line of symmetry

2. Is the dashed line a line of symmetry?

a)

b)

c)

yes   _____   _____

d)

e)

f)

_____   _____   _____

g)

h)

i)

_____   _____   _____

COPYRIGHT © 2016 JUMP MATH: NOT TO BE COPIED.

3. Use a ruler. Draw 1 line of symmetry.

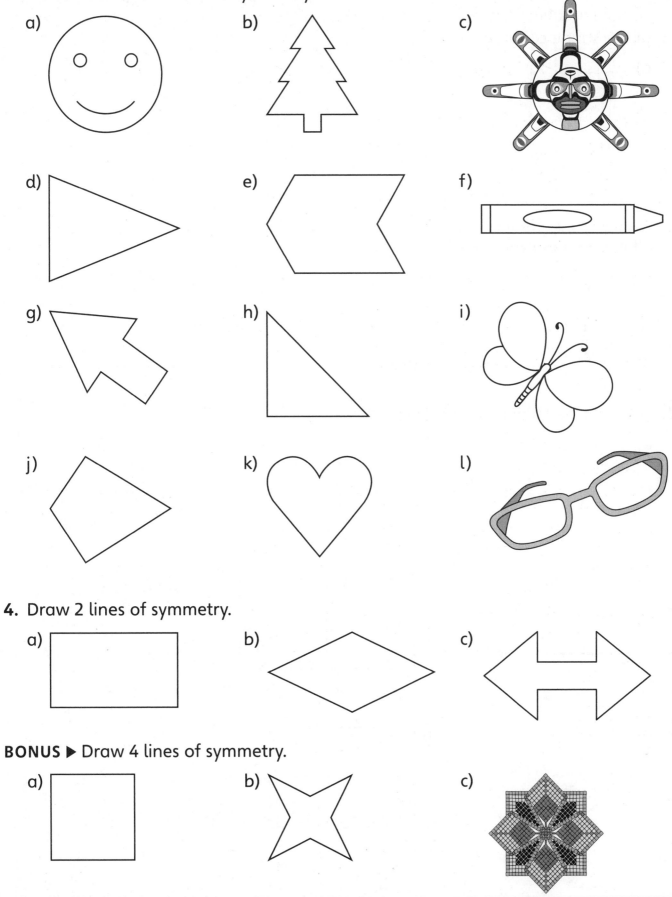

a)

b)

c)

d)

e)

f)

g)

h)

i)

j)

k)

l)

4. Draw 2 lines of symmetry.

a)

b)

c)

BONUS ▶ Draw 4 lines of symmetry.

a)

b)

c)

COPYRIGHT © 2016 JUMP MATH: NOT TO BE COPIED.

5. The dashed line is the line of symmetry. Draw the missing part of the picture. Use a ruler.

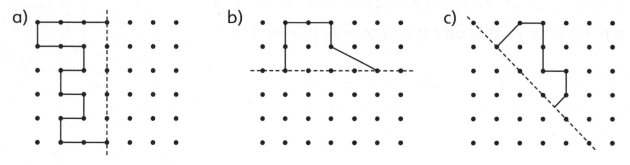

a)　　　　　　　　b)　　　　　　　　c)

6. Sketch the missing part of the picture so that it has a line of symmetry. Hint: First draw the line of symmetry.

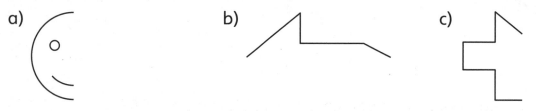

a)　　　　　　　　b)　　　　　　　　c)

7. Sketch the missing part of the picture so that it has 2 lines of symmetry. Draw both lines of symmetry.

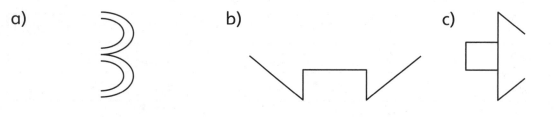

a)　　　　　　　　b)　　　　　　　　c)

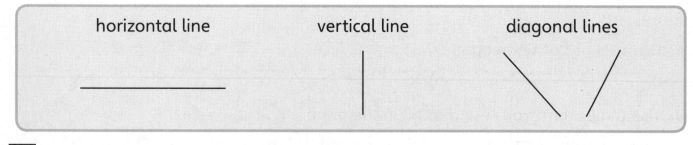

| horizontal line | vertical line | diagonal lines |

8. Draw a picture that has a line of symmetry in the given direction.

　　a) horizontal　　　　　b) vertical　　　　　c) diagonal

9. Draw a figure with more than one line of symmetry. How many lines of symmetry does it have? What lines of symmetry are they?

COPYRIGHT © 2016 JUMP MATH: NOT TO BE COPIED.

> The number of dots is **even** if you can pair all the dots.
> The number of dots is **odd** if you cannot pair all the dots.

1. Circle two dots at a time. Then write "even" or "odd."

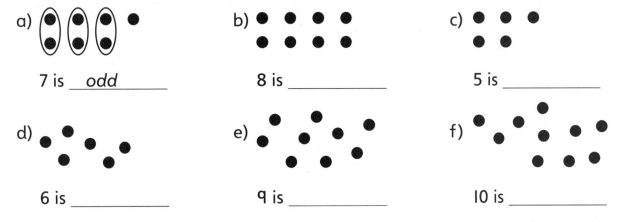

a)

7 is ___odd___

b)

8 is _____

c)

5 is _____

d)

6 is _____

e)

9 is _____

f)

10 is _____

> You say the even numbers when you count by 2s starting from 0.
> The even numbers are 0, 2, 4, 6, 8, and so on.

2. a) Underline the ones digit of the even numbers.

1	2	3	4	5	6	7	8	9	10
11	12	13	14	15	16	17	18	19	20
21	22	23	24	25	26	27	28	29	30

b) What pattern do you see in the ones digits of the even numbers?
Write the pattern.

___2__ , __4__ , _____, _____, _____, _____, _____, _____, _____, _____, _____, _____

3. Use the pattern you found to fill in the blanks.

a) 46, 48, 50, ___52__, _____, _____

b) 76, 78, 80, _____, _____, _____

c) 52, 54, 56, _____, _____, _____

d) 82, 84, 86, _____, _____, _____

e) 72, 70, 68, _____, _____, _____

f) 98, 96, 94, _____, _____, _____

g) 324, 326, _____, _____, _____

h) 490, 488, _____, _____, _____

BONUS ▶ 706, 704, _____, _____, _____, _____, _____

COPYRIGHT © 2016 JUMP MATH: NOT TO BE COPIED.

Odd numbers are the numbers that are not even: 1, 3, 5, 7, 9, and so on.

4. a) Underline the ones digit of the odd numbers.

1	2	3	4	5	6	7	8	9	10
11	12	13	14	15	16	17	18	19	20
21	22	23	24	25	26	27	28	29	30

b) What pattern do you see in the ones digits of the odd numbers?
Write the pattern.

___1___, ___3___, _____, _____, _____, _____, _____, _____, _____, _____, _____, _____

5. Use the pattern you found to fill in the blanks.

a) 47, 49, 51, ___53___, _____, _____

b) 67, 69, 71, _____, _____, _____

c) 53, 55, 57, _____, _____, _____

d) 81, 83, 85, _____, _____, _____

e) 81, 79, 77, _____, _____, _____

f) 49, 47, 45, _____, _____, _____

g) 241, 239, _____, _____, _____

h) 755, 753, _____, _____, _____

6. Fill in the missing even or odd numbers.

a) 22, ___24___, _____, 28

b) 29, 31, _____, 35

c) _____, 92, 94, _____

d) _____, 67, 69, _____

e) _____, 39, _____, 43

f) _____, 40, _____, 44

g) 34, _____, 30, _____

h) 427, _____, _____, 421

i) 866, _____, _____, 860

j) _____, 79, 77, _____

7. Add. Is the answer even or odd?

a) 7 + 3 = ___10___, ___even___

b) 4 + 8 = _____, _____

c) 2 + 9 = _____, _____

d) 5 + 4 = _____, _____

e) 6 + 2 = _____, _____

f) 1 + 4 = _____, _____

8. If you add two even numbers, will the sum be odd or even? Explain.

COPYRIGHT © 2016 JUMP MATH: NOT TO BE COPIED.

NS3-28 Repeated Addition

REMINDER ▶ You can use boxes to keep track of the sums.

☐ $\xrightarrow{\text{add } 2 + 2 = 4}$ 4 $\xrightarrow{\text{add } 4 + 2 = 6}$ 4

$2 + 2 + 2 =$ _____ $2 + 2 + 2 =$ _____ $2 + 2 + 2 = \underline{\ 6\ }$

I. Add the numbers. Use boxes to keep track.

6

a) $3 + 3 + 3 = \underline{\ 9\ }$ b) $4 + 4 + 4 =$ _____   c) $6 + 6 + 6 =$ _____

d) $3 + 3 + 3 + 3 =$ _____   e) $4 + 4 + 4 + 4 =$ _____   f) $5 + 5 + 5 + 5 =$ _____

g) $2 + 2 + 2 + 2 =$ _____   h) $5 + 5 + 5 =$ _____   i) $6 + 6 + 6 + 6 =$ _____

2. Write an addition sentence for the picture. Add to find the number of apples.

a) 2 apples in each box   3 boxes

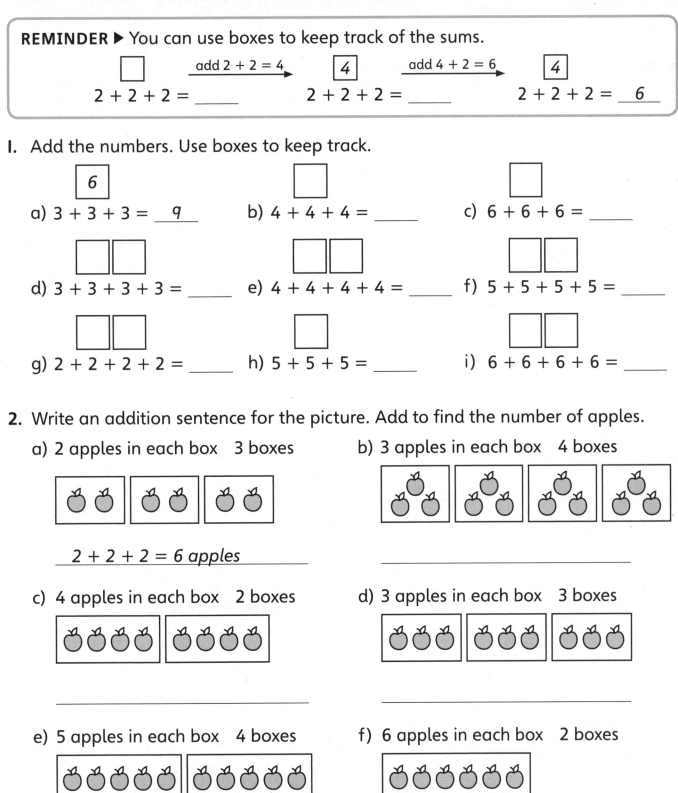

$\underline{\quad 2 + 2 + 2 = 6 \text{ apples} \quad}$

b) 3 apples in each box   4 boxes

_____

c) 4 apples in each box   2 boxes

_____

d) 3 apples in each box   3 boxes

_____

e) 5 apples in each box   4 boxes

f) 6 apples in each box   2 boxes

_____

COPYRIGHT © 2016 JUMP MATH: NOT TO BE COPIED.

3. Draw a picture and write an addition sentence for your picture.

a) 2 boats

3 campers in each boat

_____

b) 4 plates

2 apples on each plate

_____

c) 3 boxes

5 pencils in each box

_____

d) 3 fish bowls

2 fish in each bowl

_____

4. Write an addition sentence.

a) 4 boxes   3 flowers in each box

_____

b) 6 wagons   3 campers in each wagon

_____

c) 5 bags   1 banana in each bag

_____

d) 5 baskets   6 oranges in each basket

_____

e) 4 boats   8 campers in each boat

_____

f) 2 vans   9 people in each van

_____

BONUS ▶ Yu sees some boxes of apples at a store. She writes a sentence for the total number of apples: $75 + 75 + 75 + 75 = 300$.

a) How many apples are in each box? _____

b) How many boxes of apples does Yu see? _____

COPYRIGHT © 2016 JUMP MATH: NOT TO BE COPIED.

Number Sense 3-28

Skip Counting by 2s and 4s

You can skip count forwards by 2s starting at 0. Add 2 each time.

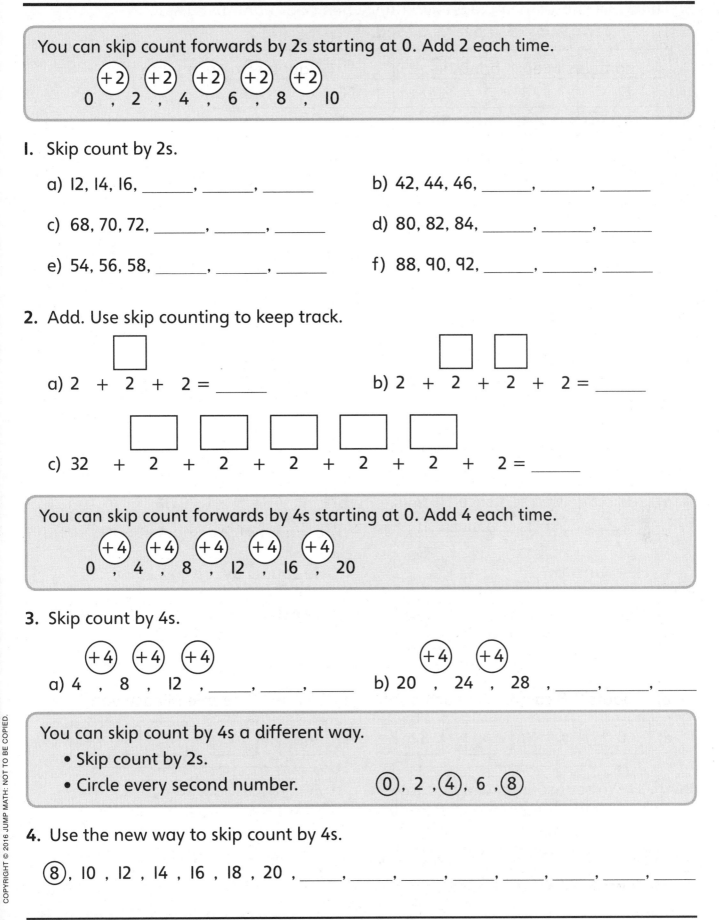

0 , 2 , 4 , 6 , 8 , 10

1. Skip count by 2s.

   a) 12, 14, 16, _____, _____, _____

   b) 42, 44, 46, _____, _____, _____

   c) 68, 70, 72, _____, _____, _____

   d) 80, 82, 84, _____, _____, _____

   e) 54, 56, 58, _____, _____, _____

   f) 88, 90, 92, _____, _____, _____

2. Add. Use skip counting to keep track.

   a) 2 + 2 + 2 = _____

   b) 2 + 2 + 2 + 2 = _____

   c) 32 + 2 + 2 + 2 + 2 + 2 + 2 = _____

You can skip count forwards by 4s starting at 0. Add 4 each time.

0 , 4 , 8 , 12 , 16 , 20

3. Skip count by 4s.

   a) 4 , 8 , 12 , _____, _____, _____

   b) 20 , 24 , 28 , _____, _____, _____

You can skip count by 4s a different way.
   • Skip count by 2s.
   • Circle every second number.   ⓪, 2 ,④, 6 ,⑧

4. Use the new way to skip count by 4s.

   ⑧, 10 , 12 , 14 , 16 , 18 , 20 , _____, _____, _____, _____, _____, _____, _____, _____

COPYRIGHT © 2016 JUMP MATH: NOT TO BE COPIED.

5. The chart shows the numbers you say when skip counting by 4s.
The first two numbers have 0s added.

04	08	12	16	20
24	28	32	36	40
44	48	52	56	60

Describe any patterns you see in the **columns** of the chart.

_____

_____

_____

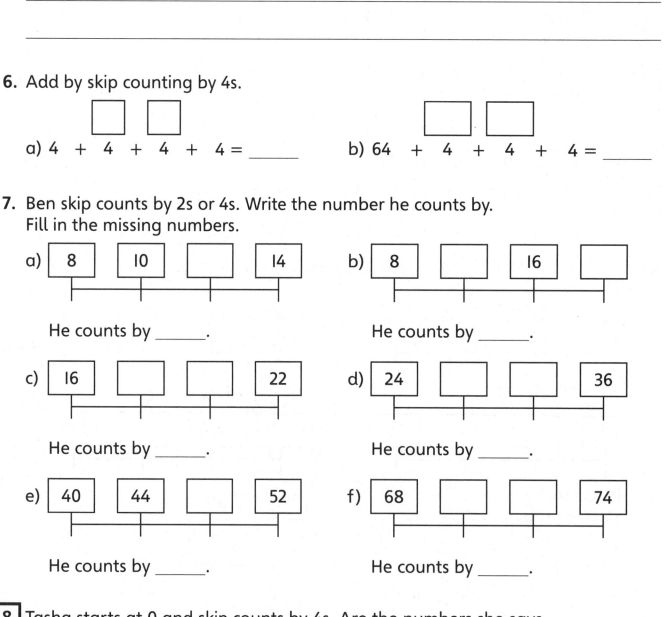

6. Add by skip counting by 4s.

a) 4 + 4 + 4 + 4 = _____

b) 64 + 4 + 4 + 4 = _____

7. Ben skip counts by 2s or 4s. Write the number he counts by.
Fill in the missing numbers.

a) | 8 | 10 | | 14 |

He counts by _____.

b) | 8 | | 16 | |

He counts by _____.

c) | 16 | | | 22 |

He counts by _____.

d) | 24 | | | 36 |

He counts by _____.

e) | 40 | 44 | | 52 |

He counts by _____.

f) | 68 | | | 74 |

He counts by _____.

8. Tasha starts at 0 and skip counts by 4s. Are the numbers she says all even? Explain.

COPYRIGHT © 2016 JUMP MATH: NOT TO BE COPIED.

1. Underline the ones digit of the numbers you say when skip counting by 5s.

   a) <u>5</u> , 1<u>0</u> , 15 , 20 , 25 , 30

   Write the pattern in the ones digits. 5 , 0 , _____, _____, _____, _____

   b) 35 , 40 , 45 , 50 , 55 , 60

   Write the pattern in the ones digits. _____, _____, _____, _____, _____, _____

2. Circle the numbers you say when skip counting by 5s starting at 5.

   17   15   23   42   75   92   80   85   33   95   14

3. Add by skip counting by 5s.

   a) 5 + 5 + 5 + 5 = _____   b) 65 + 5 + 5 + 5 = _____

4. a) Skip count by 10s.   0 , 10 , 20 , _____, _____, _____, _____, _____, _____

   b) Describe any patterns you see in the ones and tens digits.

   _____

5. Amir skip counts by 5s or 10s. Write the number he counts by.
   Fill in the missing numbers.

   a) | 15 | 25 | | 45 | b) | 35 | | 45 | |

   He counts by _____.   He counts by _____.

   c) | 75 | | | 90 | d) | | 270 | | 290 |

   He counts by _____.   He counts by _____.

   e) | | 455 | | 475 | f) | | 560 | | 570 |

   He counts by _____.   He counts by _____.

6. Explain how you knew which numbers to circle in Question 2.

COPYRIGHT © 2016 JUMP MATH: NOT TO BE COPIED.

1. Skip count forwards by 3s.

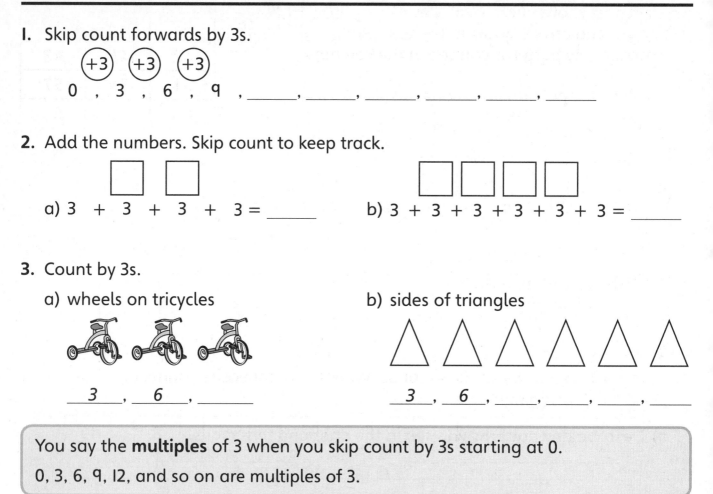

  0 , 3 , 6 , 9 , _____, _____, _____, _____, _____, _____

2. Add the numbers. Skip count to keep track.

☐ ☐

a) 3 + 3 + 3 + 3 = _____

☐ ☐ ☐ ☐

b) 3 + 3 + 3 + 3 + 3 + 3 = _____

3. Count by 3s.

   a) wheels on tricycles

   __3__ , __6__ , _____

   b) sides of triangles

   __3__ , __6__ , _____, _____, _____, _____

> You say the **multiples** of 3 when you skip count by 3s starting at 0.
>
> 0, 3, 6, 9, 12, and so on are multiples of 3.

4. The chart shows some multiples of 3. The first three numbers
   have a 0 in the tens place.

03	06	09
12	15	18
21	24	27
30	33	36

Describe any patterns you see in the columns.
Hint: Look at the ones digits and the tens digits.

_____

_____

_____

5. The chart shows more multiples of 3.
Look at the ones digits and the tens digits.
Describe any patterns you see in the columns.

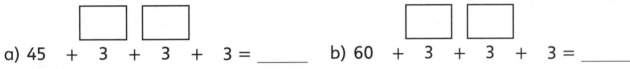

30	33	36	39
	42	45	48
	51	54	57
	60	63	66

_____

_____

_____

6. Add by skip counting by 3s.

a) 45 + 3 + 3 + 3 = _____   b) 60 + 3 + 3 + 3 = _____

7. Karen skip counts by 2s, 3s, 4s, or 5s. Write the number she counts by.
Fill in the missing numbers.

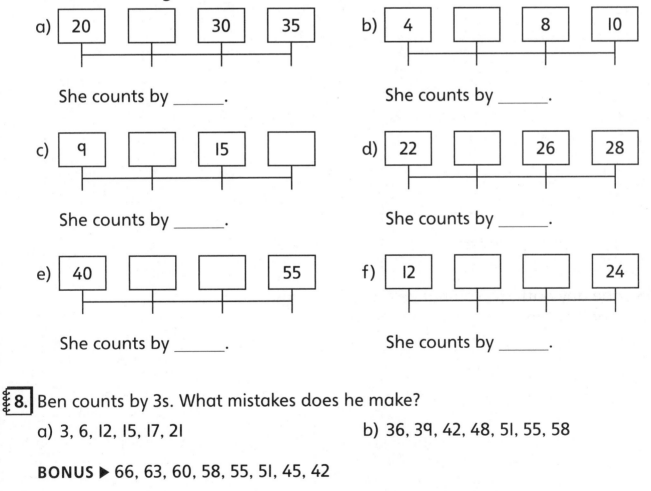

a) | 20 | | 30 | 35 |

She counts by _____.

b) | 4 | | 8 | 10 |

She counts by _____.

c) | 9 | | 15 | |

She counts by _____.

d) | 22 | | 26 | 28 |

She counts by _____.

e) | 40 | | | 55 |

She counts by _____.

f) | 12 | | | 24 |

She counts by _____.

8. Ben counts by 3s. What mistakes does he make?

a) 3, 6, 12, 15, 17, 21   b) 36, 39, 42, 48, 51, 55, 58

BONUS ▶ 66, 63, 60, 58, 55, 51, 45, 42

COPYRIGHT © 2016 JUMP MATH: NOT TO BE COPIED.

NS3-32 Multiplication and Repeated Addition

We use **multiplication** as a short way to write addition of the same number.

$$4 \times 3 = \underbrace{3 + 3 + 3 + 3}$$
$$\text{add 3 four times}$$

This is **repeated addition**.

1. Complete the number sentence using repeated addition.

   a) $4 \times 2 = $ _2 + 2 + 2 + 2_____   b) $3 \times 2 = $ _____

   c) $3 \times 4 = $ _____   d) $4 \times 5 = $ _____

   e) $2 \times 3 = $ _____   f) $1 \times 5 = $ _____

   g) $5 \times 2 = $ _____   h) $3 \times 5 = $ _____

   i) $2 \times 10 = $ _____   j) $4 \times 7 = $ _____

2. Complete the number sentence using multiplication.

   a) $2 + 2 + 2 = $ _3 × 2_____   b) $4 + 4 = $ _____

   c) $6 + 6 + 6 = $ _____   d) $3 + 3 + 3 = $ _____

   e) $9 + 9 + 9 = $ _____   f) $7 + 7 + 7 + 7 + 7 = $ _____

   g) $8 + 8 + 8 + 8 = $ _____   h) $5 + 5 + 5 + 5 + 5 + 5 = $ _____

   i) $4 + 4 + 4 + 4 = $ _____   j) $1 + 1 + 1 = $ _____

   BONUS ▶ $100 + 100 + 100 + 100 + 100 + 100 + 100 = $ _____

3. Circle the additions that cannot be written as multiplications.

$2 + 2 + 2 + 2$	$3 + 4 + 3 + 3 + 3$	$2 + 5 + 7$	$7 + 7 + 7 + 7$
$4 + 4 + 4 + 4 + 4$	$9 + 9 + 9 + 9 + 9$	$5 + 5 + 5 + 8$	$6 + 6 + 6$
$17 + 17 + 17$	$101 + 101 + 101$	$4 + 4 + 9 + 4$	$3 + 3$

COPYRIGHT © 2016 JUMP MATH: NOT TO BE COPIED.

4. Write an addition sentence. Then write a multiplication sentence.

a) 3 boxes   2 pencils in each box

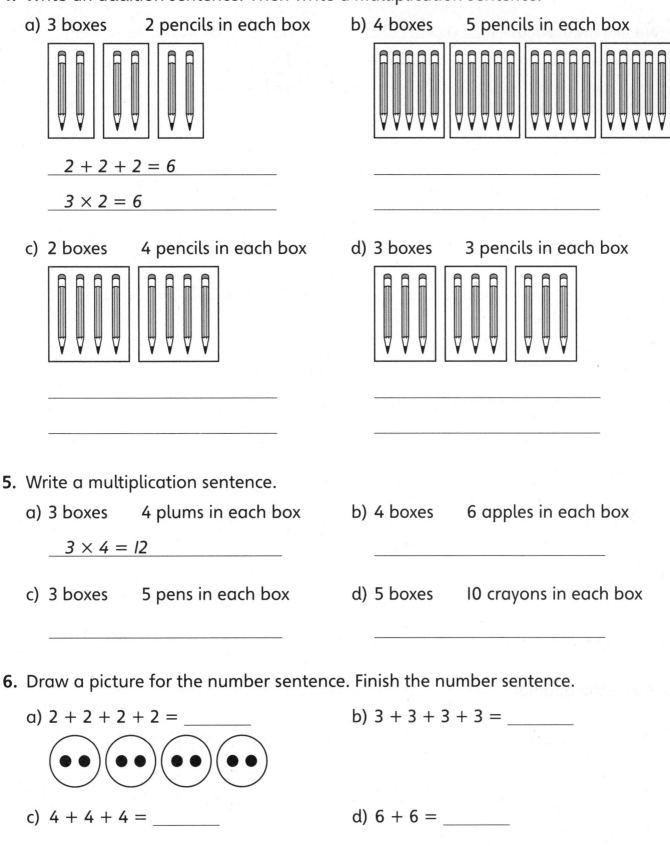

$\underline{2 + 2 + 2 = 6}$

$\underline{3 \times 2 = 6}$

b) 4 boxes   5 pencils in each box

_____

_____

c) 2 boxes   4 pencils in each box

_____

_____

d) 3 boxes   3 pencils in each box

_____

_____

5. Write a multiplication sentence.

a) 3 boxes   4 plums in each box

$\underline{3 \times 4 = 12}$

b) 4 boxes   6 apples in each box

_____

c) 3 boxes   5 pens in each box

_____

d) 5 boxes   10 crayons in each box

_____

6. Draw a picture for the number sentence. Finish the number sentence.

a) 2 + 2 + 2 + 2 = _____

b) 3 + 3 + 3 + 3 = _____

c) 4 + 4 + 4 = _____

d) 6 + 6 = _____

COPYRIGHT © 2016 JUMP MATH: NOT TO BE COPIED.

NS3-33 Multiplication and Equal Groups

Show **equal groups** of objects.

• Use big circles for the groups.

• Use dots for the objects.

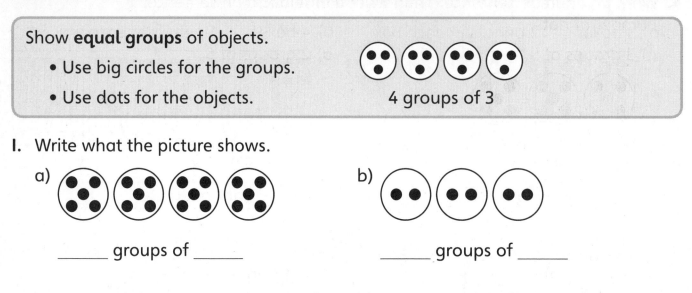

4 groups of 3

I. Write what the picture shows.

a)

_____ groups of _____

b)

_____ groups of _____

2. Draw equal groups. Use big circles for the groups and dots for the objects.

a) 4 groups of 2

b) 3 groups of 4

3. Write an addition sentence for the picture. Then write a multiplication sentence.

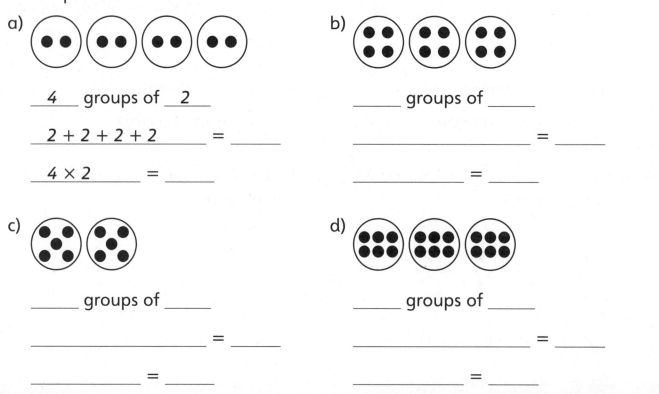

a)

___4___ groups of ___2___

___2 + 2 + 2 + 2___ = _____

___4 × 2___ = _____

b)

_____ groups of _____

_____ = _____

_____ = _____

c)

_____ groups of _____

_____ = _____

_____ = _____

d)

_____ groups of _____

_____ = _____

_____ = _____

COPYRIGHT © 2016 JUMP MATH: NOT TO BE COPIED

4. Draw a picture. Then write a multiplication sentence. Find the total
   number of dots.

a) 3 groups of 5

_____ big circles

_____ dots in a circle

_3 × 5 = 15_____

b) 2 groups of 6

_____ big circles

_____ dots in a circle

_____

c) 5 groups of 4

_____ big circles

_____ dots in a circle

_____

d) 6 groups of 3

_____ big circles

_____ dots in a circle

_____

e) 2 groups of 4

_____ big circles

_____ dots in a circle

_____

f) 3 groups of 3

_____ big circles

_____ dots in a circle

_____

g) 4 groups of 3

_____ big circles

_____ dots in a circle

_____

h) 5 groups of 2

_____ big circles

_____ dots in a circle

_____

COPYRIGHT © 2016 JUMP MATH: NOT TO BE COPIED.

You can draw a picture for a multiplication sentence.

┌─ number of big circles

3 × 4 = 12 ◄─── total number of dots

└─ number of dots in a circle

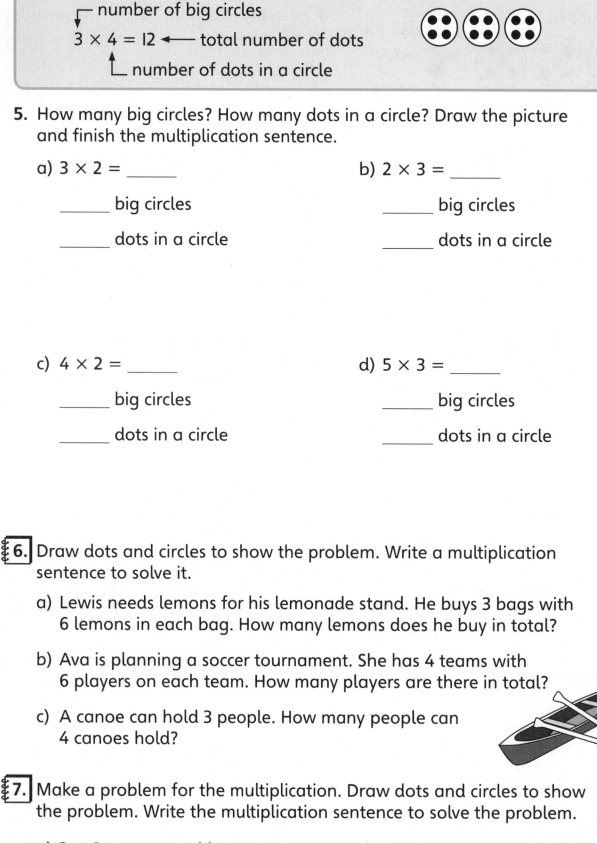

5. How many big circles? How many dots in a circle? Draw the picture and finish the multiplication sentence.

a) 3 × 2 = _____

_____ big circles

_____ dots in a circle

b) 2 × 3 = _____

_____ big circles

_____ dots in a circle

c) 4 × 2 = _____

_____ big circles

_____ dots in a circle

d) 5 × 3 = _____

_____ big circles

_____ dots in a circle

6. Draw dots and circles to show the problem. Write a multiplication sentence to solve it.

a) Lewis needs lemons for his lemonade stand. He buys 3 bags with 6 lemons in each bag. How many lemons does he buy in total?

b) Ava is planning a soccer tournament. She has 4 teams with 6 players on each team. How many players are there in total?

c) A canoe can hold 3 people. How many people can 4 canoes hold?

7. Make a problem for the multiplication. Draw dots and circles to show the problem. Write the multiplication sentence to solve the problem.

a) 2 × 3   b) 4 × 5   c) 2 × 5   d) 3 × 10

COPYRIGHT © 2016 JUMP MATH: NOT TO BE COPIED.

NS3-34 Multiplying by Skip Counting

When you multiply two numbers, the result is called the **product** of the numbers.

Rob finds the product 3 × 4 by skip counting on a number line. He counts off three 4s.

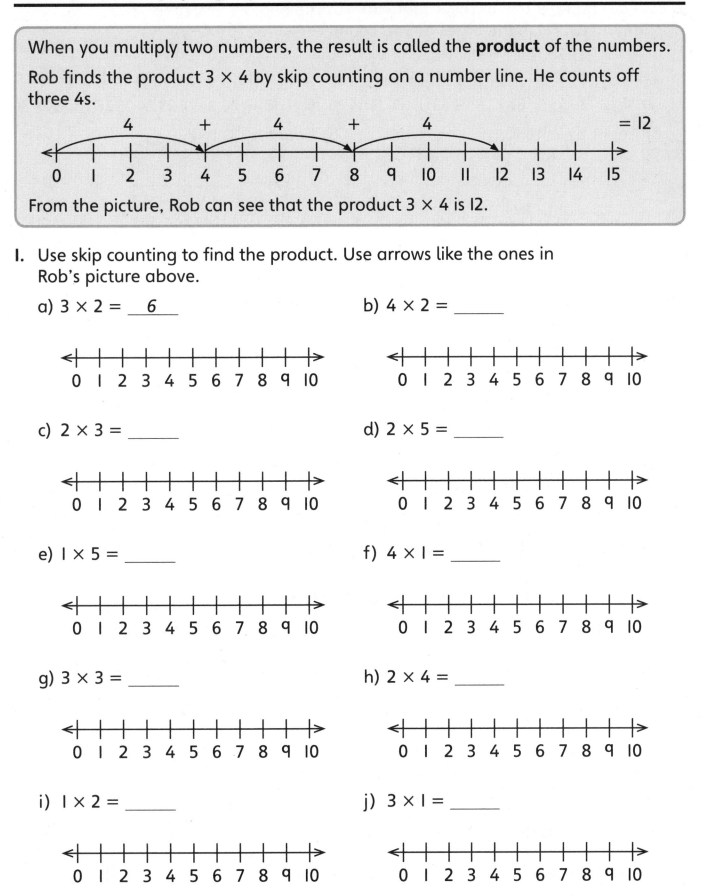

From the picture, Rob can see that the product 3 × 4 is 12.

1. Use skip counting to find the product. Use arrows like the ones in Rob's picture above.

a) 3 × 2 = ___6___

b) 4 × 2 = _____

c) 2 × 3 = _____

d) 2 × 5 = _____

e) 1 × 5 = _____

f) 4 × 1 = _____

g) 3 × 3 = _____

h) 2 × 4 = _____

i) 1 × 2 = _____

j) 3 × 1 = _____

COPYRIGHT © 2016 JUMP MATH: NOT TO BE COPIED.

2. Use the number line to skip count. Start at the number you are skip counting by. Fill in the boxes as you count.

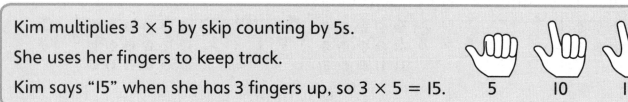

0 1 2 3 4 5 6 7 8 9 10 11 12 13 14 15 16 17 18 19 20 21 22 23 24 25 26 27 28 29 30

a) Count by 2s to 10.

b) Count by 3s to 15.

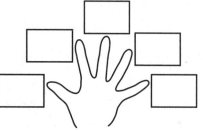

c) Count by 4s to 20.

d) Count by 5s to 25.

Kim multiplies 3 × 5 by skip counting by 5s.

She uses her fingers to keep track.

Kim says "15" when she has 3 fingers up, so 3 × 5 = 15.

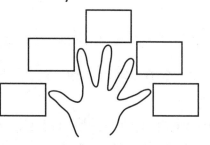

5   10   15

3. Skip count to multiply. Use your fingers to keep track.

a) 2 × 5 = _____   b) 3 × 5 = _____   c) 4 × 2 = _____   d) 3 × 2 = _____

e) 5 × 5 = _____   f) 2 × 3 = _____   g) 4 × 3 = _____   h) 2 × 4 = _____

i) 5 × 4 = _____   j) 4 × 4 = _____   k) 3 × 3 = _____   l) 1 × 2 = _____

4. Skip count by 10s to multiply.

a) 3 × 10 = _____   b) 2 × 10 = _____   c) 4 × 10 = _____   d) 5 × 10 = _____

BONUS ▶ Use both hands to keep track.

e) 8 × 10 = _____   f) 6 × 10 = _____   g) 9 × 10 = _____   h) 10 × 10 = _____

COPYRIGHT © 2016 JUMP MATH: NOT TO BE COPIED.

NS3-35 Arrays

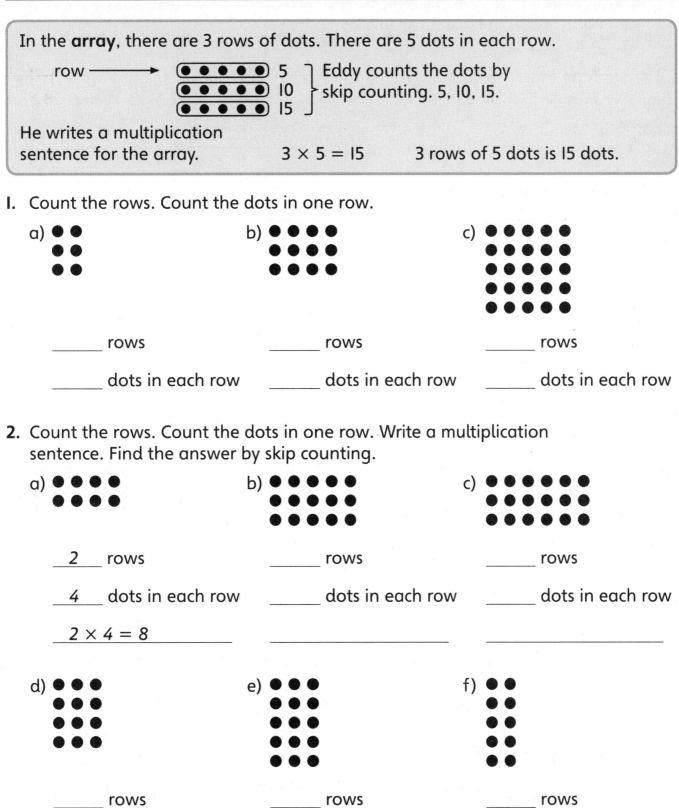

In the **array**, there are 3 rows of dots. There are 5 dots in each row.

row ⟶ 〔• • • • •〕 5
　　　 〔• • • • •〕 10 ⎬ Eddy counts the dots by skip counting. 5, 10, 15.
　　　 〔• • • • •〕 15

He writes a multiplication sentence for the array.　　　$3 \times 5 = 15$　　　3 rows of 5 dots is 15 dots.

1. Count the rows. Count the dots in one row.

a)
_____ rows

_____ dots in each row

b)
_____ rows

_____ dots in each row

c)
_____ rows

_____ dots in each row

2. Count the rows. Count the dots in one row. Write a multiplication sentence. Find the answer by skip counting.

a)
___2___ rows

___4___ dots in each row

___$2 \times 4 = 8$___

b)
_____ rows

_____ dots in each row

_____

c)
_____ rows

_____ dots in each row

_____

d)
_____ rows

_____ dots in each row

_____

e)
_____ rows

_____ dots in each row

_____

f)
_____ rows

_____ dots in each row

_____

COPYRIGHT © 2016 JUMP MATH: NOT TO BE COPIED.

3. Draw an array. Write a multiplication sentence.

a) 2 rows   3 dots in each row   b) 3 rows   7 dots in each row

_____   _____

c) 5 rows   6 dots in each row   d) 4 rows   5 dots in each row

_____   _____

4. Draw an array. Write a multiplication sentence.

a) On a bus, 4 people can sit in a row.
There are 5 rows of seats on the bus.
How many people can ride on the bus?

_____ × _____ = _____

b) Liz puts 6 stamps in each row of her stamp book.
There are 3 rows of stamps.
How many stamps are there altogether?

_____ × _____ = _____

c) John plants 3 rows of trees with 5 trees in each row.
How many trees did he plant?

_____ × _____ = _____

d) There are 4 rows of candles on a shelf.
There are 6 candles in each row.
How many candles are there altogether?

_____ × _____ = _____

COPYRIGHT © 2016 JUMP MATH: NOT TO BE COPIED.

5. Write a multiplication sentence for each array.

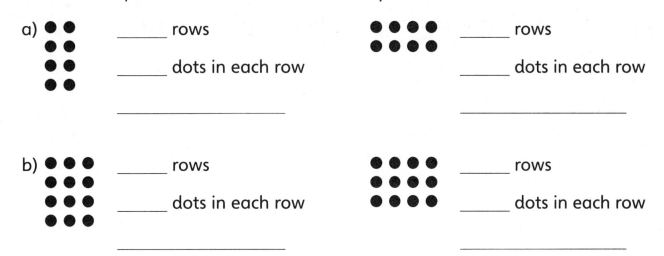

a) _____ rows

_____ dots in each row

_____

_____ rows

_____ dots in each row

_____

b) _____ rows

_____ dots in each row

_____

_____ rows

_____ dots in each row

_____

> **REMINDER ▶** The result of multiplying two numbers is called a **product**.
>
> The product of 3 and 4 is 3 times 4 or 12.

6. Explain why the products in Question 5.a) are the same.

_____

_____

When you multiply the same numbers in a different order, you get the same answer.

$5 \times 3 = 3 \times 5$

This is called the **commutative property** of multiplication.

7. Find the product using the commutative property.

a) $6 \times 3 =$ _____

so $3 \times 6 =$ _____

b) $7 \times 4 =$ _____

so $4 \times 7 =$ _____

c) $8 \times 6 =$ _____

so $6 \times 8 =$ _____

d) $9 \times 4 =$ _____

so $4 \times 9 =$ _____

8. Draw an array to show the product.

a) 5×4

b) 5×2

c) 4×7

d) 6×3

9. Draw an array showing 2×3 and 3×2. Are the products 2×3 and 3×2 the same or different? How do you know?

COPYRIGHT © 2016 JUMP MATH: NOT TO BE COPIED.

You can write the multiples of 4 in a chart with 2 rows of 5 boxes.

row ──▶

04	08	12	16	20
24	28	32	36	40

You can use the patterns in the chart to help remember the multiples of 4.

1. Describe any patterns you see in the chart above.

_____

_____

¹ 04	² 08	³ 12	⁴ 16	⁵ 20
⁶ 24	⁷ 28	⁸ 32	⁹ 36	¹⁰ 40

12 is the third number in the chart. It is in position 3.

2. a) 24 is in position _____   b) 8 is in position _____   c) 40 is in position _____

3. a) 28 is in position _____   b) 32 is in position _____   c) 16 is in position _____

  __7__ × 4 = 28   _____ × 4 = 32   _____ × 4 = 16

  d) 36 is in position _____   e) 4 is in position _____   f) 20 is in position _____

  _____ × 4 = 36   _____ × 4 = 4   _____ × 4 = 20

4. Use the patterns in the chart to help remember the multiples of 4.
Try each question without looking at the chart.

a) 4	b) 4	c) 4	d) 4	e) 4	f) 4
× 1	× 3	× 5	× 6	× 2	× 9

COPYRIGHT © 2016 JUMP MATH: NOT TO BE COPIED.

You can write the multiples of 6 in a chart with 2 rows of 5 boxes.

0 6	1 2	1 8	2 4	3 0
3 6	4 2	4 8	5 4	6 0

You can use the patterns in the chart to help remember the multiples of 6.

5. Describe any patterns you see in the chart above.

_____

_____

¹ 0 6	² 1 2	³ 1 8	⁴ 2 4	⁵ 3 0
⁶ 3 6	⁷ 4 2	⁸ 4 8	⁹ 5 4	¹⁰ 6 0

48 is in position 8 in the chart.

6. a) 42 is in position _____   b) 18 is in position _____   c) 30 is in position _____

7. a) 54 is in position _____   b) 36 is in position _____   c) 12 is in position _____

_____ × 6 = 54   _____ × 6 = 36   _____ × 6 = 12

d) 24 is in position _____   e) 60 is in position _____   f) 6 is in position _____

_____ × 6 = 24   _____ × 6 = 60   _____ × 6 = 6

8. Use the patterns in the chart to help remember the multiples of 6.
Try each question without looking at the chart.

a)   6   b)   6   c)   6   d)   6   e)   6   f)   6
    × 5   × 4   × 7   × 3   × 1   × 8

9. Write the multiples of 8 in a chart with 2 rows of 5 boxes.
What patterns do you see?

COPYRIGHT © 2016 JUMP MATH: NOT TO BE COPIED.

NS3-37 Patterns in Multiplication of Odd Numbers

You can write the multiples of 3 in a chart with 3 rows of 3 boxes.

You can use the patterns in the chart to help remember the multiples of 3.

03	06	09
12	15	18
21	24	27

1. Describe any patterns you see in the chart above.

_____

_____

18 is in position 6 in the chart.

^{1} 03	^{2} 06	^{3} 09
^{4} 12	^{5} 15	^{6} 18
^{7} 21	^{8} 24	^{9} 27

2. a) 12 is in position _____   b) 27 is in position _____   c) 6 is in position _____

3. a) 24 is in position _____   b) 15 is in position _____   c) 21 is in position _____

　　__8__ × 3 = 24　　　　　_____ × 3 = 15　　　　　_____ × 3 = 21

d) 3 is in position _____   e) 18 is in position _____   f) 9 is in position _____

　　_____ × 3 = 3　　　　　_____ × 3 = 18　　　　　_____ × 3 = 9

4. Use the patterns in the chart to help remember the multiples of 3.
   Try each question without looking at the chart.

   a)　　3　　b)　　3　　c)　　3　　d)　　3　　e)　　3　　f)　　3
   　×　2　　　　×　4　　　　×　6　　　　×　1　　　　×　9　　　　×　3
   　―――　　　　―――　　　　―――　　　　―――　　　　―――　　　　―――

5. Fred saw 4 tricycles at a park. How many wheels did he see?

_____

COPYRIGHT © 2016 JUMP MATH: NOT TO BE COPIED.

You can write the multiples of 7 in a chart with 3 rows of 3 boxes.

You can use the patterns in the chart to help remember the multiples of 7.

07	14	21
28	35	42
49	56	63

6. Describe any patterns you see in the chart above.

_____

_____

28 is in position 4 in the chart.

¹ 07	² 14	³ 21
⁴ 28	⁵ 35	⁶ 42
⁷ 49	⁸ 56	⁹ 63

7. a) 7 is in position _____   b) 56 is in position _____   c) 49 is in position _____

8. a) 14 is in position _____   b) 21 is in position _____   c) 63 is in position _____

_____ × 7 = 14   _____ × 7 = 21   _____ × 7 = 63

d) 28 is in position _____   e) 42 is in position _____   f) 35 is in position _____

_____ × 7 = 28   _____ × 7 = 42   _____ × 7 = 35

9. Use the patterns in the chart to help remember the multiples of 7.
Try each question without looking at the chart.

a)   7   b)   7   c)   7   d)   7   e)   7   f)   7
   × 6   × 4   × 5   × 8   × 1   × 7
   ____   ____   ____   ____   ____   ____

10. Write the multiples of 9 in a chart with 3 rows of 3 boxes.
What patterns do you see?

COPYRIGHT © 2016 JUMP MATH: NOT TO BE COPIED.

I. Use skip counting to find out how many legs the animals have.

Animal	Number of Animals						
	1	2	3	4	5	6	7
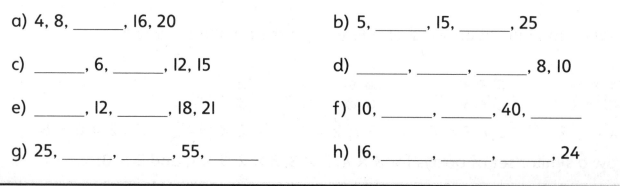	2						
	4						
	6						
	8						

2. A hockey line has 5 players. Fill in the missing information.

__4__ lines	5 + 5 + 5 + 5	4 × 5
3 lines	5 + 5 + 5	
5 lines		
_____ lines		2 × 5

3. Fill in the missing numbers.

a) 4, 8, _____, 16, 20

b) 5, _____, 15, _____, 25

c) _____, 6, _____, 12, 15

d) _____, _____, _____, 8, 10

e) _____, 12, _____, 18, 21

f) 10, _____, _____, 40, _____

g) 25, _____, _____, 55, _____

h) 16, _____, _____, _____, 24

COPYRIGHT © 2016 JUMP MATH: NOT TO BE COPIED.

4. Mandy practices guitar twice a week. How many times will she practice in 4 weeks?

_____

5. The table shows the price of tickets in dollars for a play.

Fill in the missing numbers.

Tickets	1	2		4	
Price	5	10			25

6. a) Can you use multiplication to find the perimeter of the playground? If yes, write a multiplication sentence. If no, use addition.

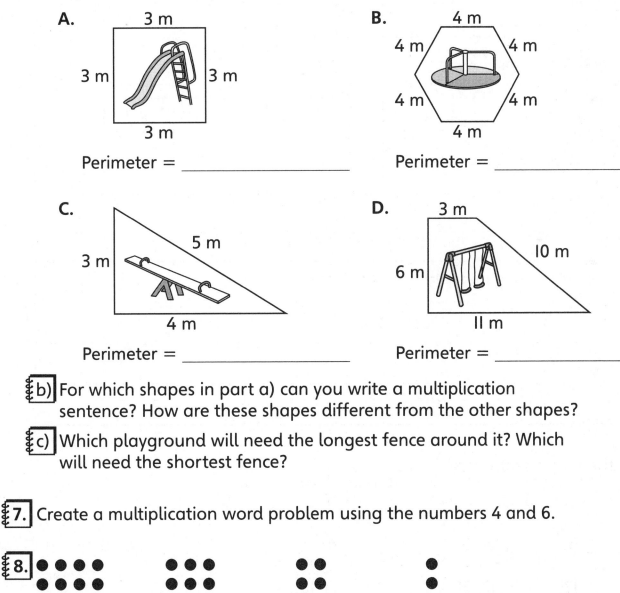

A.
3 m

3 m   3 m

3 m

Perimeter = _____

B.
4 m

4 m   4 m

4 m   4 m

4 m

Perimeter = _____

C.
5 m

3 m

4 m

Perimeter = _____

D.
3 m

6 m   10 m

11 m

Perimeter = _____

b) For which shapes in part a) can you write a multiplication sentence? How are these shapes different from the other shapes?

c) Which playground will need the longest fence around it? Which will need the shortest fence?

7. Create a multiplication word problem using the numbers 4 and 6.

8.
● ● ● ●   ● ● ●   ● ●   ●
● ● ● ●   ● ● ●   ● ●   ●

$2 \times 4 = 8$ $2 \times 3 = 6$ $2 \times 2 = 4$ $2 \times 1 = 2$ $2 \times 0 = 0$

Draw a similar set of arrays for 3×4, 3×3, 3×2, 3×1, and 3×0.

COPYRIGHT © 2016 JUMP MATH: NOT TO BE COPIED.

1. Write an addition sentence and a multiplication sentence to double the number.

   a) 7   b) 5   c) 9

   ___ 7 + 7 = 14 ___   _____   _____

   ___ 2 × 7 = 14 ___   _____   _____

2. Double the tens and the ones. Add the answers to double the number.

   a)
Number	42	31	14	23	44	21
Double	84					

   b)
Number	73	53	94	82	61	74
Double	146					

   c)
Number	65	99	56	78	67
Addition	120 + 10				
Double	130				

3. Double 2 times the number to find 4 times the number.

   a) 2 × 4 = __8__   b) 2 × 5 = _____   c) 2 × 7 = _____

   so 4 × 4 = __16__   so 4 × 5 = _____   so 4 × 7 = _____

   d) 2 × 8 = _____   e) 2 × 6 = _____   f) 2 × 9 = _____

   so 4 × 8 = _____   so 4 × 6 = _____   so 4 × 9 = _____

4. Double 3 times the number to find 6 times the number.

   a) 3 × 2 = _____   b) 3 × 4 = _____   c) 3 × 8 = _____

   so 6 × 2 = _____   so 6 × 4 = _____   so 6 × 8 = _____

   d) 3 × 5 = _____   e) 3 × 6 = _____   f) 3 × 9 = _____

   so 6 × 5 = _____   so 6 × 6 = _____   so 6 × 9 = _____

COPYRIGHT © 2016 JUMP MATH: NOT TO BE COPIED.

5. Use doubles to find the products.

a)

If	$2 \times 7 = 14$	$3 \times 7 = 21$	$4 \times 7 = 28$	$2 \times 6 = 12$
Then	$4 \times 7 = \underline{\hspace{1cm}}$	$6 \times 7 = \underline{\hspace{1cm}}$	$8 \times 7 = \underline{\hspace{1cm}}$	$4 \times 6 = \underline{\hspace{1cm}}$

b)

If	$3 \times 6 = 18$	$4 \times 6 = 24$	$2 \times 8 = 16$	$4 \times 8 = 32$
Then	$6 \times 6 = \underline{\hspace{1cm}}$	$8 \times 6 = \underline{\hspace{1cm}}$	$4 \times 8 = \underline{\hspace{1cm}}$	$8 \times 8 = \underline{\hspace{1cm}}$

c)

If	$2 \times 9 = 18$	$3 \times 9 = 27$	$4 \times 9 = 36$	$2 \times 12 = 24$
Then	$4 \times 9 = \underline{\hspace{1cm}}$	$\underline{\hspace{0.5cm}} \times 9 = \underline{\hspace{1cm}}$	$\underline{\hspace{0.5cm}} \times 9 = \underline{\hspace{1cm}}$	$\underline{\hspace{0.5cm}} \times 12 = \underline{\hspace{1cm}}$

6. Double 2 times the number to find 4 times the number. Then find 8 times the number.

a) $2 \times 7 = \underline{\hspace{1.5cm}}$

so $4 \times 7 = \underline{\hspace{1.5cm}}$

and $8 \times 7 = \underline{\hspace{1.5cm}}$

b) $2 \times 8 = \underline{\hspace{1.5cm}}$

so $4 \times 8 = \underline{\hspace{1.5cm}}$

and $8 \times 8 = \underline{\hspace{1.5cm}}$

c) $2 \times 6 = \underline{\hspace{1.5cm}}$

so $4 \times 6 = \underline{\hspace{1.5cm}}$

and $8 \times 6 = \underline{\hspace{1.5cm}}$

7. a) A prairie skink lizard is 20 cm long. A tiger salamander is 2 times as long as a prairie skink. How long is the tiger salamander?

b) A rubber boa snake is 2 times as long as a tiger salamander. How long is the rubber boa?

c) A prairie rattlesnake is 2 times as long as a rubber boa. How long is a prairie rattlesnake?

BONUS ▶ Is the prairie rattlesnake longer than 1 m?

BONUS ▶ Use doubles to find 12×4.

$3 \times 4 = \underline{\hspace{2cm}}$

so $6 \times 4 = \underline{\hspace{2cm}}$

and $12 \times 4 = \underline{\hspace{2cm}}$

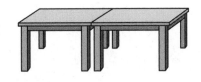

8. A table is 82 cm long. How long are two tables?

COPYRIGHT © 2016 JUMP MATH: NOT TO BE COPIED.

NS3-40 Brackets

We call addition, subtraction, and multiplication **operations**.
Brackets tell you which operation to do first.

Examples: $3 \times (7 + 2)$ $(8 - 2) \times 5$
              Do this first.   Do this first.

I. Do the operation in brackets. Write the question with only one operation.

a) $3 \times (4 + 2)$

= _3 × 6_____

b) $(3 \times 4) + 2$

= _____

c) $7 + (3 + 1)$

= _____

d) $3 \times (7 + 2)$

= _____

e) $(5 - 1) \times 6$

= _____

f) $(9 - 2) \times 6$

= _____

2. Do the operation in brackets first.

a) $4 \times (2 + 3)$

= _4 × 5_____

= _20_____

b) $(3 + 3) \times 2$

= _____

= _____

c) $7 + (4 \times 2)$

= _____

= _____

d) $2 \times (5 + 3)$

= _____

= _____

e) $(5 - 3) \times 5$

= _____

= _____

f) $8 \times (7 - 4)$

= _____

= _____

g) $(2 \times 3) - 1$

= _____

= _____

h) $(3 + 4) + 8$

= _____

= _____

i) $7 + (9 \times 2)$

= _____

= _____

3. Which sentence is correct? $3 \times (2 + 1) = 9$ or $2 \times (2 + 1) = 5$
Explain how you know.

BONUS ▶ Find the answer.

a) $(3 \times 2) + (6 \times 1)$

b) $(5 - 1) + (3 \times 3)$

c) $7 + (3 \times 1) + 4$

COPYRIGHT © 2016 JUMP MATH: NOT TO BE COPIED.

NS3-4l Multiplying by Adding On

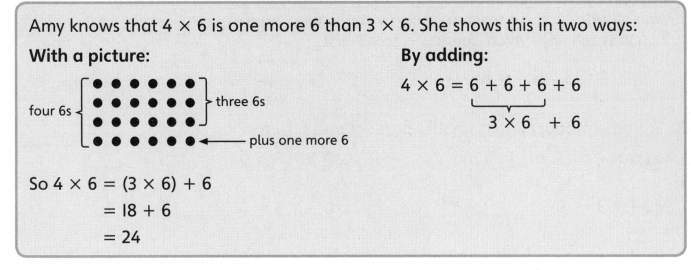

Amy knows that 4 × 6 is one more 6 than 3 × 6. She shows this in two ways:

With a picture:

four 6s ⎰ ⎱ three 6s

plus one more 6

So 4 × 6 = (3 × 6) + 6

= 18 + 6

= 24

By adding:

4 × 6 = 6 + 6 + 6 + 6

3 × 6 + 6

1. Write a product for the array.

a)

$\underline{\quad 4 \times 3 \quad}$

↑ rows   ↑ dots in each row

b)

$\underline{\qquad\qquad}$

c)

$\underline{\qquad\qquad}$

d)

$\underline{\qquad\qquad}$

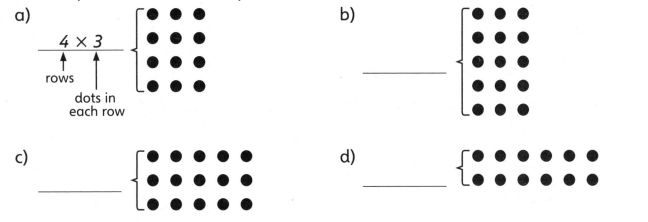

2. Fill in the missing products and numbers.

a)

$\underline{\quad 4 \times 5 \quad}$

↑ rows   ↑ dots in each row

} 3×5

+ $\underline{\;5\;}$

b)

$\underline{\qquad\qquad}$ {

} $\underline{\qquad}$

+ $\underline{\qquad}$

c)

$\underline{\qquad\qquad}$ {

$\underline{\qquad\qquad}$

+ $\underline{\qquad}$

d)

$\underline{\qquad\qquad}$ {

} $\underline{\qquad\qquad}$

+ $\underline{\qquad}$

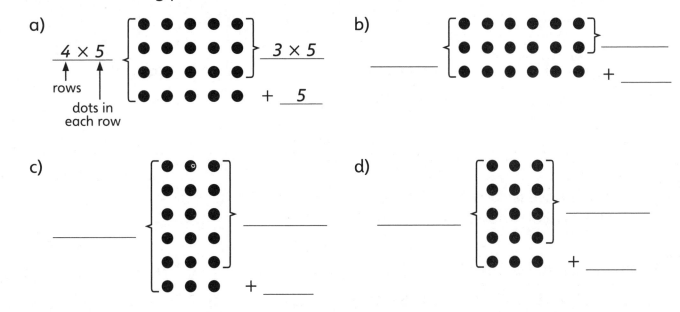

COPYRIGHT © 2016 JUMP MATH: NOT TO BE COPIED.

You can turn a product into a smaller product and a sum.

$$5 \times 3 = (4 \times 3) + 3 \qquad 9 \times 4 = (8 \times 4) + 4$$

Take I away from 5.   Add an extra 3.   Take I away from 9.   Add an extra 4.

3. Turn the product into a smaller product and a sum.

a) $6 \times 7 = (5 \times \underline{\ \ 7\ \ }) + \underline{\ \ 7\ \ }$

b) $5 \times 7 = (4 \times \underline{\ \ \ \ }) + \underline{\ \ \ \ }$

c) $9 \times 3 = (8 \times \underline{\ \ \ \ }) + \underline{\ \ \ \ }$

d) $3 \times 6 = (2 \times \underline{\ \ \ \ }) + \underline{\ \ \ \ }$

e) $9 \times 4 = (\underline{\ \ \ \ } \times \underline{\ \ \ \ }) + \underline{\ \ \ \ }$

f) $8 \times 6 = (\underline{\ \ \ \ } \times \underline{\ \ \ \ }) + \underline{\ \ \ \ }$

g) $6 \times 8 = \underline{\hspace{4cm}}$

h) $8 \times 7 = \underline{\hspace{4cm}}$

i) $7 \times 6 = \underline{\hspace{4cm}}$

j) $9 \times 6 = \underline{\hspace{4cm}}$

4. Find the answer by turning the product into a smaller product and a sum.

a) $5 \times 3 = \underline{\ \ (4 \times 3) + 3\ \ }$

$= \underline{\ \ 12 + 3\ \ }$

$= \underline{\ \ 15\ \ }$

b) $6 \times 4 = \underline{\hspace{3cm}}$

$= \underline{\hspace{3cm}}$

$= \underline{\hspace{1.5cm}}$

c) $6 \times 8 = \underline{\hspace{3cm}}$

$= \underline{\hspace{3cm}}$

$= \underline{\hspace{1.5cm}}$

d) $6 \times 9 = \underline{\hspace{3cm}}$

$= \underline{\hspace{3cm}}$

$= \underline{\hspace{1.5cm}}$

e) $6 \times 6 = \underline{\hspace{3cm}}$

$= \underline{\hspace{3cm}}$

$= \underline{\hspace{1.5cm}}$

f) $7 \times 8 = \underline{\hspace{3cm}}$

$= \underline{\hspace{3cm}}$

$= \underline{\hspace{1.5cm}}$

g) 8×3 h) 7×6 i) 7×7 j) 3×6

COPYRIGHT © 2016 JUMP MATH: NOT TO BE COPIED.

7 groups of 2 =   4 groups of 2   +   3 groups of 2

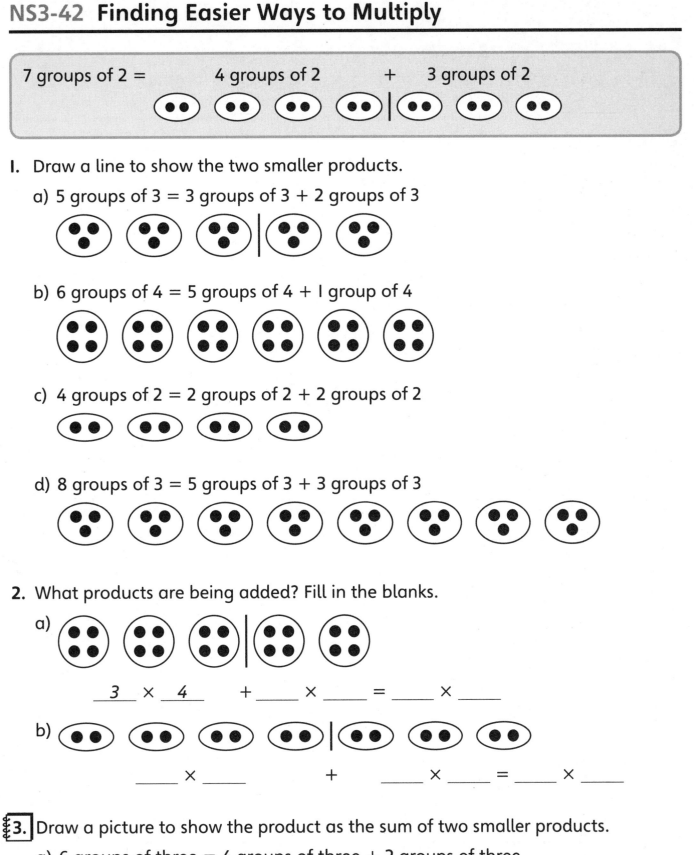

1. Draw a line to show the two smaller products.

   a) 5 groups of 3 = 3 groups of 3 + 2 groups of 3

   b) 6 groups of 4 = 5 groups of 4 + 1 group of 4

   c) 4 groups of 2 = 2 groups of 2 + 2 groups of 2

   d) 8 groups of 3 = 5 groups of 3 + 3 groups of 3

2. What products are being added? Fill in the blanks.

   a)

   $\underline{\ \ 3\ \ } \times \underline{\ \ 4\ \ } \quad + \underline{\ \ \ } \times \underline{\ \ \ \ } = \underline{\ \ \ } \times \underline{\ \ \ \ }$

   b)

   $\underline{\ \ \ \ } \times \underline{\ \ \ \ } \quad\quad + \quad \underline{\ \ \ \ } \times \underline{\ \ \ } = \underline{\ \ \ } \times \underline{\ \ \ \ }$

3. Draw a picture to show the product as the sum of two smaller products.

   a) 6 groups of three = 4 groups of three + 2 groups of three

   b) 8 groups of four = 5 groups of four + 3 groups of four

   c) $5 \times 3 = (3 \times 3) + (2 \times 3)$

COPYRIGHT © 2016 JUMP MATH: NOT TO BE COPIED.

8 = 5 + 3, so	8 sevens	=	5 sevens	+	3 sevens

$$7 + 7 + 7 + 7 + 7 + 7 + 7 + 7 = 7 + 7 + 7 + 7 + 7 \ + \ 7 + 7 + 7$$

4. Fill in the blank.

a) 7 eights = 5 eights + _____ eights   b) 6 nines = 5 nines + _____ nine

c) 9 sixes = 5 sixes + _____ sixes   d) 8 fours = 5 fours + _____ fours

5. Write the product as the sum of two smaller products. Use 5 in one of the products. Then find the final product.

a) $7 \times 8 = \underbrace{8 + 8 + 8 + 8 + 8}_{} \ + \ \underbrace{8 + 8}_{}$

$\quad = \quad\quad (5 \times 8) \quad\quad + \ (\underline{\ 2\ } \times 8)$

$\quad = \quad\quad \underline{\ 40\ } \quad\quad + \quad \underline{\ 16\ }$

$\quad = \quad\quad \underline{\ 56\ }$

b) $8 \times 6 = \underbrace{6 + 6 + 6 + 6 + 6}_{} \ + \ \underbrace{6 + 6 + 6}_{}$

$\quad = \quad\quad (5 \times 6) \quad\quad + \ (\underline{\quad} \times 6)$

$\quad = \quad\quad \underline{\quad\quad} \quad\quad + \quad \underline{\quad\quad}$

$\quad = \quad\quad \underline{\quad\quad}$

c) $7 \times 9 = \underbrace{9 + 9 + 9 + 9 + 9}_{} \ + \ \underbrace{9 + 9}_{}$

$\quad = \quad\quad (5 \times 9) \quad\quad + \ (\underline{\quad} \times 9)$

$\quad = \quad\quad \underline{\quad\quad} \quad\quad + \quad \underline{\quad\quad}$

$\quad = \quad\quad \underline{\quad\quad}$

d) 8×7 e) 7×7 f) 9×6 g) 7×6 h) 8×8

6. Which parts of Question 5 have the same answer? How could you have predicted that?

COPYRIGHT © 2016 JUMP MATH: NOT TO BE COPIED.

NS3-43 Multiplying by 1 and 0

Any number times 1 is the number itself.

Example: $7 \times 1 = 1 + 1 + 1 + 1 + 1 + 1 + 1 = 7$

7 ones

1. Multiply.

a) $3 \times 1 =$ _____

b) $8 \times 1 =$ _____

c) $2 \times 1 =$ _____

d) $4 \times 1 =$ _____

e) $5 \times 1 =$ _____

f) $6 \times 1 =$ _____

BONUS ▶

g) $100 \times 1 =$ _____

h) $400 \times 1 =$ _____

i) $1 \times 1000 =$ _____

$4 \times 3 = 3 + 3 + 3 + 3$ and $1 \times 3 = 3$

Add 4 threes. Add 1 three.

So 1 times any number is the number itself.

2. Multiply.

a) $1 \times 9 =$ _____

b) $1 \times 6 =$ _____

c) $12 \times 1 =$ _____

d) $7 \times 1 =$ _____

e) $1 \times 17 =$ _____

f) $1 \times 20 =$ _____

BONUS ▶

g) $153 \times 1 =$ _____

h) $1 \times 500 =$ _____

i) $1 \times 999 =$ _____

3. Add or multiply.

a) $8 + 1 =$ _____

b) $8 \times 1 =$ _____

c) $1 + 4 =$ _____

d) $1 \times 4 =$ _____

e) $1 \times 5 =$ _____

f) $1 + 5 =$ _____

g) $9 \times 1 =$ _____

h) $9 + 1 =$ _____

i) $1 \times 1 =$ _____

j) $1 + 1 =$ _____

BONUS ▶ $999 + 1 =$ _____

COPYRIGHT © 2016 JUMP MATH: NOT TO BE COPIED.

4. Multiply.

a) $3 \times 0 = 0 + 0 + 0$

  $= $ _____

b) $4 \times 0 = 0 + 0 + 0 + 0$

  $= $ _____

c) $2 \times 0 = 0 + 0$

  $= $ _____

d) $5 \times 0 = 0 + 0 + 0 + 0 + 0$

  $= $ _____

e) $19 \times 0 = $ _____

f) $183 \times 0 = $ _____

5. Continue the pattern to find 0 times the number. Fill in the circles.

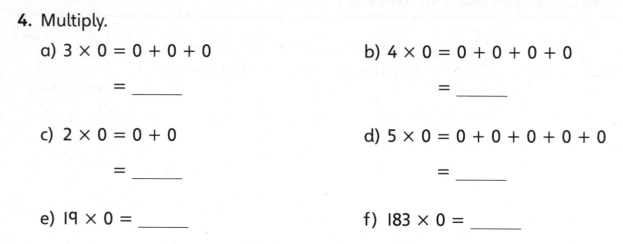

a)

5×2	10
4×2	8
3×2	6
2×2	
1×2	
0×2	

b)

5×5	
4×5	
3×5	
2×5	
1×5	
0×5	

6. Multiply.

a) $0 \times 7 = $ _____
b) $8 \times 0 = $ _____
c) $0 \times 17 = $ _____
d) $9 \times 0 = $ _____

e) $12 \times 0 = $ _____
f) $30 \times 0 = $ _____
g) $0 \times 25 = $ _____
h) $0 \times 11 = $ _____

BONUS ▶ $0 \times 1000 = $ _____

7. Add or multiply.

a) $8 \times 0 = $ _____
b) $8 + 0 = $ _____
c) $0 \times 9 = $ _____
d) $0 + 9 = $ _____

e) $5 + 1 = $ _____
f) $5 \times 1 = $ _____
g) $0 \times 1 = $ _____
h) $0 + 1 = $ _____

BONUS ▶ Put the same number in each box. Write three different answers.

☐ $\times 1 = $ ☐ $+ 0$ ☐ $\times 1 = $ ☐ $+ 0$ ☐ $\times 1 = $ ☐ $+ 0$

COPYRIGHT © 2016 JUMP MATH: NOT TO BE COPIED.

1. Count the number of squares in the rectangle. Write your answer in the bottom right square. Then write the multiplication sentence.

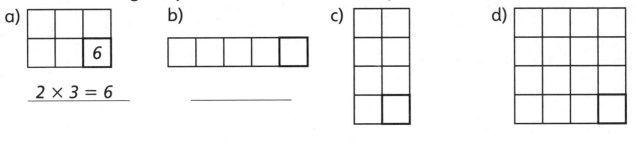

a)

		6

$2 \times 3 = 6$

b)

_____

c)

d)

_____   _____

2. Draw a rectangle for the product of the two numbers. Count the number of squares in the rectangle. Write the answer in the bottom right square of the rectangle.

a) 2 × 3

×	1	2	3	4	5
1					
2			6		
3					
4					
5					

b) 3 × 4

×	1	2	3	4	5
1					
2					
3					
4					
5					

c) 4 × 2

×	1	2	3	4	5
1					
2					
3					
4					
5					

d) 2 × 5

×	1	2	3	4	5
1					
2					
3					
4					
5					

COPYRIGHT © 2016 JUMP MATH: NOT TO BE COPIED.

Tony wants to use the chart to find 3×4.

He draws a rectangle starting at the dot.
The rectangle has 3 rows of 4 squares.

The answer is the number in the bottom
right corner of the rectangle.

So $3 \times 4 = 12$.

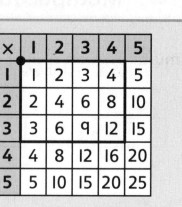

×	1	2	3	4	5
1	1	2	3	4	5
2	2	4	6	8	10
3	3	6	9	12	15
4	4	8	12	16	20
5	5	10	15	20	25

3. Use Tony's method to multiply.

a) 2×4

×	1	2	3	4	5
1	1	2	3	4	5
2	2	4	6	8	10
3	3	6	9	12	15
4	4	8	12	16	20
5	5	10	15	20	25

So $2 \times 4 = $ _____.

b) 5×3

×	1	2	3	4	5
1	1	2	3	4	5
2	2	4	6	8	10
3	3	6	9	12	15
4	4	8	12	16	20
5	5	10	15	20	25

So $5 \times 3 = $ _____.

c) 4×2

×	1	2	3	4	5
1	1	2	3	4	5
2	2	4	6	8	10
3	3	6	9	12	15
4	4	8	12	16	20
5	5	10	15	20	25

So $4 \times 2 = $ _____.

d) 5×4

×	1	2	3	4	5
1	1	2	3	4	5
2	2	4	6	8	10
3	3	6	9	12	15
4	4	8	12	16	20
5	5	10	15	20	25

So $5 \times 4 = $ _____.

4. Which two answers from Question 3 are the same? Why is that
the case?

COPYRIGHT © 2016 JUMP MATH: NOT TO BE COPIED.

A **multiplication chart** shows the product of two numbers.

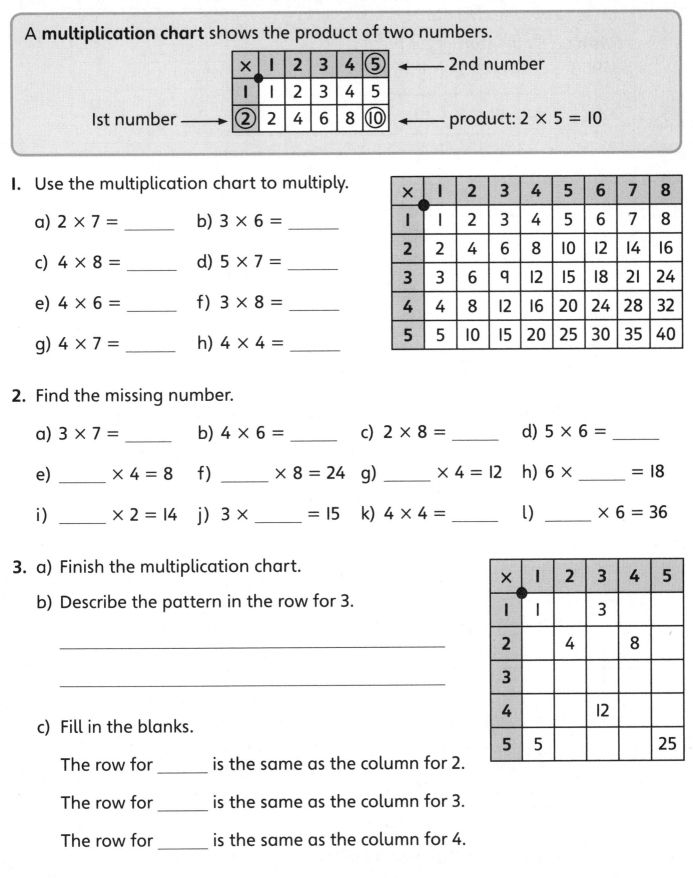

1. Use the multiplication chart to multiply.

   a) $2 \times 7 =$ _____   b) $3 \times 6 =$ _____

   c) $4 \times 8 =$ _____   d) $5 \times 7 =$ _____

   e) $4 \times 6 =$ _____   f) $3 \times 8 =$ _____

   g) $4 \times 7 =$ _____   h) $4 \times 4 =$ _____

×	1	2	3	4	5	6	7	8
1	1	2	3	4	5	6	7	8
2	2	4	6	8	10	12	14	16
3	3	6	9	12	15	18	21	24
4	4	8	12	16	20	24	28	32
5	5	10	15	20	25	30	35	40

2. Find the missing number.

   a) $3 \times 7 =$ _____   b) $4 \times 6 =$ _____   c) $2 \times 8 =$ _____   d) $5 \times 6 =$ _____

   e) _____ $\times 4 = 8$ f) _____ $\times 8 = 24$ g) _____ $\times 4 = 12$ h) $6 \times$ _____ $= 18$

   i) _____ $\times 2 = 14$ j) $3 \times$ _____ $= 15$ k) $4 \times 4 =$ _____   l) _____ $\times 6 = 36$

3. a) Finish the multiplication chart.

   b) Describe the pattern in the row for 3.

   _____

   _____

   c) Fill in the blanks.

   The row for _____ is the same as the column for 2.

   The row for _____ is the same as the column for 3.

   The row for _____ is the same as the column for 4.

×	1	2	3	4	5
1	1		3		
2		4		8	
3					
4			12		
5	5				25

COPYRIGHT © 2016 JUMP MATH: NOT TO BE COPIED.

4. a) Use the completed half to quickly finish the empty half.

×	1	2	3	4	5	6	7	8	9	10
1	1	2	3	4	5	6	7	8	9	10
2		4	6	8	10	12	14	16	18	20
3			9	12	15	18	21	24	27	30
4				16	20	24	28	32	36	40
5					25	30	35	40	45	50
6						36	42	48	54	60
7							49	56	63	70
8								64	72	80
9									81	90
10										100

b) Describe any patterns you see in the row for 8.

_____

_____

c) Look for even and odd numbers in the column for 7. What do you notice?

_____

_____

5. Compare the row for 2 with the row for 4. What do you notice?

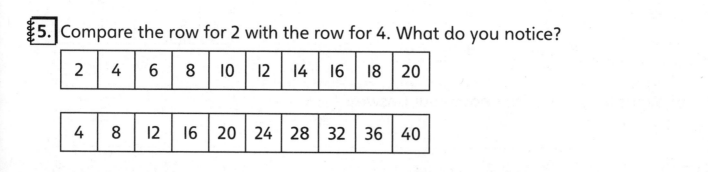

2	4	6	8	10	12	14	16	18	20

4	8	12	16	20	24	28	32	36	40

COPYRIGHT © 2016 JUMP MATH: NOT TO BE COPIED.

NS3-46 The Associative Property

> **REMINDER** ▶ Brackets tell you which operation to do first.
>
> Examples: $3 \times (4 \times 2)$ $(3 \times 4) \times 2$
>
>   Do this first.   Do this first.

1. Do the operation in brackets. Write the question with only one operation.

   a) $3 \times (4 \times 2)$

      = ___3 × 8___

   b) $(3 \times 4) \times 2$

      = _____

   c) $7 \times (3 \times 1)$

      = _____

   d) $5 \times (1 \times 4)$

      = _____

   e) $(3 \times 2) \times 5$

      = _____

   f) $6 \times (2 \times 4)$

      = _____

2. Do the operation in brackets first.

   a) $5 \times (2 \times 2)$

      = ___5 × 4___

      = ___20___

   b) $5 \times (2 \times 5)$

      = _____

      = _____

   c) $(3 \times 2) \times 2$

      = _____

      = _____

   d) $(1 \times 8) \times 4$

      = _____

      = _____

   e) $(3 \times 2) \times 7$

      = _____

      = _____

   f) $7 \times (1 \times 7)$

      = _____

      = _____

3. a) Find the product two ways.

      $(3 \times 2) \times 4$ $3 \times (2 \times 4)$

      = _____   = _____

      = _____   = _____

   b) What do you notice about your answers?

   _____

COPYRIGHT © 2016 JUMP MATH: NOT TO BE COPIED.

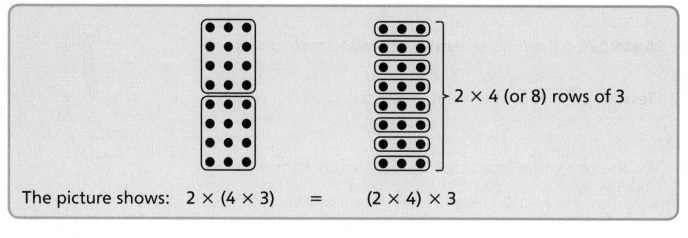

The picture shows: $2 \times (4 \times 3)$ $=$ $(2 \times 4) \times 3$

4. Circle 5×2 or 2×5. Find that product. Then find the answer.

a) $3 \times \boxed{5 \times 2}$

= ___3 × 10___

= ___30___

b) $7 \times 5 \times 2$

= _____

= _____

c) $3 \times 2 \times 5$

= _____

= _____

d) $2 \times 5 \times 8$

= _____

= _____

e) $6 \times 5 \times 2$

= _____

= _____

f) $9 \times 2 \times 5$

= _____

= _____

5. Write the two products. Then use the easier one to find the answer.

$(8 \times 3) \times 3$

= _____

$8 \times (3 \times 3)$

= _____

So $8 \times 3 \times 3 =$ _____.

6. Circle the product you would find first. Then find the answer.

a) $4 \times \boxed{3 \times 3}$

= _____

= _____

b) $2 \times 4 \times 6$

= _____

= _____

c) $7 \times 2 \times 2$

= _____

= _____

BONUS ▶ What number makes the sentence true?

a) $2 \times 3 \times 5 = \boxed{}$

b) $\boxed{} \times 2 \times 3 = 30$

c) $\boxed{} \times 2 \times 3 = 24$

d) $\boxed{} \times 2 \times 5 = 20$

e) $2 \times 2 \times \boxed{} = 28$

f) $\boxed{} \times 1 \times 9 = 54$

COPYRIGHT © 2016 JUMP MATH: NOT TO BE COPIED.

NS3-47 Concepts in Multiplication (2)

1. A stool has 3 legs. How many legs will 6 stools have? _____

2. Tessa multiplies 5 by a number less than 4.
   The ones digit of her answer is 0.

   What number did she multiply 5 by? _____ What is her answer? _____

3. a) There are 10 crayons in a box. How many crayons are in 5 boxes? _____

   b) Pens come in packages of 4. How many pens are in 4 packages? _____

4. Find two numbers (△ and ☐) so that the multiplication

   sentence ☐ × △ = ☐ is true. The two numbers in the

   squares have to be the same.

5. Find the sum and product of each pair of numbers.

	Sum	Product
3 and 4		
2 and 5		
1 and 7		
2 and 2		
Make your own: _____ and _____		

6. Fill in the blanks.

   a) Two numbers whose product is bigger than their sum. _____ and _____

   b) Two numbers whose sum is bigger than their product. _____ and _____

   c) Two numbers whose sum and product are equal. _____ and _____

7. What do you get when you multiply a number by 1?
   What is 1 × 100? What is 1 × 732?

COPYRIGHT © 2016 JUMP MATH: NOT TO BE COPIED.

8.

Vehicle	Number of Wheels
Bicycle	2
Tricycle	3
Go-Cart	4

a) How many wheels do 6 bicycles have?

b) Do 5 tricycles have more wheels than 4 go-carts?

c) Jim counted 11 wheels on 3 vehicles. How many of each type of vehicle did he count?

9. Write an addition and multiplication sentence for the perimeter.

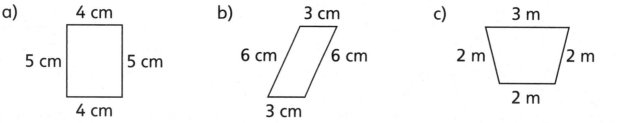

a) 4 cm / 5 cm / 5 cm / 4 cm

b) 3 cm / 6 cm / 6 cm / 3 cm

c) 3 m / 2 m / 2 m / 2 m

10. Iva says the rectangle has perimeter 2 × (3 + 4) cm.
Tristan says the rectangle has perimeter 2 × 3 + 2 × 4 cm.
Who is correct? Explain.

4 cm / 3 cm / 3 cm / 4 cm

11. Find the perimeter. Write a multiplication sentence if you can.

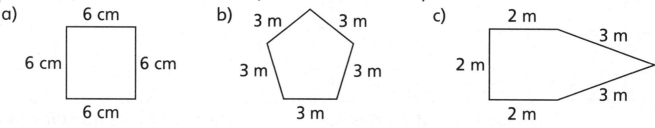

a) 6 cm / 6 cm / 6 cm / 6 cm

b) 3 m / 3 m / 3 m / 3 m / 3 m

c) 2 m / 3 m / 2 m / 2 m / 3 m

BONUS ▶ Mary draws a polygon on grid paper. She finds the perimeter of her polygon by writing 4 × 5 = 20 cm. Draw Mary's polygon.

BONUS ▶ A box of 2 pencils costs 8 cents. A box of 3 pencils costs 10 cents. What is the cheapest way to buy 6 pencils?

BONUS ▶ Use the numbers 2, 3, and 4 to fill in the boxes.

a) (☐ × △) + ⬠ = 10

b) (☐ × △) − ⬠ = 10

COPYRIGHT © 2016 JUMP MATH: NOT TO BE COPIED.

ME3-9 Shapes and Area

Two pattern block squares cover this rectangle.

The squares are the same size.

There are no gaps or overlaps.

The **area** of the rectangle is 2 squares.

1. Bill measured the area of a book with squares. Write ✓ for what he did correctly. Write ✗ for what he did wrong.

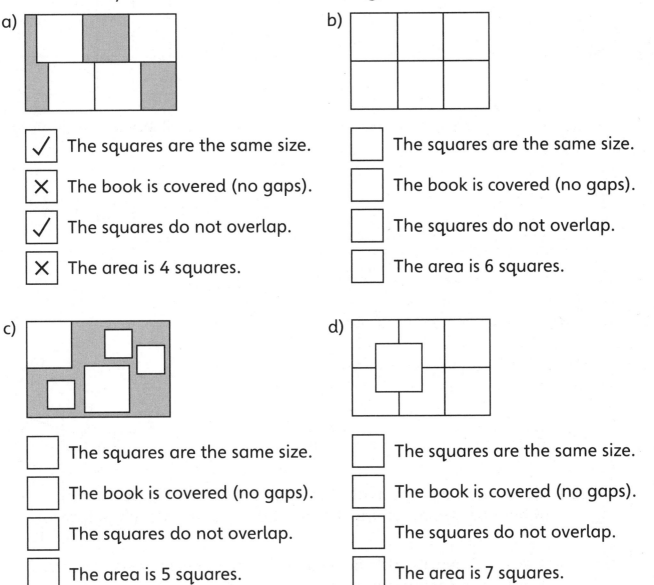

a)

✓	The squares are the same size.
✗	The book is covered (no gaps).
✓	The squares do not overlap.
✗	The area is 4 squares.

b)

	The squares are the same size.
	The book is covered (no gaps).
	The squares do not overlap.
	The area is 6 squares.

c)

	The squares are the same size.
	The book is covered (no gaps).
	The squares do not overlap.
	The area is 5 squares.

d)

	The squares are the same size.
	The book is covered (no gaps).
	The squares do not overlap.
	The area is 7 squares.

COPYRIGHT © 2016 JUMP MATH: NOT TO BE COPIED.

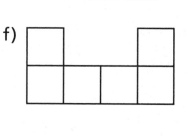

A **square centimetre** is a square with sides 1 cm long.

We write **cm²** for short.

You can measure area in square centimetres.

1 cm

1 cm

2. Find the area in square centimetres.

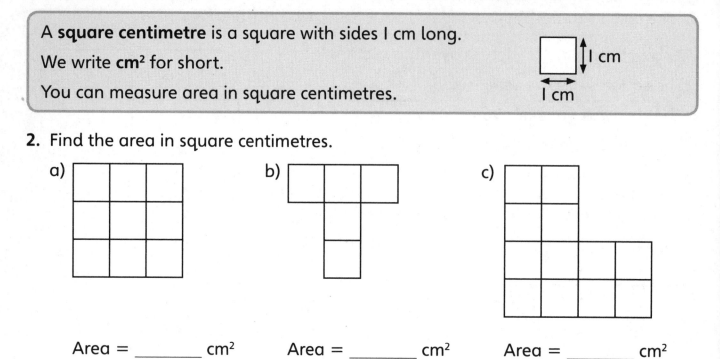

a)

Area = _____ cm²

b)

Area = _____ cm²

c)

Area = _____ cm²

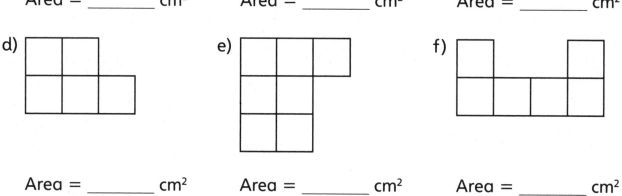

d)

Area = _____ cm²

e)

Area = _____ cm²

f)

Area = _____ cm²

3. Use a ruler to join the marks and divide the rectangle into square centimetres. Then find the area in cm².

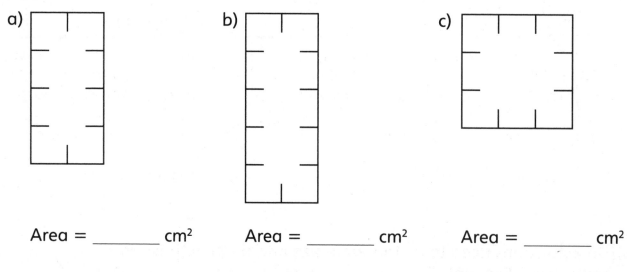

a)

Area = _____ cm²

b)

Area = _____ cm²

c)

Area = _____ cm²

COPYRIGHT © 2016 JUMP MATH: NOT TO BE COPIED.

4. The small squares on the grid are each I cm². Find the areas in square units.

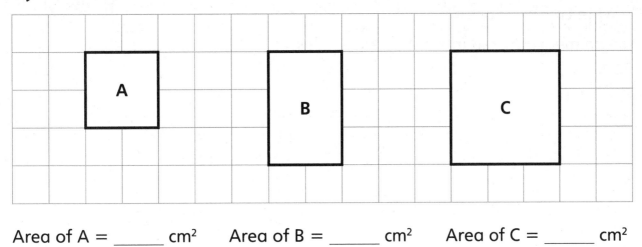

Area of A = _____ cm²   Area of B = _____ cm²   Area of C = _____ cm²

5. Draw 3 shapes on the grid lines. Find the area of each shape.

6. a) Draw 3 different shapes on the grid lines, each with an area of 6 cm².

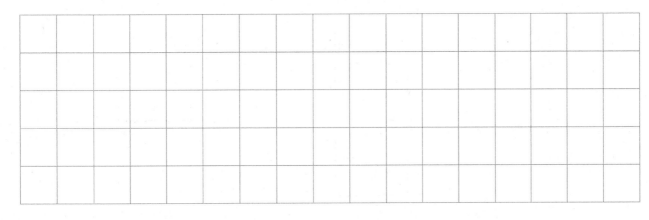

b) Do 2 polygons need to be the same size and shape to have the same area? Explain.

COPYRIGHT © 2016 JUMP MATH: NOT TO BE COPIED.

ME3-10 Measuring Area with Different Units

You can use pattern blocks to measure area. Cover the shape with blocks of the same type without gaps and overlaps. Then count the blocks.

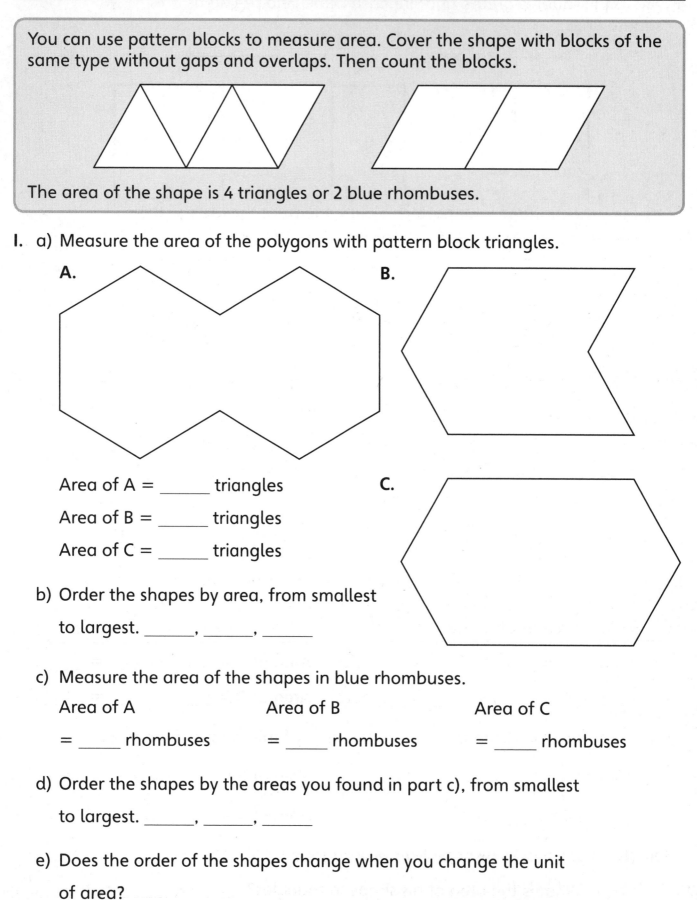

The area of the shape is 4 triangles or 2 blue rhombuses.

I. a) Measure the area of the polygons with pattern block triangles.

A.

B.

Area of A = _____ triangles

Area of B = _____ triangles

Area of C = _____ triangles

C.

b) Order the shapes by area, from smallest

to largest. _____, _____, _____

c) Measure the area of the shapes in blue rhombuses.

Area of A   Area of B   Area of C

= _____ rhombuses   = _____ rhombuses   = _____ rhombuses

d) Order the shapes by the areas you found in part c), from smallest

to largest. _____, _____, _____

e) Does the order of the shapes change when you change the unit

of area? _____

COPYRIGHT © 2016 JUMP MATH: NOT TO BE COPIED.

2. a) How many pattern block triangles cover each block?

rhombus

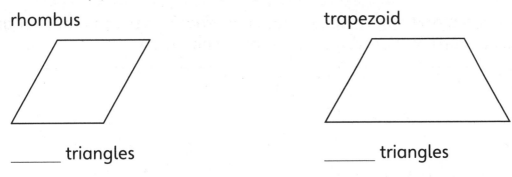

_____ triangles

trapezoid

_____ triangles

b) Make each shape with pattern blocks. Measure the area of the shape you made in the given pattern block unit.

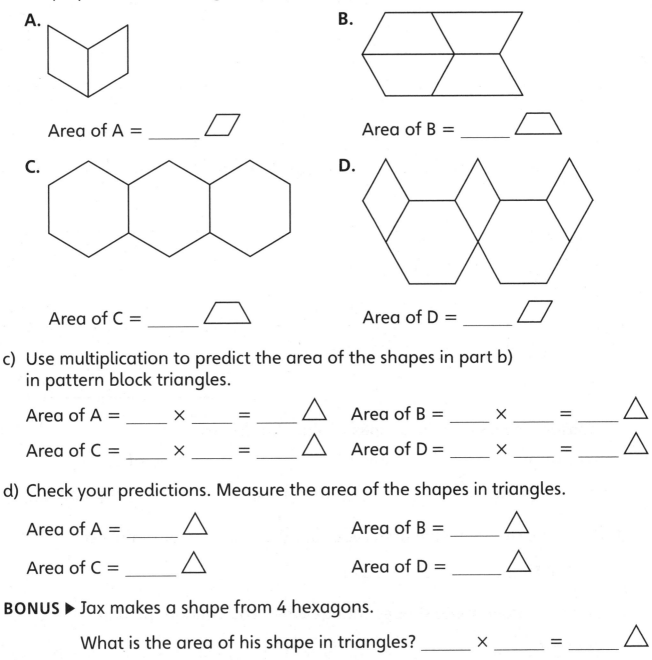

A.

Area of A = _____ ▱

B.

Area of B = _____ ⏢

C.

Area of C = _____ ⏢

D.

Area of D = _____ ▱

c) Use multiplication to predict the area of the shapes in part b) in pattern block triangles.

Area of A = ____ × ____ = ____ △   Area of B = ____ × ____ = ____ △

Area of C = ____ × ____ = ____ △   Area of D = ____ × ____ = ____ △

d) Check your predictions. Measure the area of the shapes in triangles.

Area of A = _____ △   Area of B = _____ △

Area of C = _____ △   Area of D = _____ △

BONUS ▶ Jax makes a shape from 4 hexagons.

What is the area of his shape in triangles? _____ × _____ = _____ △

COPYRIGHT © 2016 JUMP MATH: NOT TO BE COPIED.

ME3-II Skip Counting to Find Area

The area is 12 square units.

1	2	3	4
5	6	7	8
9	10	11	12

The area is 10 square units.

1	2	3	4	5
6	7	8	9	10

1. Josh covered a rectangle with small squares. Count the number of squares to find the area.

a)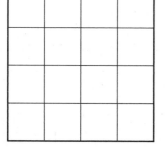

_____ square units

b)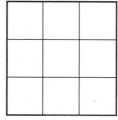

_____ square units

c)

_____ square units

2. Count the number of small squares to find the area.

a)

_____ square units

b)

_____ square units

c)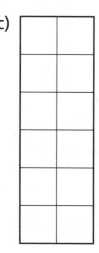

_____ square units

d)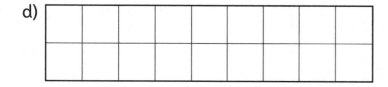

_____ square units

COPYRIGHT © 2016 JUMP MATH: NOT TO BE COPIED.

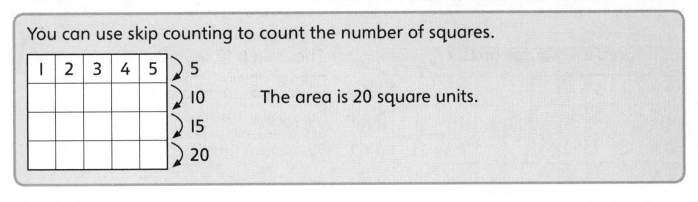

You can use skip counting to count the number of squares.

1	2	3	4	5

5
10
15
20

The area is 20 square units.

3. Use skip counting to find the area.

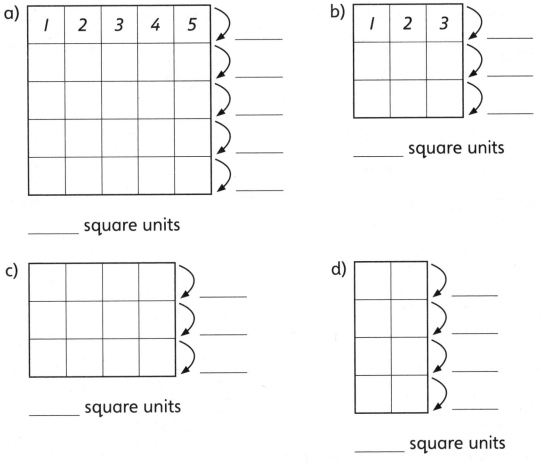

a)

1	2	3	4	5

_____
_____
_____
_____
_____

_____ square units

b)

1	2	3

_____
_____
_____

_____ square units

c)

_____
_____
_____

_____ square units

d)

_____
_____
_____
_____

_____ square units

e)

_____
_____
_____
_____

_____ square units

COPYRIGHT © 2016 JUMP MATH: NOT TO BE COPIED.

ME3-12 Multiplying to Find Area

1	2	3	4	5	6	7	8	9	10	⟩ 10
2										⟩ 20
3										⟩ 30
4										⟩ 40
5										⟩ 50

10 square units in each row

5 rows

50 square units

1. Count the number of square units in each row. Count the number of rows. Write the area in square units.

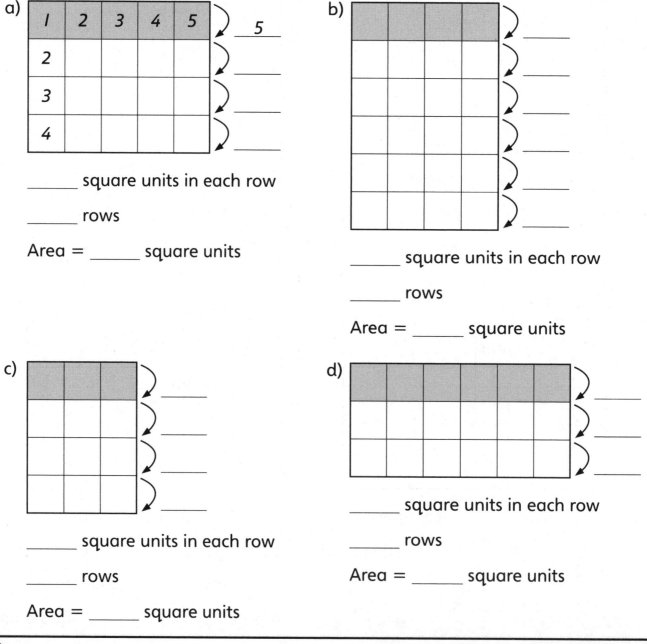

a)

1	2	3	4	5
2				
3				
4				

⟩ 5

⟩ _____

⟩ _____

⟩ _____

_____ square units in each row

_____ rows

Area = _____ square units

b)

_____ square units in each row

_____ rows

Area = _____ square units

c)

_____ square units in each row

_____ rows

Area = _____ square units

d)

_____ square units in each row

_____ rows

Area = _____ square units

COPYRIGHT © 2016 JUMP MATH: NOT TO BE COPIED.

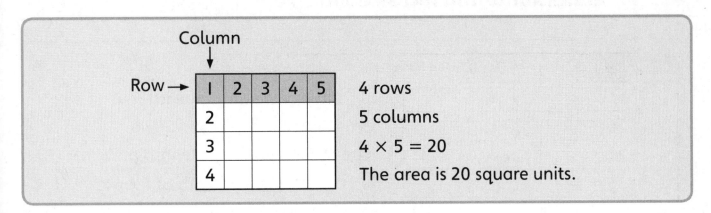

Column

Row →	1	2	3	4	5
2					
3					
4					

4 rows

5 columns

$4 \times 5 = 20$

The area is 20 square units.

2. Count the number of rows and the number of columns. Multiply to find the total number of square units.

a)

1	2	3	4
2			
3			
4			
5			

__5__ rows __4__ columns

Area = __$5 \times 4 = 20$__ square units

b)

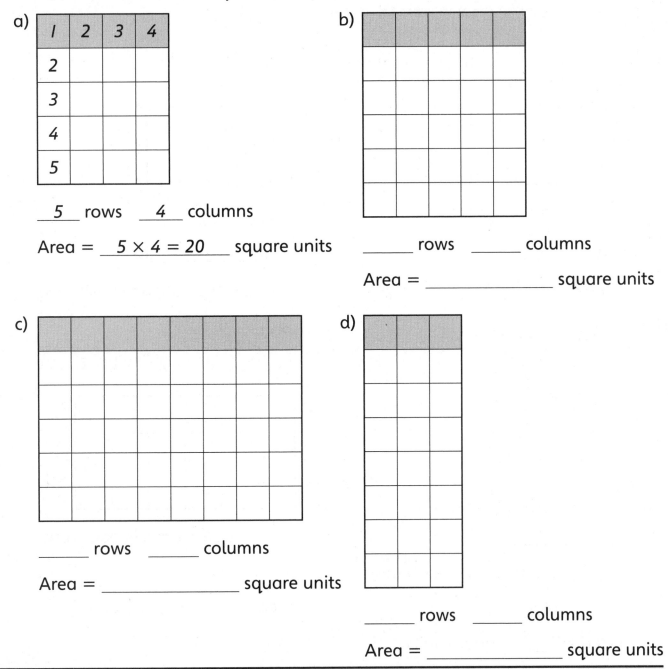

_____ rows _____ columns

Area = _____ square units

c)

_____ rows _____ columns

Area = _____ square units

d)

_____ rows _____ columns

Area = _____ square units

COPYRIGHT © 2016 JUMP MATH: NOT TO BE COPIED.

ME3-I3 Estimating and Measuring Area

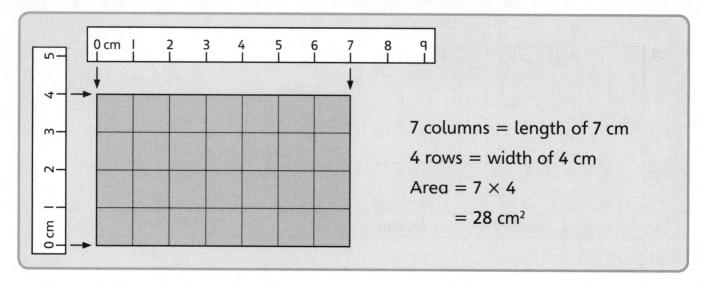

7 columns = length of 7 cm

4 rows = width of 4 cm

Area = 7 × 4

= 28 cm²

I. Measure the length and width of the rectangle in centimetres.
Multiply them to find the area in cm².

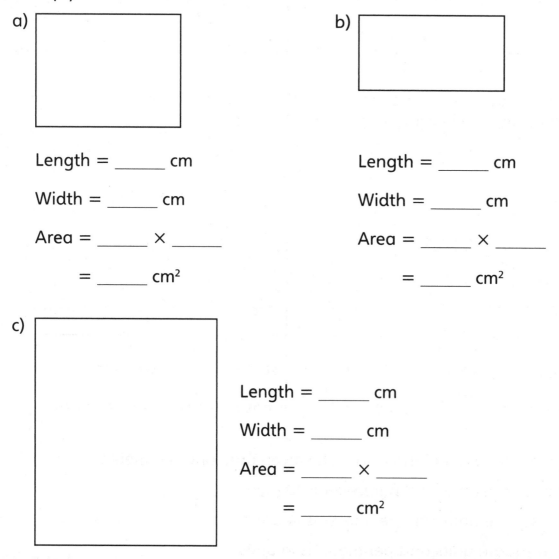

a)

Length = _____ cm

Width = _____ cm

Area = _____ × _____

= _____ cm²

b)

Length = _____ cm

Width = _____ cm

Area = _____ × _____

= _____ cm²

c)

Length = _____ cm

Width = _____ cm

Area = _____ × _____

= _____ cm²

COPYRIGHT © 2016 JUMP MATH: NOT TO BE COPIED

2. Estimate and measure the length and width of the rectangle in centimetres. Find the area in cm².

a)

b)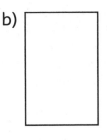

	Estimate	Actual
Length	_____ cm	_____ cm
Width	_____ cm	_____ cm
Area		

	Estimate	Actual
Length	_____ cm	_____ cm
Width	_____ cm	_____ cm
Area		

3. Estimate the area of the shape in pattern block squares. Cover the shape with pattern block squares to measure the area.

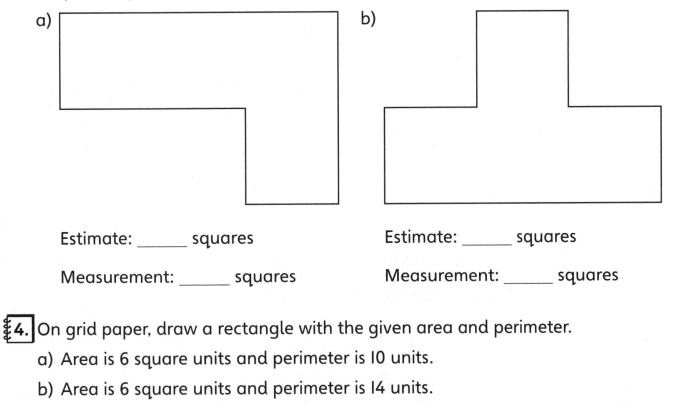

a)

Estimate: _____ squares

Measurement: _____ squares

b)

Estimate: _____ squares

Measurement: _____ squares

4. On grid paper, draw a rectangle with the given area and perimeter.

a) Area is 6 square units and perimeter is 10 units.

b) Area is 6 square units and perimeter is 14 units.

c) Area is 10 square units and perimeter is 14 units.

COPYRIGHT © 2016 JUMP MATH: NOT TO BE COPIED.

5. a) The shaded regions are the same size and shape. Find the area
  of the shaded regions in large squares and in square centimetres.

A.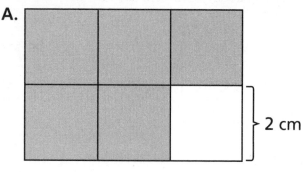

         2 cm

B.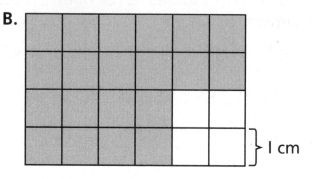

            I cm

   Area of A = _____ large squares   Area of B = _____ cm²

  b) I large square = _____ cm²

  c) Zara makes a rectangle using 6 squares
  that are each larger than I cm². Is the
  area of Zara's rectangle more than 6 cm²?
  Explain.

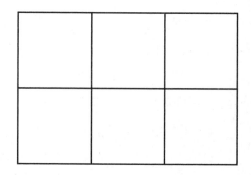

  d) Zara's squares have sides that are
  2 cm long. What is the area of Zara's
  rectangle in square centimetres? Explain.

6. Each grid square has a side length
  of I cm.

  a) Find the area of the shaded parts.

  b) What is the total area of the grid?

  c) What is the area that is
  not shaded?

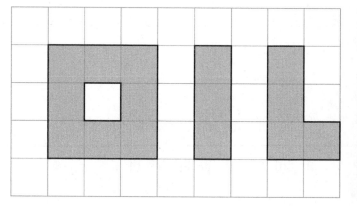

7. Can you build or draw a square with
  the given area using square blocks?
  Use grid paper, a geoboard, or square
  pattern blocks to find your answer.

  a) 4 square units   b) 6 square units

  c) 7 square units   d) 9 square units

8. Estimate the area of the top of your desk in JUMP Math books.
  Explain your answer.

COPYRIGHT © 2016 JUMP MATH· NOT TO BE COPIED

PDM3-1 Tally Charts

You can use **tallies** to count and record data. Each line stands for I.
Draw the 5th line across the others.

| = I || = 2 ||| = 3 |||| = 4   ℍℍ = 5   ℍℍ| = 6   ℍℍ|| = 7   ℍℍ ℍℍ = 10

I. What number does the tally show?

a) ℍℍ |||| = ___9___

b) ℍℍ ℍℍ | = _____

c) ℍℍ ||| = _____

2. Count by 5s to find the number the tally shows.

a) ℍℍ ℍℍ ℍℍ ℍℍ

___5, 10, 15, 20___

b) ℍℍ ℍℍ ℍℍ ℍℍ ℍℍ

_____

c) ℍℍ ℍℍ ℍℍ

_____

d) ℍℍ ℍℍ ℍℍ
ℍℍ ℍℍ ℍℍ = ___30___

e) ℍℍ ℍℍ ℍℍ ℍℍ ℍℍ
ℍℍ ℍℍ ℍℍ = _____

f) ℍℍ ℍℍ ℍℍ ℍℍ ℍℍ
ℍℍ ℍℍ ℍℍ ℍℍ = _____

3. Multiply by 5 to find the number the tally shows.

a) ℍℍ ℍℍ ℍℍ ℍℍ

___4 × 5 = 20___

b) ℍℍ ℍℍ ℍℍ ℍℍ ℍℍ ℍℍ

_____

c) ℍℍ ℍℍ

_____

4. Count by 5s, then count on by Is to find the number the tally shows.

a) ℍℍ ℍℍ ℍℍ ℍℍ |||

___5, 10, 15, 20, 21, 22, 23___

b) ℍℍ ℍℍ ℍℍ ||

_____

c) ℍℍ ℍℍ ℍℍ ℍℍ ℍℍ ℍℍ | = _____

d) ℍℍ ℍℍ ℍℍ ℍℍ ℍℍ |||| = _____

e) ℍℍ ℍℍ ℍℍ ℍℍ ℍℍ ℍℍ ℍℍ || = _____

f) ℍℍ ℍℍ ℍℍ ℍℍ ℍℍ ℍℍ ℍℍ ||| = _____

5. Multiply by 5, then add the leftover tally marks to find the number
the tally shows.

a) ℍℍ ℍℍ ℍℍ ℍℍ |||

___(4 × 5) + 3 = 23___

b) ℍℍ ℍℍ ||

_____

c) ℍℍ ℍℍ ℍℍ ℍℍ |

_____

d) ℍℍ ℍℍ ℍℍ ||||

_____

COPYRIGHT © 2016 JUMP MATH: NOT TO BE COPIED.

6. Draw the tally for the number.

a) 12 = _~~||||~~ ~~||||~~ ||_   b) 3 = _____   c) 5 = _____

d) 6 = _____   e) 10 = _____   f) 11 = _____

g) 14 = _____   h) 15 = _____   i) 20 = _____

BONUS ▶ 53 = _____

7. Students chose favourite fruits in a survey. The tally chart shows the results.

a) Write the number each tally shows.

Favourite Fruit	Tally	Number of Students
Apples	~~||||~~ ||	7
Bananas	~~||||~~ ~~||||~~	
Oranges	~~||||~~		
Grapes	||||	
Peaches	|||	

b) How many students chose oranges? _____

c) How many students chose grapes? _____

d) Which fruit is the most popular? _____

e) Which fruit is the least popular? _____

f) Which fruit is more popular, oranges or grapes? _____

g) Add the data to find the answer. Write the addition sentence.

How many students answered the survey in total?

How many students chose apples or bananas?

h) Subtract the data to find the answer. Write the subtraction sentence.

How many more students chose bananas than peaches?

How many fewer students chose peaches than apples?

i) Which fruit is twice as popular as peaches? Write a multiplication sentence.

Probability and Data Management 3-1

COPYRIGHT © 2016 JUMP MATH: NOT TO BE COPIED.

Line Plots

1. Measure the heights of the flowers to the nearest centimetre.

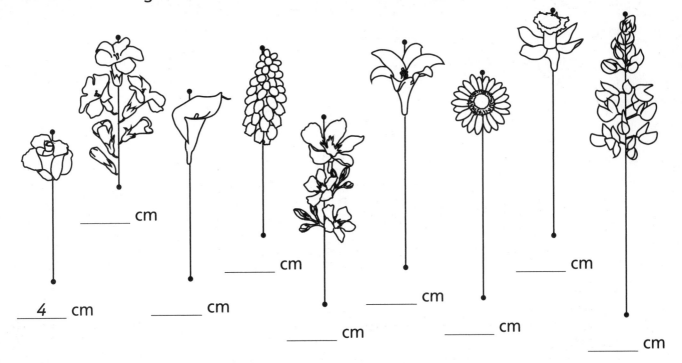

_____ cm

__4__ cm

_____ cm

_____ cm

_____ cm

_____ cm

_____ cm

_____ cm

_____ cm

_____ cm

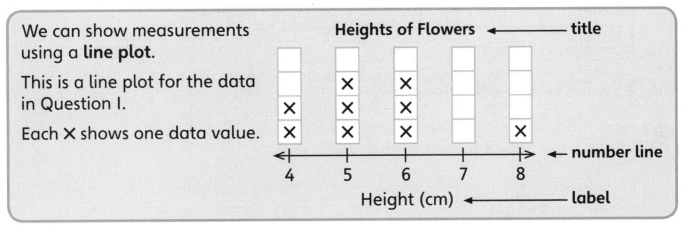

We can show measurements using a **line plot**.

This is a line plot for the data in Question 1.

Each ✗ shows one data value.

Heights of Flowers ← title

← number line

Height (cm) ← label

2. a) Use the line plot in the grey box to fill in the table.

   b) How many flowers are 7 cm tall? _____

   How does the line plot show this?

   _____

   _____

   c) Where is it easier to see the number of flowers of each length, on the line plot

   or in the table? _____

Height (cm)	Number of Flowers
4	2
5	
6	
7	
8	

COPYRIGHT © 2016 JUMP MATH: NOT TO BE COPIED.

3. a) Measure the lengths of the pencils to the nearest centimetre.

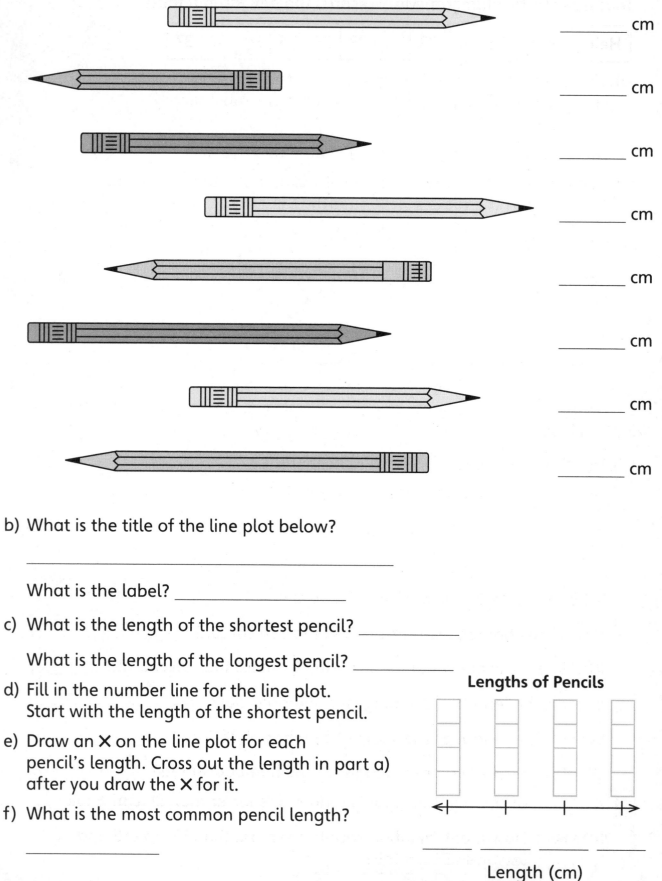

_____ cm

_____ cm

_____ cm

_____ cm

_____ cm

_____ cm

_____ cm

_____ cm

b) What is the title of the line plot below?

_____

What is the label? _____

c) What is the length of the shortest pencil? _____

What is the length of the longest pencil? _____

d) Fill in the number line for the line plot.
Start with the length of the shortest pencil.

e) Draw an ✕ on the line plot for each
pencil's length. Cross out the length in part a)
after you draw the ✕ for it.

f) What is the most common pencil length?

_____

Lengths of Pencils

_____ _____ _____ _____

Length (cm)

COPYRIGHT © 2016 JUMP MATH: NOT TO BE COPIED

4. The students in Mary's class measure the heights of 10 bamboo shoots to the nearest centimetre. Mary records the heights in a table.

Height (cm)	32	32	33	33	33	35	35	36	37	37

a) The line plot below will show the heights of the bamboo shoots. Write a title and a label for the line plot. Include the unit in the label.

b) Complete the number line for the line plot.

c) Draw an ✗ in the line plot for each height in the table. Cross out the height in the table after you draw the ✗ for it.

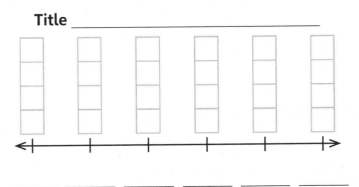

Title _____

Label _____

d) Use the line plot to answer the questions.

How many bamboo shoots have a height of 33 cm? _____

How many bamboo shoots are 34 cm tall? _____

How many bamboo shoots have a height of 36 cm? _____

What is the total number of bamboo shoots? _____

How many bamboo shoots are less than 34 cm tall? _____

BONUS ▶ How many bamboo shoots are more than 35 cm tall? _____

e) What is the length of the longest bamboo shoot? _____

What is the length of the shortest bamboo shoot? _____

What is the most common length of the bamboo shoots? _____

f) Are most of the bamboo shoots longer or shorter than 34 cm? Explain.

   BONUS ▶ How many bamboo shoots are more than 33 cm tall and less than 36 cm tall?

COPYRIGHT © 2016 JUMP MATH: NOT TO BE COPIED.

1. Students count the pockets on their clothes. The line plot shows how many students have each number of pockets.

   Pockets on Our Clothes Today

   a) How many people have each number of pockets?

   1 pocket _____

   5 pockets _____

   0 pockets _____

   3 pockets _____

   7 pockets _____

   b) What is the largest number of pockets? _____

   What is the smallest number of pockets? _____

   c) What is the most common number of pockets? _____

   d) How many students counted their pockets in total? _____

   How do you know? _____

   > In the line plot in Question 1, the 4 ✗s above number 2 on the number line show that 4 students have 2 pockets on their clothes.

2. Students count the buttons on their clothes.

   Buttons on Our Clothes Today

   a) One student has 3 buttons. Circle the ✗ that shows this.

   b) The thick ✗s show that _____ students

   have _____ buttons on their clothes.

   c) What is the largest number of buttons

   on students' clothes in the line plot? _____

   d) What is the most common number of buttons

   on the clothes in the line plot? _____

   How many students have that many buttons? _____

   e) How many students counted their buttons for the line plot? _____

COPYRIGHT © 2016 JUMP MATH: NOT TO BE COPIED

> The **mode** is the most common data value.
>
> In the set 2, 3, 4, 4, 5, 5, 5, the mode is 5.

3. Circle the mode in the set of data values.

   a) 2, 3, 3, 4, 5   b) 10, 10, 10, 13, 14, 14   c) 1, 3, 5, 5, 7, 7, 7

4. Write the data in order from least to greatest. Circle the mode.

   a) 1, 3, 5, 7, 3, 5, 3   b) 10, 15, 13, 11, 21, 15   c) 321, 321, 87, 903

   _____   _____   _____

5. Look at the line plots in Questions 1 and 2.

   a) What is the mode in Question 1? _____ pockets

   b) What is the mode in Question 2? _____ buttons

   c) How can you find the mode from a line plot? _____

   _____

> The data set 3, 3, 4, 4, 5, 6, 7 has two modes, the numbers 3 and 4.
>
> The data set 3, 3, 5, 5 has no mode. Each value appears the same number of times.

6. Jake collected 12 birch leaves. The table shows the lengths of the leaves.

Length (cm)	3	5	4	7	3	5	5	3	7	7	4	8

   a) Make a line plot showing the lengths of the leaves.

   b) What are the modes of the data set?

   c) How many more 7 cm leaves than 8 cm leaves are there?
   How can you see that from the line plot?

   d) Jake places all the leaves of the same length end to end. How long is each chain of leaves? Use multiplication to find the answers.

   3 cm leaves   4 cm leaves   5 cm leaves   7 cm leaves

   e) Jake places all 12 leaves end to end. What is the total length of all the leaves?